S0-BIP-250

JAPAN'S HIGH TECHNOLOGY

An Annotated Guide To English - Language Information Sources

By
Dawn E. Talbot

ORYX PRESS
1991

The rare Arabian Oryx is believed to have inspired the myth of the unicorn. This desert antelope became virtually extinct in the early 1960s. At that time several groups of international conservationists arranged to have 9 animals sent to the Phoenix Zoo to be the nucleus of a captive breeding herd. Today the Oryx population is nearly 800, and over 400 have been returned to reserves in the Middle East.

The Oryx Press
4041 North Central at Indian School Road
Phoenix, AZ 85012-3397

Published simultaneously in Canada

Printed and Bound in the United States of America

∞ The paper used in this publication meets the minimum requirements of American National Standard for Information Science—Permanence of Paper for Printed Library Materials, ANSI Z39.48, 1984.

Library of Congress Cataloging-in-Publication Data

Talbot, Dawn E., 1950–
Japan's high technology : an annotated guide to English-language information sources / by Dawn E. Talbot.
p. cm.
Includes index.
ISBN 0-89774-528-0
1. High technology—Japan—Bibliography—Catalogs. 2. English imprints—Catalogs. I. Title.
Z7916.T35 1990
[T27.J3] 90-7968
016.6'0952—dc20 CIP

To my husband, Don L. Bosseau, for his patience, understanding, and help.

Table of Contents

Acknowledgements

Obtaining the myriad of detail required in a guide such as this is clearly not a singular effort. I have been aided by colleagues at a number of the University of California campuses. Many other librarians have also provided information, as have professional societies and publishers. Special thanks are due to Jan Neumann, Center for Magnetic Recording Research, and Kathleen Wright, Naval Ocean Systems Center, for their help in locating relevant materials. In Japan, Tamiyo Togasaki and Junko Kurita, International House of Japan, also provided invaluable assistance, and I thank them for their help. Mr. Sumio Saito, United Publishers Services Limited, Tokyo, kindly supplied bibliographic details for a number of titles. Thanks also to The Oryx Press for the encouragement and patience during the extended gestation period it took to bring this work to completion.

Introduction

With Japan maintaining a progressively higher position in the universal trade market, technical information from and about Japan is vital to the world's business culture. This guide to over 500 English-language sources of information in science, technology, and business should be a useful first step for those with a need to access the vast store of published technical information from Japan. That there exists a significant body of English-language material published in Japan is often not widely known. There is also an increasing number of titles about Japan published outside of Japan. This guide reveals some of those sources. Although this is by no means an exhaustive listing, it is a good representation of the wide variety of materials available.

For those with a need to stay abreast of cutting-edge technologies, reliance on purely English-language sources is not sufficient. Many publications listed in this guide will provide an overview and the direction for more in-depth research using Japanese-language materials.

Prior to 1986, it was very difficult to find guides to Japanese publications in science and technology that were published in English. Today, those that are available (listed in the first chapter, Guides to Sources of Japanese Information) take a variety of approaches. They cover the printed English-language sources in varying detail. Some are concerned more with personal contacts, others with electronic databases; still others focus on a narrow subject approach.

This collection aims to be as comprehensive as possible within its scope—that of published sources (including electronically published as well as print) in the English language. The subject focus is broadly defined as science, technology, and business materials with an emphasis on the high-technology areas where Japan is achieving its preeminence. Most of the information sources are secondary—that is, they act as guides or pointers to the primary literature or are publications containing directory information such as names, addresses, telephone and telefacsimile numbers, and statistical information.

No attempt has been made to cover the primary journal literature for example. Although one cannot ignore the published journal literature in the vernacular, keeping current with some 10,000 journal titles presently published in Japan in science and technology would be a daunting task well beyond the scope of this book. However, guides to the journal literature can be found in the Bibliographies chapter. Also, many of the abstracting and indexing services listed in Chapter 3 will provide access to the journal literature. The proceedings of conferences, symposia, and technical meetings are also out of scope for this guide. Again, the abstracting and indexing services listed in Chapter 3 will provide some access to this type of information.

Brief explanations are provided at the beginning of each chapter to introduce the reader to the type of materials contained in the chapter. Almost all listed titles are in print and, therefore, readily available. However some out-of-print sources are listed because there was no more current source available and because they can be consulted in many of the large libraries in the United States.

Every effort has been made to ensure that all publications are still beneficial entities. The newsletters category is a particularly volatile area (see Chapter 8). Many of these titles only remain active for a relatively short period of time. Because their production costs are high, the subscription fees also tend to be high. Attracting and retaining a sufficiently large subscriber base is often difficult for these publishers.

For each entry, the publisher's address or that of a distributor is listed, along with a telephone number and, wherever possible, a telefacsimile number. Telefacsimile is a very timely and effective method of communicating with most Japanese companies. In the descriptive section, a date and frequency of publication, if appropriate, is indicated. The number of pages and the International Standard Book Number (ISBN) or International Standard Serial Number (ISSN), distinct identifying numbers useful for ordering purposes, are also given. Prices are indicated in U.S. dollars or pounds sterling. All Japanese yen prices have been converted using an exchange rate of 136 yen to the dollar. These prices are provided only as a guide because prices become outdated very quickly, especially with the fluctuations of the international monetary situation.

Brief annotations provide descriptions of the content of each work. These have been derived from the works themselves wherever possible. In some instances content information was obtained from the publisher. The guides listed in Chapter 1 also provide helpful information, particularly for verification purposes. The Subject Dictionaries chapter is the only area where some annotations are missing. This proved to be a particularly difficult area since many of these specialized technical dictionaries are not held in academic library collections. Working with unofficial translated titles also presents some problems for verification since these can differ markedly from one translation to another.

The appendixes provide some suggestions for gaining access to the material found within this guide. The booksellers listed specialize in Japanese titles. This is an advantage because they understand the Japanese book trade and can obtain titles more efficiently than others not well versed in this area. The libraries listed have been selected because of their Japanese science, technology, and business collections. There are other excellent East Asian collections throughout the United States; however, their collections focus generally on the humanities and social sciences and are also primarily published in Japanese. Because of the expense of industry reports, holdings of the titles listed in this guide are patchy throughout the libraries of this country. However, because they are all in English, there is a good chance that many of them will be held in the larger libraries, certainly in the case of the more generalized directories and handbooks. Libraries may not hold the more specialized titles, nor the more expensive newsletters.

In the Other Sources of Information appendix, a few non-profit organizations are listed that can provide information from and about Japan. No attempt has been made to include the large number of commercial consulting firms which offer a variety of services to access information from Japan. The title index provides a very useful starting point for locating details of a known title. If the title is unknown then the subject index will provide the most useful reference point. An author index has been included for those publications with named individuals indicated as being resposible for the work. In many cases there is no author since the publication is produced by a corporate body. Names of these corporate bodies are included in the Publisher and Related Organizations index.

This work began as a way to organize the diverse array of information I had begun to collect from and about Japan. Working at the Center for Magnetic Recording Research, in an area of high technology where the Japanese were making significant progress, I was expending more and more effort getting information from Japan. At the time, there were no published guides to current science and technical information from Japan, and frequently I had to rely solely on announcements of new publications. These started to appear with greater regularity as Japan's influence on the U.S. economy gained in importance and many publishers tried to seize the opportunity to convert this interest in Japan into a profitable venture. It is hoped that the current work will act as a convenient guide to the increasing number of publications, which provide information in English about science, technology, and business in Japan.

Chapter 1
Guides to Sources of Japanese Information

The following titles will broaden the category of sources available to the reader. Some of the guides listed in this section will provide help in seeking out information sources other than those in published format. Some ongoing publications (newsletters, annuals) are provided to keep the Japan researcher current. By consulting a number of these guides, one can improve one's approach and discover resources that are especially relevant to a particular field of interest.

1. *Asian Markets: A Guide to Company and Industry Information Sources.* Washington Researchers, Ltd., 2612 P St. NW, Washington, DC 20007. (202) 333-3533. (202) 625-0656 Fax. 1st ed., 1988. 371 p. ISBN 0-934940-73-8. $195.00.

Lists information sources such as organizations, personal contacts, publications, databases for Asian markets, industries, and companies. Gives contacts both in the U.S. and Asia with addresses and telephone numbers. Provides product and ownership information for 140,000 foreign companies. Gives foreign investment in the U.S. and U.S. investment in Asia. Lists translation agencies capable of handling technical reports. As the title indicates, the coverage of this publication is not limited to Japan.

2. *Directory of Japanese Technical Resources in the U.S.* U.S. Department of Commerce, National Technical Information Service (NTIS), Office of International Affairs, 5285 Port Royal Rd., Springfield, VA 22161. (703) 487-4650. (703) 321-8199 Fax. Annual. ISBN 0-934213-19-4. 208 p. NTIS Order No. PB89-158869. $36.00.

This annual was begun in 1987 in response to the Japanese Technical Literature Act of 1986 (Public Law 99-382). This law directs the Department of Commerce to compile, publish, and disseminate an annual directory, listing all programs and services in the U.S. that collect, abstract, translate, and distribute Japanese scientific and technical information. It also includes all translations of Japanese technical documents performed by the federal government for the preceeding 12 months. The main body of work consists of the listings of information services, Japanese online databases, and federally funded translations. The information services section is further indexed by name of organization, types of services, type of expertise offered, and geographic areas. Some background articles are also included that discuss issues of interest to those concerned with monitoring information from Japan. Essays from the now out-of-print 1987 and 1988 directories have been republished as *Accessing Japanese Technical Information* (see Chapter 2, Conferences, Reports on Access to Japanese Information).

3. *EC-Japan Centre Directory of Sources of Japanese Information.* EC-Japan Centre for Industrial Cooperation, Information Service, Ichibancho Eight One Bldg., 5th Fl., 6-4 Ichibancho, Chiyoda-ku, Tokyo 102. (03) 221-6161. (03) 221-6226 Fax. 1988. 89 p. ISBN 4-931240-00-3. Gratis.

A selective directory of sources judged by the compilers to be the most important sources for the foreign business representative in Japan. Many of the entries are concerned with online electronic databases. Both Japanese- and English-language sources are included. The directory is divided into two major sections. The first is an alphabetical list of producers and publishers of Japanese information, and the second lists database organizations and publications on Japanese databases. Access to the information in these two sections is best approached from one of the four indexes: producers and organizations, databases and publications, online host systems, or subject list of sources divided into 21 subject areas.

4. *English-Language Japanese Business Reference Guide.* Jeffries, Francis M. Jeffries and Associates Inc., 17200 Hughes Rd., Poolesville, MD 20837. (301) 428-8204. 1988. 218 p. $48.00.

Provides an extensive index with which the author suggests you begin to locate useful information. The guide is divided into 37 sections, each covering a different industry. There are 14 appendixes containing information on library collections, publishers, bibliographies, business journals, U.S. insurance companies in Tokyo, Japanese directories, U.S. banks in Japan, state representatives, U.S. shipping companies in Japan, U.S. accounting firms in Japan, lawyers and patent attorneys in Japan, and a bibliography of articles from popular business periodicals on U.S.-Japan business issues.

5. *How to Find Information about Japanese Companies and Industries.* Washington Researchers Ltd., 2612 P St., NW, Washington, DC 20007. (202) 333-3533. (202) 625-0656 Fax. 1984. 331 p. ISBN 0-9349-4029-0. $100.00.

This how-to book is designed as a comprehensive guide to business information sources from Japan. The first section contains a very general introduction on research methodology, whereas the main sections list sources available in the U.S. and those available in Japan. There is a section on worldwide organizations and a selective listing of published information sources.

6. *Identifying and Acquiring Grey Literature in Japan on High Definition Television (HDTV).* Ruhl, Mary Jane. U.S. Department of Commerce, National Technical Information Service (NTIS), Office of International Affairs, 5285 Port Royal Rd., Springfield, VA 22161. (703) 487-4650. (703) 321-8199 Fax. 1989. 72 p. NTIS Order No. PB 90-135302. $16.95.

Report of a one-month study to investigate acquiring so-called grey literature from Japan, i.e., information that is unavailable through regular commercial sources. The investigator documents experiences in visiting various organizations in Japan to solicit grey literature in a targeted field—High Definition Television (HDTV). Appendixes provide information on the organizations visited, descriptions of the visits, a bibliography of information obtained, and an analysis of the publication of HDTV grey literature.

7. *Information Gathering on Japan: A Primer.* Search Associates, Inc., International Research, 3422 Q St., NW, Washington, DC 20007. (202) 337-3656. 1988. 90 p. $50.00.

Lists sources of information from Japan especially for the business researcher. Emphasizes personal contacts rather than printed sources. Organized into 12 chapters: Department of Commerce, U.S. Government, U.S. Congress, Research and Academic Organizations, Japan in the U.S., Japan, Information Services, Business Associations, Lobbyists, Consultants and Translators, and Non-U.S. Organizations. The final chapter provides a bibliography of background reading on Japan.

8. *Introduction to Japanese Government Publications.* Kuroki, Tsutomu. Pergamon Press Ltd., Maxwell House, Fairview Park, Elmsford, NY 10523. (914) 592-7700. 1st ed. in English, 1981. 214 p. ISBN 0-08-024679-6. (Guides to official publications. vol. 10). $65.00.

General references are to older materials, mostly in Japanese. Includes useful introductory sections on how government publications are created and disseminated by the different agencies.

9. *Japanese Business Publications in English.* Edwards, Shiela, and Thompson, Karen. The British Library, Science Reference and Information Service, 25 Southampton Bldgs., Chancery Lane, London WC2A 1AW. (071) 323-7472. 2d ed. 1987. 55 p. ISBN 0-7123-0743-5. $20.00.

A listing of over 200 English-language publications held in the British Library, this guide is arranged in five sections by the form of the publications: Directories; Statistics, Market Information and Industry Surveys; Trade and Business Journals; Bibliographies and Abstracting Journals; and Company Reports. The first three sections are further subdivided by subject into General, Manufacturing, Chemical, Electronics, and Energy. A brief description is provided together with publisher and cost. The British Library call number is also given. Addresses for publishers are not given. An alphabetical index of titles and organizations is included.

10. *The Japanese Market. A Directory of Sources of Information and Business Services.* Japan External Trade Organization (JETRO), 2-2-5 Toranomon, Minato-ku, Tokyo 105. (03) 582-3518. (03) 587-2485 Fax. 1989. 86 p. ISBN 8224-0440-4. $20.00.

Compiled by members of the Opportunity Japan Campaign Task Force of the British Market Council, this directory is aimed at British companies wanting to increase their access to Japanese markets. Although it has a British bias, it is a very useful directory. Information sources are listed within broad categories: general information; market information; trade fairs and exhibitions; importers, agents and distribution channels; standards, products approvals, other government laws and regulations; financing for imports and investment; industrial property rights; business services; immigration procedures; office and residential accommodation; employment of staff; Japanese-language training; investment; and background information. While most of the references are to printed sources, particularly JETRO publications, names and addresses of appropriate agencies and companies are also provided.

11. *The Japanese Market. Information Sources for Overseas Companies.* Carr, Jennifer L. Warwick Statistics Service, University of Warwick Library, Coventry CV4 7AL. In the U.S. and Canada, contact Addor Associates, Inc., 115 Roseville Rd., P.O. Box 2128, Westport, CT 06880. 1984. 106 p. ISBN 0-903220-18-0. (Warwick Statistics Service Occasional Review No. 5). $28.00.

Part 1 lists principal sources of information on Japan in the U.K., e.g., libraries, information services, consultants, and government agencies. Part 2 lists similar sources in Japan that are accessible to the visiting foreigner. Part 3 lists selected English-language publications and Japanese and English databases that contain business information. An index of all organizations listed in the publication is provided.

12. *Japanese Technical Information Sources.* Technical Insights, Inc., Department J01389, P.O. Box 1304, Fort Lee, NJ 07024-9967. (201) 568-4744. (201) 568-8247 Fax. 1989. 200 p. $295.00.

Section 1, an index guide by type of service provided, and Section 2, an index guide by technology area, refer to Section 3 which contains the entries for 170 sources of information including technical translation companies, consultants and publishers of Japanese research and development, and companies able to provide information on new technologies and licensing opportunities. Some information on publications and databases is included although the major focus is on translators and translation agencies and commercial services offering Japanese information services for a fee.

13. *Japanese Technical Literature Bulletin.* Japanese Technical Literature Program, #4817, H.C. Hoover Bldg., 14th and Constitution Ave., NW, Washington, DC 20230. (202) 377-1288. (202) 377-4498 Fax. Bimonthly. 4 p. Gratis.

This newsletter highlights U.S. government activities in areas of Japanese scientific and technical information. It includes citations of recent Japanese reports and studies of potential interest to U.S. industry. Recently completed U.S. government translations available through the National Technical Information Service (NTIS) are also listed. Notices of upcoming meetings either sponsored by the Japanese Technical Literature program or NTIS or of potential interest to the readership are included.

14. *Science Information in Japan.* Japan Documentation Society, NIPDOK, 2-5-7 Koisikawa, Bunkyo-ku, Tokyo 112. (03) 813-3791. (03) 813-3793 Fax. 2d ed. 1967. 192 p. ISSN 6800-4702. Out of print.

Although this is a dated publication, much of the general data on scientific and technical information in Japan remains relevant and would not be easy to find elsewhere. It provides a thorough investigation of the topic from policies on scientific and technical research in Japan to scientific and technical publications, to libraries and library policies and organizations in Japan involved in science and technology. A large number of appendixes give more detailed statistical information. The data were prepared under a National Science Foundation program grant.

15. *Sources of Electronics Information in Japan.* American Electronics Association, 520 Great American Pkwy., Santa Clara, CA 95054. (408) 987-4200. 1985. 72 p. $45.00.

The work is organized into six chapters covering Organizations, Databases and Databanks, Publications, Research Laboratories, Libraries, and Trade Fairs and Exhibitions. Published sources listed can be in English or Japanese. Sometimes it is unclear whether the language of the publication mentioned is in Japanese or English. Bibliographic information is often limited, and ordering information is generally not given. It is an insightful listing of useful sources, however, which may necessitate further inquiries before one can acquire the publications.

16. *Tapping Japanese Database Resources; An American Strategy.* Satoh, Tom. U.S. Department of Commerce, Japanese Technical Literature Program, 14th and Constitution Ave., NW, Washington, DC 20230. (202) 377-1288. (202) 377-4498 Fax. 1990.

Tom Satoh has been involved in Japanese scientific and technical literature access for a number of years, most recently with the now defunct *Japanese Technical Abstracts* published by University Microfilms International. This report appears in the *Directory of Japanese Databases—1990.* For complete details see under this title in Chapter 11, Online Databases.

17. *Understanding the Japanese Industrial Challenge: From Automobiles to Software.* Jeffries, Francis M. Jeffries and Associates Inc., 17200 Hughes Rd., Poolesville, MD 20837. (301) 428-8204. 1987. 404 p. $49.00.

Covers the following industries: pharmaceutical and medical, electronics, communications and semiconductors, computer, data processing services and software, fiberoptics, automobiles and automotive parts, and manufacturing automation equipment and robotics. Indexes contain information on Japanese information sources and a U.S.-Japan Business Chronology from 1984–1987. The main body of the work is devoted to extensive discussions of Japanese industry and reasons that it is proving problematical for U.S. competition. Appendix A is an extensive section listing sources for obtaining information.

Chapter 2
Conferences, Reports on Access to Japanese Information

This section has been included for those interested in gaining some background on the various meetings that have taken place during the past four to five years on the subject of improving access to Japanese scientific and technical information. By consulting some of these works, one can gain valuable insights into available sources and the processes involved in accessing that information. Many sources exist that are readily available but are generally unknown to many researchers. Although not limited to the U.S., many of the meetings were held in the U.S. under the sponsorship of U.S. government agencies. Access to Japanese information, particularly in science and technology, is perceived by many to be a key to improved competitiveness with Japan. Some sources have been listed here even though they do not represent reports of meetings but because they discuss the issue of access to Japanese information.

18. *Accessing Japanese Technical Information.* U.S. Department of Commerce, National Technical Information Service (NTIS), Port Royal Rd., Springfield, VA 22161. (703) 487-4650. (703) 321-8199 Fax. 1989. 69 p. NTIS Order No. PB90-100165. $15.95.

Collection of essays that originally appeared in the now out-of-print 1987 and 1988 editions of the *Directory of Japanese Technical Information Resources in the United States.*

19. *Assessment of Technical Strengths and Information Flow of Energy Conversation Research in Japan.* Prepared for the U.S. Department of Energy by Battelle Pacific Northwest Laboratory, P.O. Box 999, Richland, WA 99352. Vol. 1 1984. 32 p. $13.95. Vol. 2 1985. 203 p. $28.95.

This study looks at technical strengths of research and development in Japan and at the technical information flow from Japan to the U.S. It reviews 10 energy-conservation-related technology areas. The researchers interviewed scientists and engineers in the U.S. who were familiar with current work in Japan. In the area of information transfer, personal contact was cited as the primary source of information. Most printed sources, particularly those in English, were thought to be too outdated and only presented a small portion of current research efforts. Volume 1 provides an executive summary, and volume 2 is the background document.

20. *Availability of Japanese Scientific and Technical Information in the United States.* Superintendent of Documents, Washington, DC 20402. Available from Documents on Demand, Congressional Information Service, Inc., 4520 East-West Hwy., #800, Bethesda, MD 20814. 1984. 407 p. CIS Order No. H702-23. $97.00.

Hearings before the Subcommittee on Science, Research, and Technology, Committee on Science and Technology, House of Representatives, 98th Congress, 2nd Session, No. 95, March 6-7, 1984. This is a verbatim transcript of the testimonies presented by witnesses from industry, academe, and government agencies to the subcommittee over a two-day period. A great deal of useful information on the issue of access to Japanese scientific and technical literature is provided. An appendix reproduces written statements submitted for the record.

21. *Availability of Japanese Scientific and Technical Information in the United States.* Miller, Nancy R. Congressional Research Service, Library of Congress, 10 First St., SE, Washington, DC 20540. (202) 287-5000. 1984. 29 p. Gratis.

Report prepared by the Congressional Research Service, for the Subcommittee on Science, Research, and Technology, Committee on Science and Technology, U.S. House of Representatives, 98th Congress, 2nd Session, November 1984.

22. *Current Status of Science and Technology in Japan: Grey Literature in Japan.* Morita, Ichiko T. U.S. Department of Commerce, National Technical Information Service (NTIS), 5285 Port Royal Rd., Springfield, VA 22161. (703) 487-4650. (703) 321-8199 Fax. 1988. 20 p. NTIS Order No. PB88-227780. $13.00.

This study of grey literature in Japan looks at the flow of information both within Japan and outside. Dr. Morita contacted public, private, and academic information sources and research facilities in Japan to study this question. The report will be used by NTIS to improve the coverage of Japanese grey literature. Advice is provided for non-Japanese interested in gaining access to Japanese grey literature publications.

23. *Electronic Databases in Japan; An Information Resource to Be Reached On-Line.* Sigurdson, Jon, and Greatrex, Roger. Research Policy Institute, Lund University, Box 2017, S-220 02 Lund, Sweden. 1986. 143 p. ISBN 91-86002-59-7. NTIS Order No. PB88-112065. $23.00.

This is a report on an exploratory project at the University of Lund to access Japanese-language databases online. It provides an overview of the Japanese online industry, giving some search examples, searching protocols, and evaluative comments for scientific, technical, and business databases from Japan. The major databases are covered. Online search costs and available search tools such as thesauri and manuals are listed. It also discusses the future of the industry in Japan and examines machine translation as a major tool in the future for unlocking the resources of Japanese-language information.

24. *Getting America Ready for Japanese Science and Technology.* Morse, Ronald A., and Samuels, Richard J., eds. University Press of America, Inc., 4720 Boston Way, Lanham, MD 20706. 1985. 216 p. ISBN 0-8191-5373-7. $28.95.

This meeting, held February 7-8, 1985, was sponsored by Massachusetts Institute of Technology's Japan Science and Technology program and the Asia Program of the Woodrow Wilson Center for Scholars. It gathered scientists, trade association representatives, government administrators, and language specialists to generate debate on national concerns between the United States and Japan.

25. *Information from Japan: Science, Technology and Industry.* King, Shirley V., ed. British Library, Japanese Information Service, 25 Southampton Bldgs., London, WC2A 1AW. (01) 323-7924. (01) 323-7495 Fax. 1985. 130 p. ISBN 0-7123-0720-6. $24.00.

These proceedings cover papers presented at a seminar on Japanese scientific, technical, and commercial information organized by the Science Reference Library, British Library on September 27, 1984. A bibliography of publications discussed is also included.

26. *International Conference on Japanese Information in Science, Technology and Commerce, Berlin, 1989.* IOS, P.O. Box 2848, Springfield, VA 22151-2848. (703) 323-9116. (703) 250-4705 Fax. 1990. 630 p. ISBN 90-5199-022-7. $97.00.

Reprints of papers presented at the second Conference on Japanese Information in Science, Technology, and Commerce held October 23-25, 1989, at the Japanische Deutsches Zentrum, Berlin.

27. *International Conference on Japanese Information in Science, Technology and Commerce, Warwick, 1987.* King, Shirley V., and Sassoon, G.J. British Library, Japanese Information Service, 25 Southampton Bldgs., London, WC2A 1AW. (01) 323-7924. (01) 323-7495 Fax. 1989. 706 p. ISBN 0-7123-0748-6. $100.00.

Collects reprints of papers presented at the first International Conference on Japanese Information held September 1987 at the University of Warwick. Also includes the discussion sessions as well as the final panel discussion. Valuable, timely information is provided in many of the presentations from speakers from Japan, the U.S., Britain, and the Economic Community of Europe.

28. *Japanese High-Tech Information; A Beckoning Market.* Kiyosaki, Wayne S. U.S. Department of Commerce, National Technical Information Service (NTIS), 5285 Port Royal Rd., Springfield, VA 22161. (703) 487-4650. (703) 321-8199 Fax. 1987. 57 p. NTIS Order No. PB87-184040/FAA. $21.50.

A comprehensive study of the Japanese scientific and technical publications market. Provides a working-level view of the problems involved in accessing Japanese high-tech literature. Focuses on a state-of-the-art report rather than providing a guidebook approach. Suggests ways to enhance the limited access at present employed by most U.S. organizations in trying to access high-tech information from Japan. Chapters include Gaining Access, Language and Translation, Sources, and Information Storage.

29. *Japanese High Technology: Questions and Answers.* Glazer, Herbert. Sophia University, Institute of Comparative Culture, 4 Yonbancho, Chiyoda-ku, Tokyo 102. (03) 238-4080. (03) 238-4088 Fax. 1987. 44 p. ISBN 4-8816-8114-1. ISSN 0913-1620. (International Management Development Seminar Series, IMDS Bulletin No. 114). $17.22.

Glazer, a visiting professor at Sophia University from 1965/1967, 1970/1971 and 1973/1974, explores the nature of Japanese research and development and where it is in relation to Western science and technology. He takes a multifaceted approach with a good deal of statistical detail provided. The Q&A approach is used to clearly set out the information. Topics covered include Japanese R&D Today, The Role of Japanese Government in R&D; International Comparison of Japanese Technology; Long-Range Future Directions of Japanese R&D, Technology Transfer to and from Japan and Processes; and Channels and Contents of Japanese Technological Transfer.

30. *Japanese Science and Technology: Some Recent Efforts to Improve U.S. Monitoring.* Miller, Nancy R. Congressional Research Service, Library of Congress, 10 First St., SE, Washington, DC 20540. (202) 287-5000. 1986. 26 p. (Congressional Research Service Report No. 86-195 SPR). Gratis.

This report describes and analyzes efforts of several federal agencies and private sector organizations to monitor Japanese science and technology developments. Areas where the federal government could take an active role are also discussed.

31. *Japanese Scientific and Technical Information.* Jacobson, C.E. Office of Information Systems and Technology, Defense Technical Information Center (DTIC), Cameron Station, Alexandria, VA 22304-6145. 1988. 30 p. Report No. DTIC/TR-88/2. $13.95.

Proceedings of a DTIC session presented at the Special Libraries Association Annual Meeting, Anaheim, CA, June 10, 1987. Papers include JICST (Japan Information Center of Science and Technology) and Access to Japanese Science and Technology in the U.S.; Becoming an Educated Buyer of Japanese Translation Services; Translation of Japanese Science and Technology Information; and Access to Japanese Sci-Tech Literature—The Users Perspective.

32. *Japanese Scientific and Technical Information in the United States.* Gillmor, Reginald B., and Samuels, Richard J., eds. U.S. Department of Commerce, National Technical Information Service (NTIS), 5284 Port Royal Rd., Springfield, VA 22161. (703) 487-4650. (703) 321-8199 Fax. 1983. 175 p. NTIS Order No. PB83-179903. $28.00.

Proceedings of a workshop on Japanese Scientific and Technical Information held at Massachusetts Institute of Technology, January 1983, sponsored by the Department of State and NTIS. Senior level people from industry, government, and academe with responsibilities for the acquisition or dissemination of Japanese scientific and technical information were brought together to discuss the current status of these activities in the U.S. They considered problems standing in the way of greater accessibility to this information and its utilization by U.S. scientists and engineers. Workshop participants sought to (1) better coordinate existing activities among various organizations; (2) improve quality and comprehensiveness of the existing coverage; and (3) improve the long-term prospects for access to Japanese sci-tech information.

33. *Japanese Technical Information: Opportunities to Improve U.S. Access.* Hill, Christopher T. Congressional Research Service, Library of Congress, 10 First St., SE, Washington, DC 20540. (202) 287-5000. 1987. 51 p. (Congressional Research Service Report No. CRS 87-818-S). Gratis.

This report develops options for improving access to Japanese and other foreign scientific and technical information. It presents rationales for and against a federal role in providing access and discusses the pros and cons of proposals for a greater federal role in the future. Legislative proposals to enhance access to foreign information are summarized. The report also describes several options for enhancing U.S. access and offers estimates of their costs.

34. *Monitoring Foreign Science and Technology for Enhanced International Competitiveness: Defining U.S. Needs.* Peters, E. Bruce, ed. National Science Foundation, 1800 G St., NW, Washington, DC 20550. (202) 357-3619. 1986. 93 p. Gratis.

Proceedings of a workshop sponsored by the Office of Naval Research and the National Science Foundation held at SRI International, Arlington, VA, October 5–7, 1986. Its purpose was to identify ways in which monitoring science and technology abroad could advance U.S. competitiveness. Although the scope was not restricted to Japan, much of the discussion did center around access to Japanese information. Representatives from U.S. industry, government, and academe were brought together for this meeting. The proceedings were prepared from an edited transcript of the taped proceedings and cover the presentations, working group sessions, and discussion sessions. The agenda and a list of attendees is provided in the appendix.

35. *Report to Congress; Activities of the Federal Government to Collect, Abstract, Translate and Disseminate Declassified Japanese Scientific and Technical Information, 1987–1988.* U.S. Department of Commerce, National Technical Information Service (NTIS), 5285 Port Royal Rd., Springfield, VA 22161. (703) 487-4650. (703) 321-8199 Fax. 1988. 87 p. NTIS Order No. PB88-194816. $15.95.

This report was prepared in accordance with the requirements of the Japanese Technical Literature Act of 1986 (Public Law 99-382). Prepared by the staff of the Office of Japanese Technical Literature which was formally established by the U.S. Department of Commerce in June 1987, information in the directory is listed alphabetically under Executive Departments, Independent Agencies, and Quasi-Governmental Agencies. Further information is contained in six appendixes: list of sources that provide report literature to NTIS from Japan; Japanese patent statistics; list of the J-TECH reports currently available; list of publications and seminars relating to Japan from the Office of Conservation; report of the current status of machine translation; and U.S. conferences on access to Japanese information. Table of contents and indexes are not provided for this publication.

36. *Role of Technical Information in U.S. Competitiveness with Japan.* Superintendent of Documents, Washington, DC 20402. Available from Documents on Demand, Congressional Information Service, Inc., 4520 East-West Hwy., #800, Bethesda, MD 20814. 1985. 295 p. CIS Order No. H701-89. $70.00.

Verbatim transcript of the hearings before the Subcommittee on Science, Research, and Technology, Committee on Science and Technology, House of

Representatives, 99th Congress, 1st Session, No. 27, June 26–27, 1985. Witnesses called represented professional organizations, academe, industry, and various government agencies. Appendix includes additional material presented to the subcommittee, including responses from various agencies that had been requested by the subcommittee to provide additional material for the record. Also includes a National Science Foundation report dated April 1985 on U.S. access to Japanese scientific and technical literature.

37. *Science in Japan: Japanese Laboratories Open to U.S. Researchers.* Cutler, Robert S., ed. Technology Transfer Society, 611 N. Capitol Ave., Indianapolis, IN 46204. (317) 262-5022. (317) 262-5044 Fax. 1989. 138 p. $20.00.

This publication presents papers delivered at a symposium held at the annual meeting of the American Association for the Advancement of Science (AAAS), 1989. The nine contributors from academic, industrial, and government institutions in the U.S. and Japan present their observations on research opportunities in Japan open to U.S. scientists.

38. *Sharing Foreign Technology: Should We Pick Their Brains.* Superintendent of Documents, U.S. Government Printing Office, Washington, DC 20402-9325. (202) 275-3030. 1989. 278 p. Report No. 149 (U.S. Congress Committee on Science, Space, and Technology Stock #552-070-05539-8). $9.00.

Verbatim transcript of the hearing before the Subcommittee on International Scientific Cooperation of the Committee on Science, Space, and Technology, U.S. House of Representatives, 100th Congress, 2nd Session, April 27, 1988. Hearing was called to look at U.S. demand for foreign scientific and technical literature and to consider whether new mechanisms should be instigated to improve U.S. monitoring of foreign technology additional to those already in place. Although the subject was foreign technology, understandably most of the discussion focused on Japan and access to Japanese scientific and technical information.

39. *Strengthening U.S. Engineering through International Cooperation: Some Recommendations for Action.* Office of Administration and Finance, National Academy of Engineering, 2101 Constitution Ave., NW, Washington, DC 20418. (202) 334-2000. 1987. 68 p. $11.75.

This report addresses ways in which U.S. participation in engineering and technological activities in centers of excellence throughout the world might advance engineering capabilities and even enhance U.S. competitiveness. As well as recommending increased worldwide cooperation and programs for U.S engineers to continue their studies abroad, the report looks at ways to improve the gathering and dissemination of technical information from non-U.S. sources.

40. *Supply and Use of Japanese Technical Information in the United States.* Shonyo, David B., and Geffner, Janet H. U.S. Department of Commerce, National Technical Information Service (NTIS), 5285 Port Royal Rd., Springfield, VA 22161. (703) 487-4650. (703) 321-8199 Fax. 1988. 33 p. NTIS Order No. PB88-230842. $13.00.

Presents the text of a paper presented at the annual meeting of the American Association of Science, February 1988. It discusses existing barriers that make it difficult to access scientific and technical literature from Japan and gives some solutions to this problem. Some case studies are cited of U.S. companies where approaches have been designed to combat these difficulties. Discusses some reasons for the low demand for this type of information in the U.S. Some interviews with users of Japanese scientific and technical literature are summarized.

41. *Survey of Supply/Demand Relationships for Japanese Technical Information in the United States: The Field of Advanced Ceramics Research and Development.* U.S. Department of Commerce, National Technical Information Service (NTIS), 5284 Port Royal Rd., Springfield, VA 22161. (703) 487-4650. (703) 321-8199 Fax. 1988. 139 p. NTIS Order No. PB88-210943. $21.95.

The Office of Japanese Technical Literature conducted a survey to examine reasons the demand for Japanese technical information has lagged behind supply. Although the survey was carried out within the advanced ceramics industry, one can extrapolate from the results to the broader scientific and technical arena to look at current U.S. efforts to use Japanese information and to look at the challenges facing providers and users of this type of information. Some of the issues include a lack of coordination of the existing resources, the absence of Japanese language skills among U.S. scientists and engineers, the need for more scientific exchanges between the U.S. and Japan, and the need for efficient and cost-effective screening methods for the vast amount of information in the vernacular originating in Japan. The survey, which was conducted under the provisions of Public Law 99-382 (Japanese Technical Literature Act, 1986), covered professional societies, small- and medium-sized companies, government laboratories, not-for-profit research institutes, and universities engaged in advanced ceramics research. The study was conducted by Justin L. Bloom, former U.S. science attaché in Tokyo.

42. *Tracking and Assimilating Japan's Progress in Science and Technology.* Rubinger, Bruce, and Yoshizaki, Kimio. Global Competitiveness Council, 1 Devonshire Pl., #1011, Boston, MA 02109. (617) 723-4947. (617) 723-4961 Fax. 1984. 70 p. $89.00.

For this study, the authors interviewed over 100 specialists in technology-intensive industries regarding their use of scientific and technical literature from Japan. Their findings indicate that English-language information was often outdated and more generalized than that published in Japanese.

43. *U.S. Access to Japanese Technical Literature: Electronics and Electrical Engineering.* Brady, E.L. U.S. Department of Commerce, National Bureau of Standards (NBS), Gaithersburg, MD 20899. (301) 975-2000. 1986. 151 p. 2 vols. NBS special publication No. 710. $21.95.

Proceedings of a seminar cosponsored by the National Bureau of Standards (now National Institute for Standards and Technology) and the Institution of Electronics and Electrical Engineers held at NBS, June 24–25, 1985. Examines the need for improved access to Japanese technical information by providing a forum for individuals representing Congress, the practicing engineering community, industry, and the academic sector to express their concerns and needs in this area. Volume 1 contains selected presentations reprinted together with the summary conclusions and recommendations of Justin L. Bloom. A list of participants in the round-table discussion is also given. Volume 2 is a compilation of the visuals presented during the seminar.

44. *U.S.-Japan Science and Technology Exchange.* Patterns of Interdependence. Uyehara, Cecil H., ed. Westview Press, Inc., 5500 Central Ave., Boulder, CO 80301. (303) 444-3541. 1988. 279 p. ISBN 0-8133-7415-4. (Westview Special Studies in International Economics and Business). $28.50.

Published in cooperation with the Japan-America Society of Washington, Inc., these are the proceedings of the second meeting of the U.S.-Japan Science and Technology Exchange held in 1986. The first such meeting was held in 1981, and those proceedings are also available. As well as discussing policy options for cooperative technology exchange between the U.S. and Japan, the issue of increased utilization of Japanese technical literature by U.S. scientists was also discussed.

Chapter 3
Abstracting and Indexing Services

The number of titles available for this section is disturbingly low. This is the area in which we see the language barrier and the high costs associated with translation to have the most effect. Bibliographic control through English-language indexing and abstracting of the 10,000 plus journals published in science and technology alone in Japan is woefully inadequate.

An early attempt by Engineering Index, a nonprofit engineering society in New York, to remedy the situation never eventuated because of the large subscription costs needed to make the publication break even. A more successful venture from University Microfilms, Inc. (UMI) began in 1986 under the title *Japanese Technical Abstracts*. This monthly publication indexed some 500 Japanese journals in science and technology. Translated bibliographic information and an informative English-language abstract was provided. With a $5,500 annual subscription cost ($2,750 for academic institutions), the subscriber base remained low. A machine-readable version was mounted on DIALOG with access rates reduced for print subscribers.

An attempt in early 1988 to repackage the information into 10 separate subject-specific publications, priced accordingly, still failed to attract the necessary subscriber base, and at the end of June 1988, the publication ceased. Since then the database has been purchased by Scan C2C Inc., Washington, DC (a new corporation in partnership with Fuji Xerox Co. Ltd.). This venture-capital company plans to begin a similar service to that formerly marketed by UMI, but Scan C2C will make some changes to the product as a result of extensive market research that the company has been conducting. Plans call for a more responsive program, possibly utilizing Japanese electronic databases to offer a comprehensive, timely window on Japanese science and technology information. Further information can be obtained from Scan C2C Inc., (202) 863-3850 or (202) 863-3855 Fax.

Some coverage of Japanese science and technology is included in major English-language abstracting and indexing services such as CHEMICAL ABSTRACTS and INSPEC. CHEMICAL ABSTRACTS has covered the Japanese chemical literature, particularly patents, in some depth for many years. INSPEC, produced by the Institution of Electrical Engineers, London, has also been increasing the coverage of Japanese-language journals, but the high costs associated with this are a factor cited by the institution when Japanese coverage is discussed. Predicasts and Newsnet, electronic publishers, are also providing coverage of the Japanese literature. INSPEC and CHEMICAL ABSTRACTS are also available in electronic formats. For more details on these services see the Chapter 11, Online Databases.

45. *Abstracts of Japanese Chemistry.* Japan Association for International Chemical Information (JAICI), Gakkai Center Bldg., 2-4-16 Yayoi, Bunko-ku, Tokyo 113. (03) 816-3462. (03) 816-7826 Fax. Biweekly. $440.00.

Indexes 118 chemical journals which account for approximately 90 percent of Japan's chemical and chemical engineering journal literature. Abstracts are issued within seven weeks of publication of the original journals. Most abstracts are in English although a few are only in Japanese. However, all bibliographic information is given in English even for those entries that are in Japanese. Document delivery and translation into English of original articles is offered through the publisher, JAICI.

46. *Abstracts of Science and Technology in Japan—Electronics and Communications.* Japan Information Center of Science and Technology (JICST), 2-5-2 Nagata-cho, Chiyoda-ku, Tokyo 100. (03) 581-6411. (03) 593-3375 Fax. In U.S. contact U.S. Department of Commerce, National Technical Information Service (NTIS), 5285 Port Royal Rd., Springfield, VA 22161. (703) 487-4650. (703) 321-8199 Fax. Quarterly. ISSN 0901-6510. $50.00 per issue.

This English-language publication began in 1985 and indexes current Japanese journal literature. The "Electronics and Communications" section is arranged in 16 categories with 55 subcategories, including Solid State Devices, Magnetic Materials and Devices, and Superconductors and Laser Applications. Each entry provides author, title, source journal, ISSN, language, and a brief abstract. Document delivery and translation of original Japanese-language articles is available through JICST.

47. *Abstracts of Science and Technology in Japan—Energy Technology.* Japan Information Center of Science and Technology (JICST), 2-5-2 Nagata-cho, Chiyoda-ku, Tokyo 100. (03) 581-6411. (03) 593-3375 Fax. In U.S., contact U.S. Department of Commerce, National Technical Information Service (NTIS), 5285 Port Royal Rd., Springfield, VA 22161. (703) 487-4650. (703) 321-8199 Fax. Quarterly. 120 p. ISSN 0912-2311. $50.00 per issue.

This section on Energy Technology began in 1981 and covers electricity; fuels; nuclear energy; solar energy; geothermal, ocean, wind, and other alternate forms of energy; energy conversion; and energy conservation. As with the "Electronics and Communication" section it indexes current journal literature and provides an informative abstract in English.

48. *C2C Abstracts: Japan.* Scan C2C, Inc., 500 E St., SW, #800, Washington, DC 20024. (202) 863-3850 or (800) 525-3865. (202) 863-3855 Fax. Monthly. $200.00/subsection.

Monthly service containing 100-150 word summaries of articles which are selected from over 500 major Japanese business, scientific, and technical journals. Appearance of these abstracts is generally less than three months after their initial publication in Japanese. Each abstract in *C2C Abstracts: Japan* was previously listed in *C2C Currents: Japan.* Within the broad fields of chemistry, materials science, computers, and electronics there are 23 subsections available for selection. A document delivery service for articles listed in *C2C Abstracts: Japan* is available from C2C Scan.

49. *C2C Alert: Japan.* Scan C2C, Inc., 500 E St., SW #800, Washington, DC 20024. (202) 863-3850 or (800) 525-3865. (202) 863-3855 Fax. Monthly. $5.00 per keyword, $1.00 per abstract retrieved.

This customized alerting service provides customers with an electronic clipping service. The service offers a systemized retrieval from Scan C2C's database according to the subscriber's interest profile. Keywords for the search profile are selected from a keyword list prepared by C2C Scan. Coverage includes the Japanese chemical industry, material science, computer industry, and electronics.

50. *C2C Currents: Japan.* Scan C2C, Inc., 500 E St., SW #800, Washington, DC 20024. (202) 863-3850 or (800) 525-3865. (202) 863-3855 Fax. Monthly. $100.00/year.

This is a looseleaf table-of-contents alerting service that delivers information within 30 days of publication. Information includes author(s), article title, date, pagination, and name of journal. There is no indexing provided, but a subject cross-reference groups journal titles under broad subject areas. Subjects covered include computers electronics, chemistry, chemical industry, materials science, and materials production. A document delivery service for articles listed in *C2C Currents: Japan* is available through C2C Scan.

51. *Current Science and Technology Research in Japan.* Japan Information Center of Science and Technology (JICST), 2-5-2 Nagata-cho, Chiyoda-ku, Tokyo 100. (03) 581-6411. (03) 593-3375 Fax. Biannual. 1,000 p. ISSN 0288-6022. $185.00.

Formerly *Science and Technology Research in Progress in Japan.* Information is selected from the database *JICST File on Current Science and Technology Research in Japan.* Latest edition provides information on 16,209 research projects from 597 research institutions—government and semigovernment research laboratories and public technical laboratories. Information on each project includes project title, brief project description, period of research, budget, names of principle investigators, and the name of the center where the research is being done. The work is arranged into 24 subject categories which are then further subdivided. Indexes include subject, researcher name, research organization, and a directory of contributing institutions.

52. *Foreign Technology Abstract Newsletter.* U.S. Department of Commerce, National Technical Information Service (NTIS), 5285 Port Royal Rd., Springfield, VA 22161. (703) 487-4650. (703) 321-8199 Fax. Weekly, annual subject index. ISSN 0884-7541. $125.00.

Provides a weekly index of foreign technical report literature. The newsletter covers all foreign report literature not just that from Japan. Abstracts selected for this publication are taken from the NTIS database. About 25 percent of the NTIS current acquisitions are abstracted and included here but the coverage from Japan is not extensive because of budgetary limitations at NTIS. Only a small percentage of the report literature received at NTIS from Japan is translated for title and abstract information, however with the recent change in format, more Japanese information is being included. An initial section before the abstract section includes brief articles on current developments in science and technology and policy issues. The newsletter includes reports that are generated as part of Project STRIDE (S&T Reporting and Information Dissemination Enhancement), an experimental program to disseminate to the public science and technology reports prepared by U.S. government overseas offices. This program is operated jointly by the Department of State, the National Science Foundation, and NTIS. The abstract section is divided into 11 major categories as follows: biomedical technology, civil construction, structural and building engineering, communications, computer technology, electro and optical technology, energy, materials sciences, applied physical sciences, transportation technology, and mining and mineral industries.

53. *Japan Auto Abstracts.* Dodwell Marketing Consultants, 3rd Fl., Kowa No. 35 Bldg., 14-14 Akasaka, 1-chome, Minato-ku, Tokyo. (03) 589-0207. (03) 589-0516 Fax. Weekly (48 issues). 10 p. (Daily or monthly delivery also available. Different rate schedules apply). $6,000 inc. fax delivery. Additional $175.00 for floppy disks.

Each 10-page weekly issue includes 30 abstracts of approximately 100 words each. A one-page index for scanning purposes is included. The information is faxed to the subscriber each Monday or for an additional charge can be provided on floppy disks or via electronic mail. Information is formatted using dBase III Plus and can be loaded into an internal database without incurring additional charges. The information is extracted from the six major Japanese daily newspapers—*Nikkan Jidosha Shimbun* (Automotive Journal), *Nihon Keizai Shimbun* (Japan Economic Journal), *Nikkei Sangyo Shimbun* (Nikkei Industrial Journal), *Nihon Kogyo Shimbun* (Japan Industrial Journal), *Nikkan Kogyo Shimbun* (Business and Technology), and *Kagaku Kogyo Nippon* (Chemical Daily). Information covers automobile industry structure and corporate strategy, latest technology developments, and international activity. Customized subject coverage is available for an additional fee. A follow-up consultation service is also available for an additional fee. This service is advertized as a "real-time information service" on the Japanese automotive industry.

54. *Japan Pharmaceutical Abstracts.* Drug Business Research Co. Ltd., 1-25-2 Koishikawa, Bunkyoku, Tokyo 112. (03) 813-0018. Monthly. 150 p. ISSN 0385-0668. $450.00/year.

The aim of this reference tool is to provide rapid, comprehensive descriptions of new drugs worldwide. 2,500 articles are covered each year from 740 pharmaceutical, medical, and related publications from Japan. Since 1986, information on drugs is taken from the Japanese patent literature, and since

1980, from world patents. The monthly abstracts are arranged into five sections: New Ethical Drugs, New Investigational Drugs, Topics, Pharmaceutical Abstracts, and Therapeutic Classifications.

55. *JICST File on Science, Technology and Medicine.* Japan Information Center of Science and Technology (JICST), Marketing Division, Service Department, CPO. Box 1478, Tokyo 100-91. (03) 581-6411. (03) 581-6446 Fax. Monthly. $400.00 per theme per year.

A printed selective dissemination of information (SDI) service is available to subscribers on a monthly basis. Each month the JICST file on Science, Technology, and Medicine is searched for new entries corresponding to 180 diverse subject profiles. Examples of these profiles are artificial intelligence, computer-aided design (CAD), gene recombination, industrial robots, utilization of ceramics in the electronic industry, etc. Bibliographic information is provided. An abstract is provided for about 30 percent of the items. This percentage will begin to increase with 1990 output because JICST is now utilizing machine translation methods to translate into English from the original Japanese.

56. *Metrology and Instrumentation Abstracts: Current Titles from the Pacific Rim.* Brooke Associates (Manchester) Ltd., Freepost Urmston, Manchester M31 2JR, U.K. Quarterly No. 1, June 1989. 300.00 pounds, 150.00 pounds for university and public libraries.

This is being published as a joint venture between the British Library (Science Reference and Information Service) and Brooke Associates. Coverage includes new developments in measurement and instrumentation reported in China, Hong Kong, Japan, Korea, Singapore, and Taiwan. The source material numbers over 1,000 journals, most of which are not available in English. Abstracts are arranged by broad subject headings on looseleaf sheets to facilitate distribution to interested scientists and engineers. Keywords, an abstract, and full bibliographic information is provided for each entry. All source material is available from the British Library, and translations of complete articles can be arranged at additional cost.

57. *NK-MEDIA.* Japan Information Center of Science and Technology (JICST), Marketing Division, Service Department, CPO Box 1478, Tokyo 100-91. (03) 581-6411. (03) 581-6446 Fax. Agent in U.S., Mitsubishi International Corp., 520 Madison Ave., New York, NY 10022. (212) 605-2659; and Mitsubishi International Corp., 50 California St., San Francisco, CA 94111. (415) 544-2700. Biweekly. $640 per theme per year.

NK-MEDIA (Nikkan Kogyo Multiple and Effective Database of Industrial Area), a database created from the *Nikkan Kogyo Shimbun,* covers articles from that industrial newspaper on new products and new technical developments. A printed SDI service in English is offered through JICST. There are five separate subject areas from which to choose: Biotechnology in Japan, New Materials in Japan, Electronics and Computer Technology in Japan, Medical and Pharmacological Technology in Japan, and Robotics and Mechatronics Engineering in Japan. Results are mailed twice a month to subscribers.

58. *Nuclear Science Information of Japan. Oral Presentation.* Japan Atomic Energy Research Institute, Department of Technical Information, Tokai-mura, Naka-gun, Ibaraki-ken 319 11. Quarterly. ISSN 0029-5620. Unpriced. Available on exchange basis.

Formerly *Nuclear Science Abstracts of Japan*, prior to 1987, this publication indexed articles from 2,000 Japanese scientific and technical journals, and some other publications, covering nuclear science. The journal entries were also being sent to the International Atomic Energy Agency in Vienna for inclusion in the International Nuclear Information System (INIS) database. With Volume 18, 1987, the editorial policy for *Nuclear Science Information of Japan* changed such that the records sent to the INIS database were no longer included. Coverage is now of presentations given at conferences, symposia, and other formal meetings in nuclear science and technology in Japan. Data for each entry include title of presentation in English, name of speaker, affiliation of speaker, abbreviated name of meeting, and name of particular session at which paper was presented. Abstracts are not included. Publication lags three to six months from date of presentation.

59. *Science and Technology Serial Reports—Japan.* Foreign Broadcast Information Service, Joint Publications Research Service (JPRS), In U.S. contact U.S. Department of Commerce, National Technical Information Service (NTIS), 5285 Port Royal Rd., Springfield, VA 22161. (703) 487-4650. (703) 321-8199 Fax. Irregular. $5.00 per issue on a standing order basis with NTIS. Need to establish a deposit account with NTIS.

Foreign Broadcast Information Service (FBIS) staff scan, select, and translate abbreviated reports from approximately 250 Japanese publications which provide information on science and technology policy and programs in Japan. FBIS, which is part of the Central Intelligence Agency, has acted since 1941 to monitor foreign media and other information sources in political, economic, technical, and scientific fields. The usual time delay ranges from two weeks to 10 months from the date of original publication. Most information is taken from news sources, commentaries, and official speeches and statements. Articles from the primary science and technical literature are not covered. In 1986, some 7,000–8,000 pages were published by JPRS, which is the domestic branch of FBIS, as part of this service, but distribution was restricted to U.S. government use because most of the material translated was taken from copyrighted Japanese material. Now two versions are published—one for public distribution and the other for U.S. government departments. The only index provided is a monthly microfiche version produced by Bell and Howell.

Chapter 4
Bibliographies

This section includes bibliographies (selective lists of publications) from and about Japan. A few international bibliographies have been included if they have significant Japanese listings. Although most of the bibliographies are current, a few older publications have been included because these may prove useful to the researcher attempting to locate earlier materials.

Trade catalogs, commercial publications, and union catalogs of libraries and professional societies have been included. Outside the scope of this reference work, bibliographies dealing with the social sciences and humanities, of which there are a significant number, have not been included.

60. *Catalog of Japanese Periodicals.* Maruzen Co., Ltd., 2-3-10 Nihonbashi, Chuo-ku, Tokyo 103. (03) 272-2458. (03) 278-9784 Fax. Annual. 78 p. Gratis.

A classified listing of current Japanese periodicals. Includes title, publisher, current volume numbering, language, frequency, and price in U.S. dollars. Also includes an alphabetical index by journal title.

61. *Check List of Japanese Periodicals Held in British University and Research Libraries.* Mandahl, S. M., and Carnell, P. W. Rev. ed. by P. W. Carnell. Sheffield University Library, Sheffield, South Yorkshire, (0742) 78-555. 1971. 244 p. Out of print.

Although dated, this periodical listing, which was issued for the Japan Library Group, can provide useful information on older journal titles and their holding libraries in Britain.

62. *Checklist Of Japanese Government Publications.* Oikawa, Akifumi, Yutani, Eiji, and Moffitt, Emiko, eds. Tsukuba Shuppankai, 34-6 Higashiarai, Yatabe-machi, Tsukuba-gun, Ibaraki 305. 1987. 2 vols. 728 p., 1147 p. ISBN 4-924753-02-5. Unpriced.

Union list of titles held at University of California, Berkeley's East Asian Library and Stanford University's Hoover Institution. Because almost 9,000 titles are listed, this provides a valuable guide to Japanese government publications. Indexes are contained in Volume 2. The keyword index is useful for someone looking for a government publication on a particular topic.

63. *Chemical Abstracts Service Source Index (CASSI).* Chemical Abstracts Service, 2540 Olentangy River Rd., P.O. Box 3012, Columbus, OH 43210. (800) 848-6538. Quarterly with annual cumulations. ISSN 0001-0634. $200.00.

An excellent source of current Japanese scientific and technical journals, although this index covers worldwide journal literature. It is also very useful for expanding abbreviated titles. Provides title, language, starting volume and date, and publisher's address. Also indicates holding libraries in the U.S. and some other countries.

64. *Current Japanese Periodicals.* Japan Publications Trading Company. 1-2-1 Sarugaku-cho, Chiyoda-ku, Tokyo 101. (03) 292-3753. (03) 292-0410 Fax. Annual. 64 p. Gratis.

Provides an alphabetical listing of current Japanese journals with indication of the language, frequency, and price in U.S. dollars. A separate section provides a classified index by subject.

65. *Directory of Japanese Scientific Periodicals, 1988.* National Diet Library, Science and Technology Section, Reference and Bibliography Division, 1-10-1 Nagata-cho, Chiyoda-ku, Tokyo. (03) 581-2331. (03) 581-0989 Fax. Distributed by Kinokuniya Co. Ltd. 1989. 2,271 p. 2 vols. ISSN 0916-1198. ISBN 4-87582-218-9. $150.00.

This is the most complete listing of Japanese sci-tech journals available covering over 11,140 titles. Information is taken from the Diet Library holdings and supplemented by the *Directory of the Research Institutes and Laboratories in Japan, Directory of Learned Societies in Japan*, other catalogs, and individual journal publishers. It lists commercially available publications, irregular publications, publications not available for sale, and those with limited circulation, published in Japan as of November 1988. The following information is provided for each entry: title (Japanese, romanji, and English), publisher or issuing body (Japanese, romanji, English), address (Japanese, romanji) year first published, frequency, pages and size, price in yen, language, indication of the presence and language of abstracts, and type of journal. Volume 1 contains full entries for each title arranged in a classified listing. Volume 2 provides a title index arranged alphabetically by romanized title or English title. Translated titles are indicated by an asterisk to denote that this is an unofficial title.

66. *Directory of Japanese Technical Reports, 1989—1990.* Japanese Technical Literature Program, #4817, H.C. Hoover Bldg., 14th & Constitution Ave., N.W., Washington, DC 20230. (202) 377-1288. (202) 377-4498 Fax. Annual. 571 p. NTIS Order No. PB90-163098. $36.50.

Lists the Japanese report literature received annually by the National Technical Information Service (NTIS). On average these number some 1,000 publications each year. Begun in 1988, this attempts to make the Japanese report literature more accessible by collecting it into a single reference guidebook. Information is divided into 38 broad subject categories which are further subdivided into 350 narrower categories. Complete bibliographic information and abstracts are included. There are indexes by keyword, personal author, corporate author, and NTIS order/report number.

67. *Doctoral Dissertations on Asia.* Association for Asian Studies Inc., 1 Lane Hall, University of Michigan, Ann Arbor, MI 48109. (313) 665-2490. Annual. ISSN 0098-4485. $20.00.

This annual publication, subtitled "an annotated bibliographical journal of current international research," is edited by Frank Joseph Shulman, a professional bibliographer and consultant on Western-language reference works on Asia. It includes entries for dissertations in Japanese science and technology.

68. *Doctoral Dissertations on Japan and on Korea 1969–1979.* Shulman, Frank Joseph, ed. and comp. University of Washington Press, Seattle, WA 98105. (206) 543-4050. 1982. 473 p. ISBN 0-295-95895-2. $35.00 cloth. ISBN 0-295-95961-4. $14.95 paper.

This annotated bibliography of doctoral dissertations in Western languages covers all subject areas including science and technology. An earlier work covered the period 1877–1969.

69. *East Asian Materials: A Brief Introduction for Researchers and Member Libraries.* Center for Research Libraries, 6050 S. Kenwood Ave., Chicago, IL 60637. (312) 955-4545. 1984. 35 p. Gratis.

East Asian titles held in the center's collections are listed alphabetically by country. All but five pages cover Japanese journals. Holdings information is not provided, but titles are given in romanji and English; and the publication frequency is provided. The OCLC number is also listed because holdings information can be obtained from the OCLC database. The subject content of the titles is focused primarily on sci-tech information.

70. *English Language Japanese Business Directories.* U.S. Department of Commerce, International Trade Administration, Office of Japan, #2318, Washington, DC 20230. (202) 377-4527. 1987. 3 p. Mimeographed. Gratis.

This pamphlet lists seven major directories published in the English language, giving the publisher's address, phone number, price, and frequency of publication. A brief description of content is provided for each title.

71. *Guide to Japanese Reference Books.* American Library Association, 50 E. Huron St., Chicago, IL 60611. (312) 944-6780. (800) 545-2433. (312) 944-9374 Fax. Sold by Superintendent of Documents, U.S. Government Printing Office, Washington, DC 20402. (202) 275-2951. 2d ed., 1966, Supplement 1979. 303 p. Out of print.

This is a classified listing by subject somewhat akin to Sheehy's *Guide to Reference Books.* Only reference books published in Japan are included. Each subject area is subdivided by the format of the work, e.g., handbooks, yearbooks. The first edition, 1962, and the third edition, 1980, were published in Japanese only. The second edition, 1966, was translated into English and published by the American Library Association. Although dated, this is the only English-language guide for some earlier reference works from Japan. Most of the works cited are in the Japanese language.

72. *Guide to Reference Books for Japanese Studies.* International House of Japan Library, 5-11-16 Roppongi, Minato-ku, Tokyo 106. (03) 470-3213. (03) 479-1738 Fax. 1989. 156 p. ISBN 4-9900022-1-0. $15.00 (includes airmail).

Covers both English- and Japanese-language reference books on contemporary Japan. Although its scope is humanities and social sciences, this guide has been included for some of the government publications, law, economics, and business materials that are included. There is also a brief section on science and technology. Part 1 covers English-language reference books arranged by subject categories; Part 2 covers Japanese-language reference books; and part 3 covers online Japanese databases. An author/title index is provided for Part 1 and a title index for Part 2.

73. *INSPEC List of Journals and Other Serial Sources.* Institution of Electrical Engineers, Savoy Place, London, WC2R OBL. (01) 240-1871. 1988. 370 p. ISSN 0264-7508. $20.00.

This listing of the journal and serial titles scanned regularly for the INSPEC database contains over 200 Japanese titles that cover the fields of physics, electrical engineering, electronics, computers, and control. Details include full title, coden, ISSN, abbreviated title and country of publication, publisher's name and address, first and last issues covered by INSPEC, frequency of publication, and the shelfmark for the British Library Document Supply Centre.

74. *JPG Letter (Japan Publications Guide Service).* Japan Publications Guide Service (JPGS), CPO Box 971, Tokyo 100-91. (03) 661-8373. (03) 667-9646 Fax. In U.S., contact Pacific Subscription Service, PO Box 811, FDR Station, New York, NY 10150. (212) 929-1629. Monthly. 6 p. 12 issues plus three current directories (Japan English Publications in Print [JEPP], Asian English Publications in Print [AEPP], Japan Publishers Directory). $300.00/year.

Newly published annuals, books, directories, magazines, newsletters, reports and other publications, and print/nonprint materials published in English, in Japan and Southeast Asia are listed. The coverage is very broad because the publishers are attempting to be comprehensive. A limited amount of science and technology material is included. Some referral/information services are offered for subscribers. The publication is also available on diskette.

75. *Japan.* Shulman, Frank Joseph. ABC-CLIO, 130 Cremona Dr., Box 1911, Santa Barbara, CA 93116-1911. (805) 968-1911. 1990. 896 p. ISBN 1-85109-074-6. (World Bibliographical Series Vol. 103). $132.00.

Covers 1,615 major books in English on Japan. Includes descriptive annotations for each entry. Arrangement is by subject categories. The sections on Science and Technology; Politics and Government; Medicine and Health; Economy; Business, Marketing, and Domestic Commerce; Energy; Finance and Banking; Industry; and International Trade and Business should be of interest to users of this guide. Author, title, and subject indexes are included. The terms "technology" and "research and development" in the subject index would be useful starting points for those requiring information on high technology areas.

76. *Japan English Publications in Print (JEPP).* Ball, Warren, ed. Intercontinental Marketing Corp., IPO Box 5056, Tokyo, Japan 100-31. (03) 661-8373. (03) 667-9646 Fax. In U.S., contact Pacific Subscription Service, PO Box 811, FDR Station, New York, NY 10150. (212) 929-1629. 1st ed., April 1985. 370 p. ISBN 4-900178-04-7. ISSN 0910-7908. Published every three years. $170.00 or subscribe to JPGS (see above, entry 74.).

Covering 1985-1987, it includes 8,300 titles from over 2,100 publishers. Lists books, substantial booklets, annuals, magazines, newsletters, and periodicals published in Japan that are in English or contain some English. It also lists proceedings, industry reports, and major brochures. Emphasis is on publications of interest to business and technical researchers. It includes some out-of-print and out-of-stock titles. As well as major publishers, small specialized publishers are included totaling 2,270. There is a subject index subdivided into 132 categories and a title index that forms the main body of the work. This includes details of title; languages other than English, if any; author/editor/translator; pages; page size; price; and ISBN or ISSN number. An author/editor/translator index is also provided.

77. *Japan Periodicals—A Guide to Business and Economic Periodicals in English Published in Japan.* Keizai Koho Center (Japan Institute for Social and Economic Affairs), Ohtemachi, Bldg., 1-6-1 Ohtemachi, Chiyoda-ku, Tokyo 100. (03) 201-1415. (03) 201-1418 Fax. 3d ed. 1989. 94 p. ISBN 4-87605-018-X. $13.75.

Covers 250 leading business and economic periodicals. Information is gathered directly from publishers and sales agents. Publisher address and a brief description of the contents is provided. There are four sections: periodicals by subject, list of publishers, list of sales agents, and list of periodicals arranged alphabetically by title.

78. *Japanese Currently Received Titles at the BLDSC.* British Library Document Supply Center (BLDSC), Boston Spa, Wetherby, West Yorks, LS23 7BQ. (937) 54-6077. July 1987. 110 p. Gratis.

A brief list giving title and shelf number for titles held at the BLDSC. There is no indication of holdings. This preliminary edition was distributed at the International Conference on Japanese Information, 1987, to gauge interest and usefulness for prospective future purchasers. Recipients were asked to indicate the information that would be useful in future editions.

79. *Japanese Journals in English: A List of Japanese Scientific, Technical and Commercial Journals Held by the British Library Science Reference Library and/or the British Library Lending Division.* Smith, Betty, and King, Shirley V. British Library, Science Reference Library, 25 Southampton Bldgs., Chancery Lane, London, WC2A 1AW. (071) 323-7472. 1985. 143 p. ISBN 0-7123-0721-4. 12 pounds.

Lists English-language Japanese journals held at the Science Reference Library and the Lending Division of the British Library. It covers titles published between 1960 and 1984. Section 1 is an alphabetical listing by keyword of English-language journals published in Japan; Section 2 is an alphabetical listing by keyword of translated journals and journals with translations. Entries are repeated under each keyword from the title. Section 3 is an original title list of the journals listed in Section 2. Coverage of translated journals may be from cover to cover or may include only selected articles as follows: full translations of selected articles and synopses of untranslated articles; and translations of selected articles from a few significant journals in a subject (may include translated table of contents, abstracts, or original articles).

80. *Japanese Journals in Science and Technology: An Annotated Checklist.* Bonn, George S., comp. Science and Technology Division, New York Public Library, 5th Ave. & 42nd St., New York, NY 10018. (212) 340-0849. 1960. 119 p. Out of print.

Although outdated, this work is included here because it may still be useful for identification of some of the major journal titles. It selectively lists 660 titles predominately in the pure and applied sciences. Arrangement is by Library of Congress subject headings. Each subject is then subdivided by the types of publishers: societies; government agencies; industries; private publishers; universities pre-1948; and universities post-1948. Under each type (except private), the publishing bodies are arranged alphabetically by romanized name. At the end of each entry, there is an alphabetical listing of the titles published by the society. Titles are given in romanji, English, and the translated title, if appropriate; also provided are frequency, date of first issue, price, size, portion of contents in English (e.g., author and title, table of contents, abstracts), subject coverage, and any other notes. Titles considered to be outstanding in their respective fields are noted. Subject, keyword, title, society or agency, and language indexes are included.

81. *Japanese Market: A Bibliography.* Exports to Japan Unit, #355, Department of Trade and Industry, 1 Victoria St., London, SW1H, OET. (01) 215-4804. 1989. 10 p. Gratis.

This bibliography is contained within a pamphlet entitled *Opportunity Japan* which outlines the information and services available from the Exports to Japan Unit of the Department of Trade and Industry, London. An order form is included for materials available through the unit, and contact information is provided for information available from other organizations. The bibliography section lists reports on Japanese markets published by the Department of Trade and Industry; the Economic Community of Europe; the Japanese External Trade Organization (JETRO); the British Embassy, Tokyo; the Export Intelligence Unit (DTI); and some trade associations. It lists major directories and yearbooks and some general articles and books on Japan of a more generalized nature, which may prove interesting to the businessperson.

82. *Japanese National Government Publications in the Library of Congress: A Bibliography.* Ohta, Thaddeus Y. Superintendent of Documents, U.S. Government Printing Office, Washington, DC 20402. (202) 783-3238 1981. 402 p. ISBN 0-8444-0326-1. Out of print.

Bibliography compiled to make the extensive Japanese official publications housed in the Library of Congress more accessible. Most of the collection at the Library of Congress is a result of a formal agreement signed in September 1956 between the Japanese and U.S. governments to exchange official publications. Description given in each entry is as follows: romanized Japanese title (or non-Japanese title if there is no Japanese title), date, title in characters, official English title if given in the publication, place of publication if not Tokyo, publisher, frequency, and call number. If the work is in English, this is noted. Of the 3,376 entries, 350 are bilingual or English-only documents. The majority of the publications are serials, but some catalogs, directories, guidebooks, handbooks, statistical surveys, census reports, and white papers are also included.

83. *Japanese Periodicals and Newspapers in Western Languages: An International Union List.* Nunn, Godfrey Raymond. Mansell Pub. Co., 3 Bloomsbury Pl., London, WC1A 2QA. (01) 837-6676. 1979. 235 p. ISBN 0-7201-0934-5. 25.00 pounds.

One of the most extensive listings of Western-language periodicals and newspapers published in Japan. It covers over 3,500 titles listed alphabetically by title. Holdings are indicated for libraries in the U.S., Canada, and Japan. Although this list is now 10 years old, it is included as a finding tool for older titles, many of which are still being published today.

84. *Japanese Science and Technology—A Bibliography with Indexes.* National Aeronautics and Space Administration (NASA), Scientific and Technical Information Branch, Washington, DC 20546. (202) 453-1000. Annual. (Foreign Technology Bibliographies Series No. 4, 1989, NASA SP-7067). Limited distribution; only for government purposes.

Bibliography of items on Japanese technology included in the NASA database. Broad based subject coverage includes lasers, electronics, semiconductor materials, crystal growth and materials processing, chemistry and materials, computer systems, and robotics.

85. *Japanese Scientific and Technical Literature: A Subject Guide.* Gibson, Robert W., Jr., and Kunkel, Barbara K. Greenwood Press, 88 Post Rd. W, Box 5007, Westport, CT 06881. (203) 226-3571. 1981. 560 p. ISBN 0-3132-2929-5. $85.00.

An exhaustive study of scientific and technical publishing in Japan. The first section provides an analysis of information activities and bibliographic control in Japan for sci-tech literature. The text is enhanced with numerous charts and tables. Section 2 is a subject guide to 9,116 Japanese scientific and technical journals, including details of where each title is indexed. An alphabetical title index completes the work.

86. *Japanese Scientific and Technical Serials Currently Received.* MIT Libraries, Massachusetts Institute of Technology, Cambridge, MA 02139. (617) 253-1000. 1985. 31 p. Gratis.

A brief guide to serials published in Japan, irrespective of language, held in MIT libraries. Gives location and call number, issuing body, holdings, and language. A subject listing includes complete details for each title. A second duplicate listing is arranged alphabetically by title.

87. *Japanese Serials in the D. H. Hill Library (North Carolina State University).* Simpson, M. Ronald, comp. Technical Information Center, North Carolina State University, D. H. Hill Library, Box 7111, Raleigh, NC 27695-7111. (919) 737-2830. 1984. 52 p. Gratis.

A list of 411 serial publications held at the D. H. Hill Library, primarily in science and technology. Each entry includes details of source language, i.e., English, Japanese, or a combination. The arrangement is alphabetical by title or name of the institution or society, if this is the main entry. It gives the Japanese transliterated title plus the English title if known.

88. *Japanese Technology.* Halasz, Hisako, comp. Science Reference Section, Science and Technology Division, Library of Congress, 10 First St. SE, Washington, DC 20540. (202) 287-5000. April 1989. 14 p. ISSN 0090-5232. (L. C. Science Tracer Bullet TB 89-2. An earlier tracer bullet TB 84-3 contained some historical works). Gratis.

Covers English-language sources that provide information on current developments in technology from Japan. Historical sources are not included. Bibliographic information only is provided, together with the Library of Congress call number. All materials listed are held in the Library of Congress. Material is organized into the following sections: introductory texts; general texts; translated titles; bibliographies; conference proceedings; government publications; abstracting and indexing services; journals; representative journal articles; technical reports; and selected materials from the Science Reading Room pamphlet boxes.

89. *Journals with Translations Held by the Science Reference Library.* Alexander, B.A. British Library, Reference Division, Science Reference Library, 25 Southampton Bldgs., Chancery Lane, London, WC2A 1AW. (071) 323-7472. 1985. 65 p. ISBN 0-7123-0717-6. 5 pounds.

Publication lists journals, both current and ceased that are translated cover to cover or selectively, as well as journals which comprise translations from various sources. Subject coverage includes biological, physical, and information science and technology. Arrangement is alphabetical by translation journal title. Original language titles are also included for each entry. A subject index is included as well as an index of original titles. Although Russian journals predominate, there are a number of Japanese translation journals.

90. *JETRO Publications.* Japan External Trade Organization (JETRO), 2-2-5 Toranomon, Minato-ku, Tokyo 105. (03) 582-5511. (03) 582-0656 Fax. In U.S., contact JETRO offices in major U.S. cities. 1989. 4 p. Gratis.

This small pamphlet lists currently available English-language publications from JETRO. Provides title, a brief description of the contents, pagination, and price in U.S. dollars. An insert provides details of suppliers outside Japan for the publications listed.

91. *List of Publications, Governmental and Similars.* Government Publications Service Center, 1-2-1, Kasumigaseki, Chiyoda-ku, Tokyo 100. (03) 504-3885. (03) 504-3889 Fax. In U.S., contact OCS America, Inc., #1186, National Press Bldg., 14th and F St., NW, Washington, DC 20045. (202) 347-4233. (202) 639-8673 Fax. Annual. 34 p. Gratis.

Covers current government publications published by the Printing Bureau, Ministry of Finance, and others. Often works are published for the various ministries by other publishers. Also includes OECD publications on Japan. Arranged in 16 sections according to the body responsible for the publication.

92. *List of Publications in English on the Industrial Technology of Japan.* Office of Industrial Cooperation and Technology Exchange, Japan Trade Centre, 10/25 Baker St., London W1M 1AE. (01) 487-4120. 1985. Version 3 unpaged. Gratis.

Published for the Technology Subcommittee of the Anglo-Japanese Industrial Cooperation Committee. This is a classified listing arranged by Standard Industrial Codes (SIC) of technical publications from Japanese companies.

Provides title, company issuing the publication, subjects covered, name and address of publisher, frequency, and cost, if available. Many of the publications listed are free; some are "one-off" publications so that distribution may be limited.

93. *National Diet Library Newsletter.* National Diet Library, Reference and Bibliography Division, 1-10-1 Nagato-cho, Chiyoda-ku, Tokyo. (03) 581-2331. (03) 581-0989 Fax. Irregular. Available on exchange basis.

Includes a section "Books on Japan in Western Languages Recently Acquired by the National Diet Library." This lists recent publications including doctoral dissertations and government publications.

94. *Periodicals in Japan.* Nihon Faxon Co., Ltd., 4th Fl., Kurihara Bldg., 7-8-13 Nishishinjuku, Shinjuku-ku, Tokyo 160. (03) 367-3081. (03) 366-0295 Fax. Annual. ISSN 0911-0240. Gratis.

Lists 955 current journal titles published in Japan, including subscription cost. Catalog was not published in 1989, but an expanded catalog is expected in 1990.

95. *Published Japanese Market Research and Selected Business Publications in English.* U.S. and Foreign Commercial Service, American Embassy, 1-10-5 Akasaka, Minato-ku, Tokyo 107. (03) 583-7141. In U.S., contact U.S. and Foreign Commercial Service, American Embassy/Tokyo, Box 204, APO San Francisco, CA 96503. April 1988. 55 p. (Supplt Nov 1988 9 p.) (Japan Market Information Reports JMIR No. 3). $15.00.

This is a revision of a 1984 edition titled *Bibliography—English Language Business Publications in English.* The new title reflects the growing demand for market information from Japan. Part 1, published Japanese market research in English, covers 27 broad categories. A good listing of available sources of business information in English. Part 2, selected business publications in English, covers General Business, Doing Business in Japan, Administration and Management, Intellectual Property, News and Regulations, Statistics, Trade Periodicals, Newspapers, and Trade Directories. Sources in the two sections cover both Japanese and U.S. publications, but all are in English. There are three appendixes that list databases and libraries in Japan which provide additional business information, major U.S. Department of Commerce publications for exporters, and an alphabetical list of publishers. The supplement updates the main work to November 1988. Note: Many cities have regional offices of the US & FCS. Direct contact is the fastest way of obtaining US & FCS publications.

Chapter 5
Subject Dictionaries

The following dictionaries represent a highly selective list of the specialized technical and scientific dictionaries which include English to Japanese capabilities. A small section of business dictionaries has been included, intended to help the English-speaking businessperson with business transactions in Japan. General language dictionaries have been excluded although there are many published. This area is also replete with audio cassette courses and even video programs for learning conversational Japanese.

Translated titles are listed alphabetically by an English title which does not appear on the publication. Where possible transliterated titles are included to facilitate searching in library catalogs.

Many of the entries listed in this chapter were provided by Associated Technical Services, Inc., a bookdealer specializing in technical dictionaries for Asian languages. For details of this very useful source of Japanese dictionaries, see Appendix A. Obtaining dictionaries directly from Japanese publishers may be difficult, so this U.S. source can be very useful. Annotations have not been included for all titles in this section since the titles were not reviewed by the author. Help with transliterated titles was provided by John Bukacek and Donald Philippi, experienced translators to and from Japanese.

SCIENCE AND TECHNOLOGY

96. *Acronym Dictionary of New Technology/Shingijutsu Ryakugo Jiten.* Aoyama, Koichi, ed. Kogyo Chosakai, 2-14-7 Hongo, Bunkyo-ku, Tokyo. 1985. 231 p. ISBN 4-7693-5013-9 (pbk). $35.00.

This is a useful reference for acronyms encountered in technical literature. Each acronym is expanded in English and then translated into Japanese.

97. *AEA English-Japanese, Japanese-English Engineering Terminology Dictionary.* American Electronics Association, 5201 Great America Pkwy., Santa Clara, CA 95054. (408) 987-4200. For sale by U.S. Department of Commerce, National Technical Information Service (NTIS), 5285 Port Royal Rd., Springfield, VA 22161. (703) 487-4650 (703) 321-8199 Fax. 1989. 69 p. NTIS Order No. PB90-100157. $59.00.

This compilation from AEA covers terms that U.S. engineers working in Japanese laboratories found useful. Subjects covered include electronics, computer science, and materials science. The English-Japanese section lists English words followed by the Japanese equivalent in the most common form (either kanji, hiragana, katakana, or a combination). Contains a bibliography to other sources.

98. *Agune's Dictionary of Metallurgy/Agune Kinzoku Jutsugo Jiten.* Owaku, Shigeo. Kabushiki Kaisha Agune, 10 Ichibancho, Chiyoda-ku, Tokyo. 1987. 370 p. $57.50.

This Japanese-English, English-Japanese dictionary for metallurgical terms provides up-to-date terminology for this subject.

99. *Analytical Chemistry Dictionary, Chinese-English-Japanese/Chu Nichi Ei Bunseki Yogo Jiten.* Cho, Kibun. Gakko Tosho Kabushiki Kaisha, Tokyo. (03) 472-2811. 1983. 546 p. ISBN 4-7625-0014-39 (soft). $140.00.

This dictionary provides indexes for each of the three languages so is usable from and into each language. Covers analytical chemistry including instrumentation, equipment, procedures, and chemicals.

100. *Chinese-English-Japanese Glossary of Chemical Terms/Chu Ei-Nichi Kagaku Yogo Jiten.* Saburo, Tamura, and Shiratori, Fumiko. Tongfang Shudian Ltd., 3-1 chome, Jinbocho, Kanda, Chiyoda-ku, Tokyo. 1986. 647 p. ISBN 4-4978-6168-6 (soft). $78.75.

Usable from and into Chinese, English, and Japanese, this is a highly regarded, authoritative translation tool for chemical terminology.

101. *Comprehending Technical Japanese.* Daub, Edward, Inoue, Nobuo, and Bird, Byron. University of Wisconsin Press, 114 N. Murray St., Madison, WI 53715. (608) 262-8782. 1975. 440 p. ISBN 0-2990-6680-0. $35.00.

This is a textbook rather than a dictionary. It aims to provide scientists and engineers the means to read technical Japanese. It uses corresponding texts from both Japanese and English technical publications as examples.

102. *Concordance to Technical Manuals/Inta Puresu Kagaku Gijutsu Katsuyo Daijiten.* Inter Press Co., Ltd., Suyama Bldg., 3-30-10, Nishi-Ikebukuro, Toshima-ku, Tokyo 171. (03) 980-7010. (03) 980-7533 Fax. 1983. 2 vols. 2,298 p. ISBN 4-87087-002-9. $445.00.

Features correct usage for selected key words in scientific and technical sentences used in engineering manuals and instruction leaflets. There are 200 selected English terms used in over 1,000 sentences to illustrate their correct usage, in Japanese. English-Japanese/Japanese-English.

103. *Dictionary of Advanced Materials/Sentan Zairyo Jiten.* Shokabo Publ. Co. Ltd., 8-1 Yomban-cho, Chiyoda-ku, Tokyo 102. (03) 262-9166. (03) 262-9130 Fax. 1987. 427 p. ISBN 4-7853-6902-7. $50.00.

Published for the Materials Science Society of Japan, this dictionary covers 4,500 terms for advanced materials and new materials. Terms are classified into seven fields: fundamental, materials testing, metals, inorganic materials, polymeric materials, composite materials, and electronics materials. Major terms have good descriptions. New abbreviations are also included. Entry terms are in English and Japanese. An English index is included.

104. *Dictionary of Biochemistry, English/Seiri Seikagaku Yogo Jiten.* Yoshio, Masuda. Kagaku Dojin, Tokyo. 1982. 487 p. ISBN 4-7598-0086-7.

Translation of the English language *Dictionary of Biochemistry* by J. Stenesh, published in 1975 by John Wiley and Sons, New York. This translated edition provides English-Japanese and Japanese-English.

105. *Dictionary of Biological Sciences/Iwanami Seibutsugaku Jiten.* Yamada, Tsuneo, ed. Iwanami Shoten, 2-5-5 Hitotsubashi, Chiyoda-ku, Tokyo 101. (03) 265-4111. (03) 261-3965 Fax. 3d ed. 1983, 1968 printing. 1,404 p. ISBN 4-0008-0018-3. $169.75.

Provides for translation into and from Japanese, English, German, French, and Russian. This work provides a comprehensive coverage of biological sciences. Extensive definitions and explanations of terms used in Japanese are provided. The work is profusely illustrated. A number of appendices add to the usefulness of this dictionary.

106. *Dictionary of Biological Terms: English-Japanese [and] Japanese-English/Ei-Wa, Wa-Ei Seibutsugaku Yogo Jiten.* Nagano, Tametake. Sankyo Shuppansha, Tokyo, Distributed by Associated Technical Services, Inc., 855 Bloomfield Ave., Glen Ridge, NJ 07028-1394. (201) 748-5673. (201) 748-5560 Fax. 1975. 573 p. $97.75.

Although an older publication, this is still a well-respected dictionary with excellent subject coverage.

107. *Dictionary of Biology and Medical Science/Baio and Medikaru Daijiten.* Inter Press Co., Ltd., Suyama Bldg., 3-30-10, Nishi-Ikebukuro, Toshima-ku, Tokyo 171. (03) 980-7010. (03) 980-7533 Fax. 1987. 1,146 p. ISBN 4-87198-205-X. $205.00.

English-Japanese dictionary of 140,000 terms covering biology, biotechnology, medical science, and medical engincering.

108. *Dictionary of Biotechnology; In English-Japanese-German.* Schmid, Rolf, and Fukui, Saburo. Springer Verlag, 175 Fifth Ave., New York, NY 10010. (212) 460-1500. 1986. 1,350 p. ISBN 0-3871-5566-X. $163.90.

The dictionary contains 6,000 terms and 300 acronyms used in biotechnology-related sources.

109. *Dictionary of Chemical Engineering/Kagaku Kogaku Jiten.* Fujita, S., ed. Maruzen Co. Ltd., 3-9-2 Nihonbashi, Chuo-ku, Tokyo 103. (03) 278-9223. (03) 274-2270 Fax. 1986. 653 p. ISBN 4-6210-3061-2 (soft). $179.50.

Published under the auspices of the Japan Society of Chemical Engineers, this authoritative work involved 56 contributors. A major dictionary in this field, it contains extensive definitions in Japanese, clear illustrations, and a number of useful tables. Terms are in Japanese and English.

110. *Dictionary of Chemical Terms, Japanese-English-German.* Distributed by Associated Technical Services, Inc., 855 Bloomfield Ave., Glen Ridge, NJ 07028. (201) 748-5673. (201) 748-5560 Fax. 1980. 924 p. $155.00.

This is a new edition compiled by the Committee on Common Usage of Chemistry Thesaurus. It contains 50 percent more terms than the former edition. Terminology is extensively defined and contains illustrations. Because this dictionary includes an English index, the dictionary can be used to translate into and from Japanese.

111. *Dictionary of Chemistry/Kagaku Jiten.* Shita, M. Morikita Shuppan Co. Ltd., 1-4-11 Fujimi, Chiyoda-ku, Tokyo 102. (03) 265-8341. (03) 264-8709 Fax. 1985. 1,528 p. $117.50.

This dictionary provides comprehensive, authoritative coverage of chemistry, chemical technology, and chemical engineering. Translation into and from Japanese and English is provided.

112. *Dictionary of Electronics and Electrical Engineering: English-Japanese-German-Russian.* Ishibashi, Seiichi, ed. Plenum Pub. Corp., 233 Spring St., New York, NY 10013-1578. (212) 620-8000 or (800) 221-9369. 1987. 2 vols. 1,795 p. ISBN 0-3064-2749-4. $195.00.

Previously published as *Ei-Wa-Doku-Ro Denki Jutsugo Daijiten* by Yuichi Ishibashi, 3d ed., 1985, Tokyo, Omusha. This third edition adds terms from the basic sciences—mathematics, physics, and chemistry as well as terms from automation, data processing, instrumentation, nucleonics, mechanical engineering, civil engineering, architecture, and economics to the terms of electrical engineering, electronics, and communications which made up the first two editions. Contains over 42,000 entries. All terms are first listed in English in alphabetical order, followed by Japanese, German, and Russian. An index to entries in Japanese, German, and Russian is included. Lists of abbreviations and standard units are contained in a supplementary section at the back of the work.

113. *Dictionary of Glass-Making: English-French-German.* Elsevier Scientific Pub. Co., 52 Vanderbilt Ave., New York, NY 10017. (212) 370-5520. 1983. 402 p. ISBN 0-4444-2048-7. $250.00. Japanese supplement $45.00.

Published for the International Commission on Glass, the work covers English, French, and German, but a Japanese supplement was added.

114. *Dictionary of Marine Engineering Terms: English-Japanese/Japanese-English/Wa-Ei, Ei-Wa Kikan Yogo Jiten.* Masuda, Masakazu. Seizando Shoten Pub. Co., 4-51 Minami Motomachi, Shinjuku-ku, Tokyo 160. (03) 357-5861. (03) 357-5867 Fax. 1984. 325 p. ISBN 4-4251-1042-0. $59.85.

Covers marine engineering and related mechanical terminology.

115. *Dictionary of Optics and Optoelectronics, Japanese-English/English-Japanese/Hikari Yogo Jiten.* Hioki, R. Ohmsha Ltd., 3-1 Kanda Nishiki-cho, Chiyoda-ku, Tokyo 101. (03) 233-0641. (03) 291-2156 Fax. 1981. 337 p. ISBN 4-2740-2019-3. $117.50.

Terms are translated, but definitions are given in Japanese only. Includes an English index.

116. *Dictionary of Physics and Chemistry/Iwanami Ri Kagaku Jiten.* Tamamuchi, E., ed. Iwanami Shoten, 2-5-5 Hitotsubashi, Chiyoda-ku, Tokyo 101. (03) 265-4111. (03) 261-3965 Fax. 4th ed. 1988. 1,629 p. $185.00.

For translation into and from Japanese, English, French, German, and Russian. The dictionary is illustrated with a number of useful tables.

117. *Dictionary of Science and Technology/Saishin Kagaku Gijutsu Yogo Jiten.* Shizuo, Fujiwara, Yuzuru, Fujiwara, and Takashi, Nakayama, eds. Sansyusha Pub. Co., Ltd., 1-5-34 Shitaya, Taitoku, Tokyo 110. (03) 842-1711. 1985. ISBN 4-38400-030-8 (3-vol. set). $600.00.

Contains 175,000 entries. Volume 1: English-German-Japanese; Volume 2: German-English; and Volume 3: Japanese-English.

118. *Dictionary of Technical Terms in Cartography/Chizugaku Yogo Jiten.* Gihodo Shuppan Co. Ltd., No. 1, Kowa Bldg., 1-11-41 Akasaka, Minato-ku, Tokyo 107. (03) 584-4784. (03) 505-5838 Fax. 1985. 459 p. ISBN 4-7655-4309-9. $30.00.

Published for the Japan Cartographer's Association, this dictionary covers 2,100 terms. Terms from the multilingual dictionary of technical terms published by the International Cartographers Association (ICA) are included. Coverage includes surveying, cartographical projection/production, drafting, type founding, and printing. There is a medium-item index and an English index.

119. *Elsevier's Dictionary of Microelectronics: In Five Languages, English, German, French, Spanish and Japanese.* Nagy, P., and Tarjan, G., comps. Elsevier Scientific Pub. Co., 52 Vanderbilt Ave., New York, NY 10017. (212) 989-5800. 1988. 944 p. ISBN 0-4444-2659-0. $192.50.

Covers 8,521 terms.

120. *Elsevier's Dictionary of the Cement Industry: In Five Languages, English, French, German, Spanish and Japanese.* Onissi, T.R., comp. Elsevier Scientific Pub. Co., 52 Vanderbilt Ave., New York, NY 10017. (212) 989-5800. 1987. 520 p. ISBN 0-4444-2629-9. $192.50.

Covers 5,495 terms.

121. *English-German-Latin-Japanese Dictionary of Chemical Terms.* Hasimoto, Kitiro. Sankyo, Tokyo. Distributed by Maruzen Co. Ltd., 2-3-10 Nihonbashi, Chuo-ku, Tokyo 103. (03) 278-9223. (03) 274-2270 Fax. 1981. 1,141 p.

122. *English-Japanese Dictionary of Computer/Ei-Wa Konpyuta Yogo Daijiten.* Nichigai Associates, Inc., Dai-3 Shimokawa Bldg., 1-23-8 Ohmori-kita, Ohta-ku, Tokyo 143. (03) 763-5241 or (03) 764-0845. 1989. 895 p. ISBN 4-8169-0829-3. $157.50.

Contains 25,000 terms used in computer-related industries such as information sciences, communication theory, office administration, and personal computing. Explanations are clear and concise with examples to illustrate the correct usage. A Japanese-English edition is also available (1989, 990 p., $180.00) which covers more terms than the English-Japanese version.

123. *English-Japanese, Japanese-English Dictionary of Computer and Data-Processing Terms.* Ferber, Gene. MIT Press, 55 Hayward St., Cambridge, MA 02142. (617) 253-2884 or (800) 356-0343. 1989. 470 p. ISBN 0-262-06114-7. $50.00.

A dictionary designed for English-speaking engineers, scientists, and marketing professionals working in computer-related fields who need access to Japanese terminology in the field of computing. In the English-Japanese section, each English word or phrase is followed by the romanized Japanese and then the Japanese characters. In the Japanese-English section, the romanized Japanese word appears first in roman alphabetical order. This is a departure from the usual Japanese alphabetical arrangement and has been done for the intended audience of non-Japanese native speakers.

124. *English-Japanese, Japanese-English Technical Terms of Microbiology/Ei-Wa Wa-Ei Biseibutsugaka Yogoshu.* Saikon Shuppan, Wada Bldg., 1-8-13 Hirakawacho, Chiyoda-ku, Tokyo 102. (03) 261-8887. (03) 263-8879 Fax. 3d ed. 1985. 353 p. ISBN 4-7820-0061-8 (soft). $79.50.

Published for the Japanese Bacteriological Society, this is an authoritative dictionary for microbiology. Includes tables of the bacteria and abbreviations.

125. *Glossary of Technical Terms in Japanese Industrial Standards/JIS Kogyo Yogo Daijiten.* Japanese Standards Association, 4-1-24 Akasaka, Minato-ku, Tokyo 107. (03) 583-8001. (03) 586-2014 Fax. 2d ed. 1987. 2,442 p. ISBN 4-5422-0123-6.

This glossary provides English translations for terms used in Japanese industrial standards. The definition of terms is in Japanese only. Basically an English-language glossary although a few terms give German and French translations.

126. *Glossary of Terms in Heat Transfer, Fluid Flow, and Related Topics: English, Russian, German, French and Japanese.* Begell, William, ed. Hemisphere Pub. Corp., 77 Madison Ave, #1110, New York, NY 10016. (212) 725-1999 or (800) 821-8312. 1983. 116, 42 p. ISBN 0-89116-261-5 (pbk).

Terms for this glossary are grouped into seven categories. Each English term is then followed by the corresponding term in Russian, German, French, and Japanese. For the Japanese entry, terms are depicted in Japanese characters. There are separate indexes for each language with the Japanese index in romanji. Bibliographical references are included.

127. *Illustrated Dictionary of Nuclear Engineering/Zukai Genshiryoku Yogo Jiten.* Nikkan Kogyo Shimbun Sha, 8-10-1 Kudankita, Chiyoda-ku, Tokyo. 3d ed. 1983. 640 p. ISBN 4-5260-1540-7. $79.95.

This is a revision of the 1974 edition of a leading dictionary in the field of nuclear engineering. Extensive explanations are provided for each entry. Useful appendixes include abbreviations.

128. *Inter Press Dictionary Based on Idiomatic Expressions/Inta Puresu Kagaku Gijutsu Jukugo Hyogen Daijiten.* Junichi, Kabe, exec. ed.; Keisuke, Fujioka, ed. Inter Press Co., Ltd., Suyama Bldg., 3-30-10, Nishi-Ikebukuro, Toshima-ku, Tokyo 171. (03) 980-7010. (03) 980-7533 Fax. Distributed in the U.S. by Taylor and Francis, 1900 Frost Rd., #101, Bristol, PA 19007. (215) 785-5800. 1984. 2 vols. ISBN 4-8708-7003-7. $630.00.

Technical Japanese and English. Contains 18,000 idiomatic expressions taken from actual scientific and technical texts. Vol. 1: Japanese-English, 1,742 p. Vol. 2: English-Japanese, 1,741 p.

129. *Inter Press Dictionary of Science and Engineering Abbreviations: English-Japanese, Japanese-English/Inta Puresu Kagaku Gijutsu Ryakugo Daijiten.* Inter Press Co., Ltd., Suyama Bldg., 3-30-10, Nishi-Ikebukuro, Toshima-ku, Tokyo 171. (03) 980-7010. (03) 980-7533 Fax. Distributed in the U.S. by Taylor and Francis, 1900 Frost Rd., #101, Bristol, PA 19007. (215) 785-5800. 1985. 1,014, 1,091, 1,053 p. 3-vol. set. ISBN 4-87087-005-3. $320.00.

Sources used include the Institute of Electrical and Electronics Engineers, Inc. (IEEE) abbreviations and acronym list, common nouns, and accepted slang from scientific and technical publications. This is published as a supplement to the *Inter Press Dictionary of Science and Engineering.* A revised one-volume edition is also available (ISBN 4-87198-214-9). Vol. 1: Abbreviation-English-Japanese; Vol. 2: English-Abbreviation-Japanese; Vol. 3: Japanese-English-Abbreviation.

130. *Inter Press Dictionary of Science and Engineering: English-Japanese, Japanese-English/Inta Puresu Kagaku Gijutsu 25-Mango Daijiten.* Keisuke, Fujioka, ed. Inter Press Co., Ltd., Suyama Bldg., 3-30-10, Nishi-Ikebukuro, Toshima-ku, Tokyo 171. (03) 980-7010. (03) 980-7533 Fax. Distributed in the U.S. by Taylor and Francis, 1900 Frost Rd., #101, Bristol, PA 19007. (215) 785-5800. Rev. ed. 1989. Japanese-English 1,793 p. ISBN 487087-008-8. $275.00. English-Japanese 1,985 p. ISBN 487087-008-7. $275.00.

Over 230 sources were used to compile this comprehensive dictionary for science and technology. Contains new coverage on scientific and data processing terms, including idioms, abbreviations, symbols, prefixes, suffixes, and linking forms. Includes science and engineering-related proper nouns used in Japan, U.K., and U.S.

131. *Inter Press Edition Dictionary of New Business and Science, English-Japanese/Inta Puresu Han Nyu Bijinesu 18-Mango Daijiten: Ei-Wa Hen.* Inter Press Co., Ltd., Suyama Bldg., 3-30-10, Nishi-Ikebukuro, Toshima-ku, Tokyo 171. (03) 980-7010. (03) 980-7533 Fax. Distributed in the U.S. by Taylor and Francis, 1900 Frost Rd., #101, Bristol, PA 19007. (215) 785-5800. 1987. 1 vol. 1,143 p. ISBN 4-87198-201-7. $100.00.

Includes 180,000 terms drawn from actual business and scientific publications. Includes verbs, idioms, and general words. Includes an Abbreviation Data Book for reference to English abbreviations and the equivalent in Japanese. A very useful set for translating business and scientific papers.

132. *Inter Press Handy Dictionary of Science Terms, English-Japanese.* Inter Press Co., Ltd., Suyama Bldg., 3-30-10, Nishi-Ikebukuro, Toshima-ku, Tokyo 171. (03) 980-7010. (03) 980-7533 Fax. 1985. 728 p. $125.00.

Contains 35,000 terms.

133. *Inter Press Specialized Dictionaries.* Inter Press Co., Ltd., Suyama Bldg., 3-30-10, Nishi-Ikebukuro, Toshima-ku, Tokyo 171. (03) 980-7010. (03) 980-7533 Fax.

Inter Press has published a number of subject-specific scientific and technical dictionaries in addition to their comprehensive dictionaries. In abbreviated format these are

Astronomy and Seismology	— E-J/J-E, 1980, 228 p.	$95.00
Atomic Power	— E-J/J-E, 1980, 262 p.	$95.00
Chemistry and Metallography	— E-J, 1985, 660 p.	$125.00
Chemistry and Spectrography	— E-J/J-E, 1980, 342 p.	$125.00
Electronics & Electron Terms	— E-J, 1985, 752 p.	$125.00
Genetics, Zoology, Botany, Dentistry	— E-J/J-E, 1980, 214 p.	$95.00
Information Processing	— E-J, 1985, 736 p.	$125.00
Mechanical Engineering	— E-J/J-E, 1985, 730 p.	$125.00
Physics, Mathematics	— E-J/J-E, 1980, 274 p.	$95.00
Textiles	— E-J/J-E, 1979, 194 p.	$75.00

134. *Japanese-Chinese-English Science and Engineering Dictionary.* Inter Press Co., Ltd., Suyama Bldg., 3-30-10, Nishi-Ikebukuro, Toshima-ku, Tokyo 171. (03) 980-7010. (03) 980-7533 Fax. 1986. 4,235 p. 3-vol. set. ISBN 4-87087-012-6. $545.00.

Covers general scientific and engineering terms. Includes jargon as well as proper nouns. Also covers common phrases, abbreviations, acronyms, symbols, prefixes, and suffixes. Priority is given to the English entry. Title also given as *Inter Press Japanese-Chinese-English Science and Engineering Dictionary.* Vol 1: Japanese-English-Chinese, 1,425 p. Vol 2: Chinese-Japanese-English, 1,367 p. Vol 3: English-Chinese-Japanese, 1,443 p.

135. *Japanese-English-Chinese-German Dictionary on the Industrial Terms/Nichi-Ei-Chu-Doku Taisho Kogyo Yogo Jiten.* Suzuki, Haivo, ed. Gijutsu Hyoronsha, 2-4-13 Kudan-Minami, Chiyoda-ku, Tokyo 102. (03) 262-9351. (03) 262-8986 Fax. 1982. 638 p. ISBN 4-8740-8138-X.

Intended for use by practicing engineers.

136. *Japanese-English, English-Japanese Dictionary of Biotechnology/Wa-Ei Ei-Wa Baiotekunoroji Yogo Jiten.* Daiyamondasha, Tokyo. 1987. 441 p. ISBN 4-4780-8092-5. $50.00.

137. *Japanese-English-German Dictionary on Mechanical Engineering/ Wa-Ei-Doku Kikai Jutsugo Daijiten.* Egusa, T. Ohmsha Ltd., 3-1 Kanda, Nishiki-cho, Chiyoda-ku, Tokyo 101. (03) 233-0641. (03) 291-2156 Fax. 1984. 1,383 p. $235.00.

Useful from and into Japanese, English, and German, this dictionary is considered to be one of the best for its comprehensive coverage of mechanical engineering terminology, particularly industrial applications. Includes a 180-page supplement.

138. *Japanese Scientific Terms/Gakujutsu Yogoshu.* Dainippon Tosho Pub. Co., 1-9-10 Ginza, Chuo-ku, Tokyo 104. (03) 561-8671.

The Ministry of Education (Monbusho) has published a number of dictionaries of scientific terms for a variety of subjects. They are

Agricultural Sciences	— J-E/E-J, 1986, 962 p.	$30.00
Chemistry	— J-E/E-J, 1986, 685 p.	$48.00
Electrical Engineering	— E-J/J-E, 1983, 676 p.	$69.95
Genetics	— E-J/J-E, 1974, 138 p.	$49.95
Mathematics	— J-E/E-J, 1954, 146 p.	$49.95
Mechanical Engineering	— E-J/J-E, 1985, 797 p.	$75.00
Meterology	— J-E/E-J, 1987, 259 p.	$35.00
Nuclear Engineering	— J-E/E-J, 1977, 282 p.	$35.00
Oceanography	— J-E/E-J, 1981, 186 p.	$55.00
Odontology	— E-J/J-E, 1975, 126 p.	$75.00
Physics	— J-E/E-J, 1954, 221 p.	$49.95
Spectroscopy	— J-E/E-J, 1974, 165 p.	$35.00

139. *Mathematics, English-Japanese and Japanese-English Dictionary/ Sugaku Ei-Wa Wa-Ei Jiten.* Komatsu, Yusaku, ed. Kyoritsu Shuppan, 4-6-19 Kohinata, Bunkyoku, Tokyo 112. (03) 947-2511. (03) 947-2539 Fax. 1987. 370 p. $61.75.

A good, current dictionary for mathematics.

140. *Multilingual Glossary of Automatic Control Technology: English, French, Russian, Italian, Spanish, Japanese.* Broadbent, David T., and Masubuchi, M., eds. Pergamon Press, Maxwell House, Fairview Park, Elmsford, NY. (914) 592-7700. 1981. 250 p. ISBN 0-08-027607-5. $61.00.

Published for the International Federation of Automatic Control, this glossary covers English, French, Russian, Italian, Spanish, and Japanese.

141. *New Computer Concise English-Japanese Dictionary/Ei-Wa Wa-Ei Joho Shori Yogo Jiten.* Toki, Hideo, comp. and ed. Ohmsha Shoten, 3-1 Kanda Nishiki-cho, Chiyoda-ku, Tokyo 101. (03) 233-0641. (03) 291-2156 Fax. 2d ed. 1983. 636 p. ISBN 4-8901-9401-1. $55.00.

Illustrated with extensive definitions in Japanese only. Japanese index enables the dictionary to be used for Japanese to English also.

142. *Pocket Dictionary of Biotechnology: English-Japanese/Baiotekunoroji Yogo Ei-Wa Shojiten.* Inter Press Co., Ltd., Suyama Bldg., 3-30-10, Nishi-Ikebukuro, Toshima-ku, Tokyo 171. (03) 980-7010. (03) 980-7533 Fax. 1987. 144 p. ISBN 4-87198-101-0. $25.00.

Lists 1,000 terms commonly used in biotechnology and medical sciences. A Japanese-English index is also included.

143. *Technical Writers' Guide.* Inter Press Co., Ltd., Suyama Bldg., 3-30-10, Nishi-Ikebukuro, Toshima-ku, Tokyo 171. (03) 980-7010. (03) 980-7533 Fax. Distributed in the U.S. by Taylor and Francis, 1900 Frost Rd., #101, Bristol, PA 19007. (215) 785-5800. 1985. 1,140 p. ISBN 4-87087-006-1. $170.00.

A guide to 1,500 essential verbs and usages essential to reading and writing scientific English/Japanese and Japanese/English information. Uses sample sentences to illustrate verb use. English-Japanese arrangement with a Japanese-English index.

BUSINESS

144. *Advanced Business English Dictionary: English-Japanese, Japanese-English/Shin Bijinesu Eigo Daijiten: Ei-Wa, Wa-Ei.* Pashifikku Manejimento Konsarutantsu, 501 Ponpian Heights, 4-4-5 Iidabashi, Chiyoda-ku, Tokyo 100. (03) 210-2121. (03) 210-8051 Fax. 1977. 2,108 p.

145. *Business Japanese: A Guide to Improved Communication* Bonjin Co., Ltd., 6-2 Kojimachi, Chiyoda-ku, Tokyo 102. (03) 265-7782. (03) 238-9125 Fax. 1984. 293 p. ISBN 4-8935-8001-9. $25.00.

Published for the International Division of the Nissan Motor Co., Ltd., this is a language textbook that combines a language course with a reader on society and business. Typical business dialogs are used as examples. These are also represented in kanji and kana for those interested in the written language. Each chapter contains a business information section which provides practical advice on a wide range of business-related subjects.

146. *Dictionary of Economic Terms English-Japanese.* Hasegawa, Hiroyuki, ed. Fujishobo, 2-20 Jinbocho Kanda, Chiyoda-ku, Tokyo 101. 4th ed., 1983. 1,098, 208, 46 p.

Covers 45,000 economics and related terms.

147. *English-Japanese, Japanese-English Advanced Business English Dictionary/Kaiteiban Ei-Wa, Wa-Ei Shin Bijinesu Eigo Daijiten.* Kobayashi, Toshio. PMC Shuppan, 501 Ponpian Heights, 4-4-5 Iidibashi, Chiyoda-ku, Tokyo 102. (03) 264-5774. (03) 269-1943 Fax. 1987. 2,128 p. ISBN 4-89368-027-7. $120.00.

148. *Glossary of Asia-Pacific Business Terminology* Aristarchus Group, PO Box 12625, Tucson, AZ 85732. (602) 620-1240. Annual. 52 p. $25.00 (including annual update).

Guide to standard business terminology, corporate name components, and acronyms commonly encountered in research on Asian business. Spin off from Asia-Pacific database (File 30 on DIALOG). This database covers business, economics, technical developments, and new industries of Pacific Rim nations, including Japan. Three classes of terminology are included: terminology used in searching the Asia-Pacific database through controlled vocabulary, local and regional terminology transliterated from local languages, and general terminology used to describe economic activity.

149. *Japanese Business Language: An Essential Dictionary.* Mitsubishi Corp., Corporate Communications Office, 2-6-3 Marunouchi, Chiyoda-ku, Tokyo 100. (03) 210-2121. (03) 210-8051 Fax. 1987. 221 p. ISBN 0-7103-0199-5.

Analyzes 500 key words essential for conducting business in Japan. This is not a phrase book. It is a study of the meanings that underlie certain words and phrases.

150. *Talking Business In Japanese.* Akiyama, Nobuo, and Akiyama, Carol. Barron's Educational Series, Inc., PO Box 8040, 250 Wireless Blvd., Hauppauge, NY 11788. (516) 434-3311 or (800) 645-3476. 1987. 425 p. ISBN 0-8120-3848-7 (soft). $8.95.

Subtitled *Dictionary and Reference for International Business: Phrases and Words You Need to Know*, this dictionary covers 3,000 terms used in business which are not easily found in general dictionaries. Subjects covered include banking, computers, finance, accounting, heavy industry, and other forms of business. Terms are translated into Japanese characters as well as into romanji transliteration.

151. *Translator's Handbook/Wa-Ei Honyaku Handobukku.* Murata, K., ed. Japan Times Ltd. 4-5-4 Shibaura, Minato-ku, Tokyo 108. (03) 453-5311. (03) 453-5265 Fax. 1987. 531 p. $59.75.

Although this is a general dictionary of hard-to-find, difficult, and new terms, it also includes useful general information such as bilingual lists of government agencies, societies, associations, corporations, and universities.

Chapter 6
Directories and Handbooks

This section has been subdivided by broad subject categories to assist the reader in sorting through the wide range of directory information available. The seven categories are general; research centers, learned societies, libraries; company, product; trade and service organizations, trade handbooks; trade fairs; biographical; and telephone directories.

The general section is a select list of titles that represent some useful sourcebooks that the foreign businessperson or researcher needing general information on Japan may find helpful. The second section, which covers research centers, learned or professional societies, and libraries, is self-explanatory.

The company and product directories section is extensive and covers a wide variety of industries. Obtaining current information about large Japanese corporations is relatively easy. Smaller or new companies are more difficult to locate. Finding a directory focused on a particular subject area will often help because it can provide deeper coverage.

The trade-related directories offer marketing information. As well as directory-type information, a number of handbooks have been included which provide useful information for those wishing to trade with Japan. A separate section lists directories of the trade fairs held in Japan. Biographical directories, relevant to those doing business in Japan or for scientists and engineers, have been included in the biographical section.

The final group is composed of telephone directories which can be a very useful source of information. Many large academic libraries will include international telephone directories in their reference collections.

GENERAL

152. *Complete Directory of Japan.* International Culture Institute, OAG House #407, 7-5-56 Akasaka, Minato-ku, Tokyo 107. (03) 505-2296. In U.S., contact Gale Research, Inc., Book Tower, Detroit, MI 48277-0748. (313) 961-2242. 1st ed. 1986–87. 1,074 p. Biennial revisions planned. $195.00.

Directory listings give address and telephone number for national and local government, commerce, and industry (21,000); foreign diplomatic corps and organizations; foreign enterprises (3,000); colleges and universities (650); trade and nonprofit organizations (600); and Japanese businesses abroad (8,000). Very little explanation of entries or of the arrangement is provided. There are no indexes. Arrangement is alphabetical by company name within each category.

153. *Guide to Things Japanese in the Washington, DC Area.* Japan-America Society of Washington, Bacon House Mews, 606 18th St., NW, Washington, DC 20006. (202) 289-8290. 1989. 40 p. $12.00.

A comprehensive directory of a wide variety of Japanese resources available in Washington, DC. Over 200 listings cover such areas as Japanese libraries, restaurants, trade associations, grant-making institutions, Japanese-speaking doctors, Japanese landscape, papermaking, and job-seeking opportunities in Japan.

154. *Japan Business Atlas.* Business International, Pola Aoyama Bldg., 4th Fl., 2-5 Minami Aoyami, Minato-ku, Tokyo 107. (03) 404-5672. In U.S., contact Business International, 1 Dag Hammarskjold Plaza, New York, NY 10017. (212) 750-6300. 1987. 166 p. $360.00.

Comprehensive coverage of the economy of Japan. Relies on charts and graphs to visually portray the information. Most are then backed up with statistical data and commentary. Covers government in Japan, major bureaucracies, the major industries, state-of-the-art technology, R&D trends, product and market share breakdowns, potential competition, land and office rents, salary levels, and regional development.

155. *Japan Directory.* Japan Press Ltd., Japan Directory Division, CPO Box 6, Tokyo 100-91. (03) 404-5164. (03) 423-2358 Fax. Annual. 1,600 p. $440.00 (2-vol. set).

Published since 1931, the 1989 edition contains 25,000 entries. Volume 1 (Social Life) provides names, addresses, telephone and Fax for hotels, stores, and restaurants; schools, hospitals, and clubs; and embassies, consulates, and government agencies. A classified telephone directory (Yellow Pages) and a list of foreign residents (Green Pages) are also included. Volume 2 (Business Circle) is an alphabetical telephone directory of business firms, including business associations and clubs.

156. *Japan Handbook.* Kodansha Ltd., 2-12-21 Otowa, Bunkyo-ku, Tokyo 112. (03) 945-1111. 1985. 478 p. $15.00.

Edited by the Japan External Trade Organization, this bilingual English/Japanese publication is a concise economic handbook of Japan.

157. *Passport to Japan: Businessman's Guide.* Business Intercommunications, Inc. (BII), Fukushima Bldg., 3-13-21 Minami Aoyama, Minato-ku, Tokyo 107. (03) 423-3971. (03) 423-3996 Fax. Irregular. 1988/89. 181 p. ISBN 4-89377-001-2. $15.00.

Very handy pocket-sized guidebook covering a wide variety of information. Part 1 provides general background information on Japan such as history, education, religion, weather, and politics. Part 2 provides statistical data on most major industry sectors. Part 3 covers practical issues such as immigration and customs, transportation, hotels, and business information.

158. *Passport's Japan Almanac: An Authoritative Reference on Japan Today and Everything Japanese.* de Mente, Boye. Passport Books, National Textbook Co., 4255 W. Touhy Ave., Lincolnwood, IL 60646-1975. (312) 679-5500. 1987. 319 p. ISBN 0-8442-8508-0. $17.95.

Comprehensive introduction to Japan. Encyclopedic in format. Good list of addresses provided in an appendix for other sources of information on Japan. Lists their publications also.

RESEARCH CENTERS, LEARNED SOCIETIES, LIBRARIES

159. *Directory of Information Sources in Japan.* Nichigai Associates, Inc., DAI-3 Shimokawa Bldg., 1-23-8 Ohmori-kita, Ota-ku, Tokyo 143. (03) 763-5241. (03) 764-0845 Fax. 1986. 390 p. ISBN 4-8169-0553-7. $118.00.

Edited by Japan Special Libraries Association, Committee of Statistical Survey and Research, information was gained by survey of 1,778 organizations including industrial corporations, private companies, universities, learned societies, trade associations, and international organizations. Directory consists of a list of specialized information sources, arranged by eight major institutional groups further subdivided by subject. Within each category, arrangement is alphabetical. There are two indexes, English names and romanji names. Each entry gives English name of organization; Japanese name of organization; romanji name of organization; address and phone number; size of staff, size of collection, subject scope, special collections, and house publications. No indication is given regarding services provided, such as interlibrary loan, document delivery, or reference service either by mail or telephone, and whether English is acceptable. Access either open or restricted is noted. Coverage is less comprehensive than the title would suggest, but the main government-related and commercial research and development organizations are well covered. This is the English-language version of the 1985 Japanese publication *Senmon Joho Kikan Soran* which is published every three years.

160. *Directory of Japanese Company Laboratories Willing to Receive American Researchers.* Shinohara, K. National Science Foundation, 1800 G St., NW, Washington, DC 20550. (202) 357-3619. 1986. 127 p. (National Science Foundation U.S. Tokyo Office. Report Memorandum No. 92). Gratis.

The directory was prepared as a guide for U.S. scientists and engineers who may be interested in a research position in a Japanese laboratory. The directory covers laboratories funded by private companies.

161. *Directory of Japanese Learned Societies.* Japan Society for the Promotion of Science/Maruzen, 5-3-1 Kojimachi, Chiyoda-ku, Tokyo 102. (03) 263-1721. (03) 237-8238 Fax. 1970. 140 p. ISBN 4-8181-7055-0. $5.00.

Revision of 1962 edition, this directory covers 412 learned societies in all fields of science at the national level. Information provided includes title in English and romanized Japanese, address, name of president, year established, number of members, and publications of the society. Indicates title of publications, frequency, and language. Index by society name included.

162. *Directory of Libraries in Japan.* Japan Library Association, 1-1-10 Taishido, Setagaya-ku, Tokyo 154. (03) 410-6411. 1986. 137 p. ISBN 4-8204-8610-1. $25.00.

Published for IFLA fifty-second General Conference, Tokyo, 1986. Covers public and academic libraries only. Lists 837 public libraries and 759 academic libraries. Each entry gives name of library in romanji, Japanese, and any official English name. Address and telephone number given. No other information such as collection size, staff, etc., is provided. Public libraries are classified into prefectural, municipal, association, town and village, and private libraries by means of a symbol at the head of each entry. Academic libraries are arranged by university, junior college, and institute of technology. Each category is classified according to national, public, and private.

163. *Directory of Selected Japanese Scientific Research Institutes: Government, National, Universities and Special Corporations.* National Science Foundation, Washington, DC 20550. Available from U.S. Department of Commerce, National Technical Information Service (NTIS), 5285 Port Royal Rd., Springfield, VA 22161. (703) 487-4650. (703) 321-8199 Fax. 1986. (NSF/Tokyo Report Memoranda No. 114). $41.00.

This is a select, rather than comprehensive list of major research establishments in Japan. There are 67 institutes included from government and national university sectors. Industry research institutes included have strong ties to the government. For private industry laboratories see NSF Report Memorandum No. 92, *Directory of Japanese Company Laboratories Willing to Receive American Researchers.* Key government institutes covered include the 12 National Inter-University Research Institutes and 11 of the most well-known research institutes of individual universities. All of the above are under the aegis of the Ministry of Education, Science and Culture (Monbusho). All six of the Science and Technology Agency (STA) institutes are included, as well as the 16 institutes under the Agency for Industrial Science and Technology (AIST). Arrangement of the entries is by agency starting with the Monbusho group, followed by STA, MITI, and then the special or private corporations. Information includes name of the institute in English as well as in transliterated format, address, telephone number, name of the director, date of establishment, number of employees, annual budget, and a mission statement for the institute.

164. *Economic and Industrial Organisations in Japan.* Tokyo Chamber of Commerce and Industry, 3-2-2 Marunouchi, Chiyoda-ku, Tokyo 100. (03) 283-7600. (03) 216-6497 Fax. Annual. 301 p. $27.50.

A bilingual directory of economic, commercial, trade, and industrial organizations in Japan. It covers a large number of specialized trade associations. Gives full name, address, and telephone number in English and in kanji.

165. *Japan Directory of Professional Associations.* Japan Publications Guide Service, CPO Box 971, Tokyo 100-91. (03) 661-8373. (03) 667-9646 Fax. Triannual. 2d ed. 1989. 400 p. ISBN 4-900178-07-1. ISSN 0287-9530. $250.00.

Covers 3,580 professional organizations in Japan—academic, business, industrial, technical, and trade. It also lists some cultural associations and government and corporate research institutes. The main body of the work is an alphabetical listing by English name. For each listing, the romanized version of the Japanese name is also given. Information for each entry includes address, telephone and fax numbers, name of contact person(s), membership size broken down by corporate and individual members, and staff size. Presence of a library, English-language publications, and whether the facility is open to nonmembers are also indicated. A three-letter code is given to indicate the subject category assigned to the organization for subject indexing purposes. There may be more than one code assigned. A brief comment is provided regarding the purpose of the organization and its activities. English-language publications of the association are indicated by a code that corresponds to a fuller listing in the Association Publications section. Three major indexes are included: (1) Japanese name index giving the English name which is used to refer to the main section for full details (if no official English name exists, JPGS requests a suitable translation or provides a translation); (2) subject category index which lists each association under one to three of the 124 categories (there is a complete list of the subject categories used on the inside back cover); and (3) association publications index which is alphabetical by the publisher code given in the main listing for each association. The directory is available on diskette for IBM compatible machines.

166. *Japan Information Resources in the United States.* Keizai Koho Center, Japan Institute for Cultural and Social Affairs, 1-6-1 Ohtemachi, Chiyoda-ku, Tokyo 100. (03) 201-1416. (03) 201-1418 Fax. Irregular. 128 p. ISBN 4-87605-012-0. $6.50.

This is a selective listing of U.S.-based information sources on the political, cultural, educational, and economic aspects of Japan. Covers Japanese government organization, U.S. government organization, Japan trade centers, chambers of commerce, industry associations, Japan societies, nonprofit organizations, university programs, research institutions, and libraries. There is an alphabetical index by title and a geographic index.

167. *Japanese Colleges and Universities.* Maruzen Co., Export and Import Department, PO Box 5050, Tokyo International 100-31. (03) 278-9223 (03) 274-2270 Fax. 1989. Irregular. 760 p. ISBN 4-621-03357-3. $92.00.

This compilation of 95 national, 36 local public, and 344 private four-year educational institutions in Japan was compiled and edited by the Association of International Education for the Ministry of Education, Science and Culture (Monbusho). Information provided includes location, faculty, enrollment, undergraduate and graduate programs, fee, admissions procedures for foreign students, research institutes and centers, and facilities and special programs for foreign students. It includes a brief summary of the institution's history and characteristic features. Lists include preparatory Japanese-language schools; scholarships; school expenses; and an index by discipline.

168. *Japanese R&D Centers in Electronics.* Egis, Inc., 22-1 Ichibancho, Chiyoda-ku, Tokyo 102. (03) 264-1060. (03) 265-2260 Fax. In U.S., contact Egis, Inc., 220 W. Mercer St., #509, Seattle, WA 98119. (206) 282-6001 or (800) 345-8926. (206) 283-4938 Fax. 5th ed. 1988/89. 332 p. $495.00.

An alphabetical list of 219 research laboratories in 130 organizations. It includes details of publications from these laboratories and the status of their current R&D programs. It covers R&D centers funded by the national government, private organizations, universities and academic institutions, and nonprofit organizations. This is a comprehensive directory for the electronics industry. Areas covered include automobile electronics; bioelectronics; computers/peripherals; computer software/information; consumer electronics; robotics; new materials; optoelectronics; superconductivity; and telecommunications. Gives address, contact person, R&D expenditures, R&D to sales ratio, number of researchers, lab achievements, fields of research, and future plans. A final section provides an overview of Japanese R&D in electronics. Included is an analysis of the overall Japanese R&D effort, R&D policies of the Japanese government, national projects, and technology forecasts. Much of the information is presented in the form of diagrams, tables, and charts.

169. *Japanese Research Institutes Funded by Ministries Other than Education.* Sakiyama, Seikoh, comp. Office of Naval Research, Scientific Liaison Group, American Embassy, APO San Francisco, CA 96503. 1981. 107 p. Gratis.

A listing of Japanese investigators and laboratories published as an aid for foreign scientists and engineers. A companion volume (ONR Scientific Monograph, No. 2, by Seikoh Sakiyama) lists research institutes funded by the Ministry of Education. Name, address, and telephone number are included for the 159 institutes covered. If the specialty of the institute is not obvious, an explanatory note is included. The size of each lab is given when available.

170. *Japanese Research Institutes Funded by Private Corporations.* Kim, Young B., and Sakiyama, Seikoh, comps. Department of the Navy, Office of Naval Research Far East, Ballston Tower No. 1, 800 N. Quincy St., Arlington, VA 22217-5000. (202) 696-4258. 1983. 210 p. Gratis.

Covers 100 research laboratories, giving name, address, telephone number, specialty field, size, and scope of activity. This information is also provided for the parent company of each lab. After the statistical information listed in tabular form, a narrative description of the laboratory's activities is given. These are selected translations of serialized reports on Japanese industrial laboratories that appeared in *Nikkei Kogyo Shimbun*, a major Japanese daily newspaper covering technology. The table of contents groups the laboratories into 30 broad subject classifications. Two additional indexes are provided—an alphabetical list of parent companies with their related laboratories and a list of companies with English and corresponding romanji names.

171. *Japanese Research Institutes Funded by the Ministry of Education.* Sakiyama, Seikoh, comp. Department of the Navy, Office of Naval Research, Ballston Tower No. 1, 800 N. Quincy St., Arlington, VA 22217-5000. (202) 696-4258. 1980. 134 p. (Scientific Monograph of the Department of the Navy, Office of Naval Research, Tokyo; Report ONRT M2). Gratis.

Listing developed for foreign visitors of investigators and laboratories in Japan. It gives name, address, and telephone number for 317 institutes supported by the Ministry of Education. A companion volume listing laboratories supported by ministries other than the Ministry of Education is *Japanese Research Institutes Funded by Private Corporations*, compiled by Young B. Kim. Information provided includes size of laboratory in terms of staff and budget with explanatory notes if laboratory specialty is not apparent in the name. Indexes by subject, institute, and city are included.

172. *Libraries in Japan.* Japan Library Association, 1-1-10 Taishido, Setagaya-ku, Tokyo 154. (03) 410-6411. 2d rev. ed. 1980. 48 p. $5.00.

A selective listing of 26 libraries chosen as being representative of all types of libraries in Japan. It is arranged by geographical location in Japan. Each entry gives address, telephone number, a description of the library, its history, details of the collection, and approximate volume counts. Access to the library, hours of opening, and circulation policies are provided.

173. *National Laboratories and Research Public Corporations in Japan.* Science and Technology Agency, 2-2-2 Kasumigaseki, Chiyoda-ku, Tokyo 100. (03) 581-5271. (03) 593-1370 Fax. 1988. Part 1, 152 p.; Part 2, 40 p. Gratis.

Listing of national laboratories and public research corporations in Japan. Publication is a result of the 1986 General Guideline for Science and Technology which aims to strengthen international cooperation and disseminate R&D results. Laboratories listed form the core of current R&D activities in Japan. Laboratories are listed under the ministries that administer them. Information provided includes address, telephone and fax numbers, date of establishment and budget, research activities, main facilities, and an organization chart. Photographs are included. This work supersedes *Government Research Institutes in Japan.* A listing for this earlier work is included also because not all information included in the earlier work has been carried over into the current publication.

174. *Science and Technology in Japan.* Sigurdson, Jon, and Anderson, Alun M. Longman Group U.K. Ltd., Westgate House, 6th Fl., The High, Harlow, Essex CM20 1YR. (0279) 44-2601. (0279) 44-4501 Fax. 2d ed. 1989. 352 p. ISBN 0-582-03684-4. (Longman Guide to World Science and Technology, Vol. 4). 63.00 pounds.

Discusses the patterns of science and technology in Japan, both current and historical. Features chapters on government science policy, the ministries and major science programs; education and academic research; and industrial research and development. It provides a comprehensive description of Japan's major government-industry cooperative research projects and efforts to stimulate basic research. There is a directory of major research establishments, including universities, university research institutes, government research institutes, private company research establishments, and independent research institutes. Learned and professional societies and associations, information sources and international cooperation in science and technology are also described. An alphabetical index of establishments and a subject index are included. This work is useful as a detailed narrative description of Japanese science and technology policy.

175. *Scientific Research Institutes under the Jurisdiction of the Ministry of Education, Science and Culture (Monbusho).* The Japan Society for Promotion of Science, 5-3-1 Kajimachi, Chiyoda-ku, Tokyo 102. (03) 263-1721. (03) 237-8238 Fax. 1987. 318 p. Unpriced.

Supervised by Monbusho, this work was edited by the Japan Society for the Promotion of Science. Data were provided by a survey on the status of research institutes, conducted by the Ministry of Education, Science and Culture in June 1979. It covers 95 research institutes grouped according to the type of controlling agency or affiliated institution. Data provided include name in English and Japanese; address; telphone number; year founded; objectives; name of the director; number of personnel; annual budget; details of publications; names of any attached facilities; and the organization of research divisions and departments. Indexes by name of institute, by university, and by subject area are included. An appendix provides the names and addresses of university research facilities not included in the main part of the directory.

176. *Survey of Japanese Collections in the United States.* Fukuda, Naomi. Center for Japanese Studies, 108 Lane Hall, University of Michigan, Ann Arbor, MI 48109. 1981. 182 p. ISBN 0-939512-09-2. $5.00.

Reports on 28 major U.S. library collections on Japan. Gives a broad view of each library's operations including holdings, coverage, staffing, and financing. Most collections described do not contain significant holdings in science and technology.

COMPANY, PRODUCT

177. *Asia-Pacific Corporate Organization.* Sanchez, James Joseph, comp. Aristarchus Group, PO Box 12625, Tucson, AZ 85732. (602) 620-1240. 1989. 40 p. $145.00.

A reference guide to private Asian corporate organizations, including their subsidiaries, joint ventures worldwide, government organizations, conglomerates, banking and financial organizations, and nongovernmental organizations. Includes name changes, ownership, and hierarchical relationships among groups of firms. This is a spinoff from the Asia-Pacific database (File 30 on DIALOG).

178. *Biotechnology Guide Japan.* Stockton Press, 15 E. 26th St., New York, NY 10010. (800) 221-2123 or (212) 481-1334. 1989. 650 p. ISBN 0-935859-66-7. $250.00.

Provides detailed information on 500 Japanese biotechnology companies. Information provided includes name, address, telephone, telex and fax numbers, key personnel, annual revenue and profit, name of organization conducting R&D, number of researchers, charts including status of R&D and merchandizing, partnerships and affiliations, and lists of recent patents.

179. *Biotechnology in Japan: The Reference Source.* Japan Pacific Associates, Bunkyo-ku, Tokyo. In U.S., contact Japan Pacific Associates, 467 Hamilton Ave., #2, Palo Alto, CA 94301. (415) 322-8441. 1984. 322 p. (1984 edition out-of-print but new edition due 1990).

Provides a historical overview of the biotechnology industry in Japan. It covers various biotechnology industries and government ministries. Assesses major players in each sector and important issues facing the industry. It tackles the industry in Japan from a foreign company perspective. Covering 200 companies, it aims at being a more "comprehensive guidebook" for executives. It is indexed by company and product.

180. *Biotechnology Japan.* Dibner, Mark D., and White, R. Steven. McGraw Hill Book Co., 1221 Ave. of the Americas, New York, NY 10020. (212) 512-2000. (800) 262-4729. 1989. 313 p. $180.00.

Primarily a listing of Japanese companies in the biotechnology area. Gives address, primary areas of interest, sales, research and development expenditures, financing, and joint ventures and partnerships. The book covers the biotechnology industry in depth and is liberally cross-referenced.

181. *Buyers Guide of Tokyo.* Tokyo Foreign Trade Association, Tokyo Boeki Kai, Tokyo Trade Center, 1-7-8 Kaigan, Minato-ku, Tokyo 105. (03) 438-2026. (03) 433-7164 Fax. Biennial. 575 p. Gratis.

Covers over 3,000 companies in Tokyo. Most are medium-sized, interested in exporting to foreign countries. There is a classified product index.

182. *Comprehensive Directory of Japanese Pharmaceutical and Related Firms.* Ohtsuka, K., ed. Technomic Information Service, Inc., CPO Box 882, Sun Bldg., 8-7 Tomizawacho Nihonbashi, Chuo-ku, Tokyo 103. (03) 666-2952. (03) 666-2730 Fax. 2d ed. 1984. 229 p. $155.00.

With this second edition, a more concerted effort was made to contact the 446 companies directly for information. These companies are estimated to represent over 90 percent of Japan's pharmaceutical production and sales. Lists type of business, sales structure, principal products (both trade and generic names), licenses, and customers and suppliers.

183. *Consumer Japan 1990.* Euromonitor. Distributed by Gale Research Inc., Book Tower, Dept. 77748, Detroit, MI 48277-0748. (800) 877-4253. (313) 961-6083 Fax. Annual. 350 p. ISBN 0-86338-326-2. $425.00.

Provides information on 150 Japanese consumer products, demographic trends, 75 major companies, and 35 retailers. The directory is arranged by subject within the following six sections—market overview, Japanese statistical facts, major consumer markets, major Japanese companies, major Japanese retailers, and sources of information. This later section lists libraries with substantial business collections, trade associations, government offices, and other organizations having a marketing focus. Company names index included.

184. *Directory, Affiliates and Offices of Japanese Firms in the ASEAN Countries.* Japan External Trade Organization (JETRO), 2-2-5 Toranomon, Minato-ku, Tokyo 105. (03) 582-3518. (03) 587-2485 Fax. 1982. 254 p. ISBN 4-8224-0147-2. $37.50.

Listing of 2,326 Japanese capital affiliated companies, branches, and liaison offices. Companies are listed within five sections by country—Indonesia, Malaysia, Philippines, Singapore, and Thailand. Within each of these sections, companies are grouped by industry type. Each entry gives name of local company, address, telephone, type of business, and names and equity share of other participants. Two indexes are provided—alphabetically by company name and by industry type.

185. *Directory: Japanese-Affiliated Companies in the U.S.A. and Canada.* Japan External Trade Organization (JETRO), 2-2-5 Toranomon, Minato-ku, Tokyo 105. (03) 582-3518. (03) 587-2485 Fax. Biennial. 677 p. ISBN 4-8224-0426-9. $150.00.

Listing of 8,200 Japanese companies and restaurants arranged by state/province. Each listing includes company name, status, parent company, address, telephone number, fax number, principal officers, primary business activity (import, export, manufacture, etc.), products and services, and year of establishment. Indexes include classified listing by type of business or product in the U.S.; alphabetical listing of companies in the U.S.; classified listing by type of business or product in Canada; alphabetical listing of companies in Canada; and listing of advertisers. Japanese government organizations in the

U.S. and Canada and representative state and provincial offices in Japan are also provided.

186. *Directory of American Electronics Companies in Japan.* American Electronics Association, Japan Office, U.S. Electronics Industries Office, 3F Nambu Bldg., 3-3 Kioicho, Chiyoda-ku, Tokyo 102. (03) 237-7195. (03) 237-1237 Fax. 1986. 105 p. $28.00.

This is a bilingual publication providing indexes by company name in Japanese/English and English/Japanese and by industry group in Japanese and English. There is a quick listing by company name giving telephone and fax numbers, and parent-to-subsidiary and subsidiary-to-parent company indexes.

187. *Directory of American Firms in Foreign Countries: Japan.* World Trade Academy Press, Inc., 50 E. 42 St., #509, New York, NY 10017-5480. (212) 697-4999. 1988. 55 p. $26.00.

This publication covers 690 Japanese companies giving name and address of parent company in the U.S., name and address of subsidiary or affiliate in Japan, and the main business activity.

188. *Directory of Foreign Capital Affiliated Enterprises in Japan.* Business Intercommunications, Inc. (BII), CPO Box 587, Tokyo 100-91. (03) 423-3971. (03) 423-3996 Fax. Annual. 1,045 p. $400.00.

This is the most complete listing of Japanese companies and their foreign capital affiliations published in English. Four thousand companies are listed. Data are included on foreign companies in Japan; Japanese and foreign investors; foreign capital ratio; date of establishment; capital; and number of employees. A cross-reference index lists enterprises in which Japanese capital was invested. Companies that suspended operations are also noted. *Monthly Report*, by the same publisher, provides more timely information.

189. *Directory of Japanese Companies in U.S.A.* Economic World Ltd., 60 E. 42 St., #734, New York, NY 10165. (212) 986-1588. (212) 557-7541 Fax. 536 p. Annual. $270.00.

A listing of 500-600 companies includes photographs of top executives. Arrangement of company listings is within 16 industry categories: auto equipment and related supplies; banking, insurance, securities, leasing; business machines, office supplies; construction, development, real estate; consumer electronics; related products and home appliances; foodstuffs and provisions; glass, ceramics and homewares; heavy industries, electrical equipment and industrial electronics; iron and steel, nonferrous metals and related products; miscellaneous products and services; petroleum, chemicals and related products; photographic, optical products and related products; retail sales and restaurants; textile, pulp and paper; trading companies; transportation, warehousing and travel. An alphabetical index by company name is included.

190. *Directory of Japanese Firms and Representatives in Hawaii.* International Services Branch, Department of Planning and Economic Development, State of Hawaii, PO Box 2359, Honolulu, HI 96804. (808) 548-3048. 1987. 28 p. (International Business Series No. 50, Nov. 1987). Gratis.

Guide to Japanese companies and organizations that maintain operational offices in Hawaii. Provides an alphabetized index by company name. There is also an index by major activity of each company. Company entries are listed alphabetically. Information includes address, contact telephone number, parent company, and main activity of the company in Hawaii.

191. *Directory of Japanese Health Care Industry.* Japan Publications, Inc., Kyodo (Akasaka) Bldg., 4-3-1 Akasaka, Minato-ku, Tokyo 107. (03) 589-3627. (03) 505-0376 Fax. In U.S., contact Japan Publications, Inc., 150 Post St., #500, San Francisco, CA 94108. (415) 772-5555. (415) 772-5659 Fax. Annual. 275 p. ISBN 0-8002-4243-2. $450.00.

Profiles 800 manufacturers, importers, and distributors. It covers private, public, and foreign capital firms, also industrial associations and organizations. Listings are cross-referenced by market segment. Each entry provides address, phone number, size, type of business, business specialization, and sales information. The business data cover the last two years.

192. *Directory of Japanese Importers by Product. U.S.A. Edition.* Business Intercommunications, Inc. (BII), CPO Box 587, Tokyo 100-91. (03) 423-3971. (03) 423-3996 Fax. 1985. Irregular. 919 p. $420.00.

A listing of U.S. manufacturers and exporters with their Japanese importers and agents. It is arranged alphabetically by the name of the U.S. company. There are two indexes containing an alphabetical listing by product type and by Japanese company name. Data were collected from U.S. embassy and market surveys conducted by Business Intercommunications, Inc., over the last 17 years. Because this method of data collection by survey was very time-consuming, much of the data is outdated in this area of constant change.

193. *Genetic Engineering and Biotechnology Related Firms Worldwide Directory.* Sittig, Marshall. Sittig and Noyes, PO Box 592, Kingston, NJ 08528. 8th ed. 1989. 606 p. ISSN 0890-0906. ISBN 0-8002-4238-6. $240.00.

Covers 265 Japanese firms and a total of 4,000 companies worldwide. Large and small companies are represented listing equity interests held by other companies, data on number of employees, and areas of concentration. Non-U.S. companies are arranged alphabetically by county name; otherwise each company is listed alphabetically. Entries give name, address, telephone, telex and fax numbers, parent/subsidiary relationships, and brief description of research interests. Any U.S. joint ventures or agreements and presence in the U.S. are also noted. Entries are not standardized. Amount of detail varies for each entry.

194. *Guide Book of Japanese Optical and Precision Instruments.* Japan Optical Industry Association, Kikai Shinko Bldg., 3-5-8 Shibakoen, Minato-ku, Tokyo 105. (03) 431-7073. Biennial. 1989/90. 190 p. $25.00.

Lists names of companies with membership in Japan's eight major associations concerned with optical precision instruments. Foreign affiliates and a substantial number of product catalogs for listed companies are included.

195. *High Tech in Japan.* High Tech Research Institute, 5th Fl. Tama Bldg., 1-3-18 Akasaka, Minato-ku, Tokyo. (03) 583-8880. 1985. 216 p. $90.00.

Provides detailed information on activities, structure, history and objectives of high-tech industries, industrial associations, and quasi-government organizations in Japan. Coverage is broad including areas such as computers and electronics, energy, space, new materials, automotive, oceanography, civil engineering, and biotechnology. Layout is glossy with full color photographs. Company and organization indexes are included. A useful table is included which sets out clearly the structure of science and technology administration in Japan.

196. *High-Tech Start-Up Ventures in Japan: An Index to 500 Selected Companies.* Nihon Keizai Shimbun Inc. (Japan Economic Journal), 1-9-5 Ohtemachi, Chiyoda-ku, Tokyo 100. (03) 270-0251. 1984. 245 p. ISBN 4532-05502-4. $149.50.

An index to the Japanese high-tech venture industry, part 1 is a narrative overview of the high-tech start-up venture situation in Japan. It discusses the changing structure, overseas strategy, venture capital, research and development, and fund raising. Part 2 is the actual listing of companies divided into 20 industrial groups. An appendix lists venture capital firms in Japan. There is an alphabetical index by company name.

197. *JCW (Japan Chemicals Week) Chemicals Guide.* Chemical Daily Co. Ltd., 3-16-8 Nihonbashi Hamacho, Chuo-ku, Tokyo 103. (03) 663-7932. (03) 663-2530 Fax. 1986. 50 p. ISSN 0047-1755. $369.00/year.

Section 1 lists 11,400 chemicals by chemical name. An ECS reference number, CAS registry number, and names of manufacturers are given. Section 2 is a list of manufacturers' addresses and a list of distributors' and traders' addresses. The guide covers inorganic and organic industrial chemicals, plastics (excludes finished products), chemical and synthetic fibers, fertilizers, dyes and pigments, pharmaceutical raw materials, pesticides, paints and varnishes, adhesives, catalysts, polymeric additives, surface active agents, food additives, metal surface treatment agents, and lubricant additives.

198. *Japan Business Directory.* Diamond Lead Co. Ltd., 1-4-2 Kasumigaseki, Chiyoda-ku, Tokyo 100. (03) 504-6792. (03) 504-6798 Fax. Annual. 1,700 p. ISBN 0-8002-4250-5. ISSN 0910-1780. $400.00.

Formerly *Diamond's Japan Business Directory*, this directory includes an alphabetical index of 1,500 companies; industry index within industry classification by company name; a directory guide that provides information on Japanese companies and brand and trade names used by Japanese companies; and financial information. The company information includes company logo; name (either romanized or a direct translation); date of establishment; capital stock; and address and telephone number. General information on the company provides background, principal officers, number of employees, and financial statements. For each company, there is a 10-year review, together with comments written by Diamond's editorial staff. Finally, there is an industry survey focusing on particular industries that drew attention in the preceding year.

199. *Japan Chemical Directory.* Chemical Daily Co. Ltd., 3-16-8 Nihonbashi Hama-cho, Chuo-ku, Tokyo 103. (03) 663-7932. (03) 663-2530 Fax. Annual. 750 p. ISSN 0075-3203. $180.00.

A comprehensive survey of 1,350 Japanese chemical companies and related organizations. Detailed descriptions include address, telephone number, capital, names of executives, turnover, main products, and branches in Japan and overseas. An appendix includes 660 chemical enterprises from Hong Kong, Korea, Singapore, Taiwan, and Australia.

200. *Japan Company Handbook.* Toyo Keizai Shinposha Ltd., The Oriental Economist, 1-4 Nihonbashi, Hongoku-cho, Chuo-ku, Tokyo 103. (03) 270-4111. Quarterly. 1,264 p. $194.00.

This is a company directory of firms listed on the First Sections of the Tokyo, Osaka, and Nagoya stock exchanges. Basic management and financial data are provided for 1,165 companies for the past five years. The section on "How to Use This Handbook" provides a detailed, well-written guide to using the data contained therein. Listings are grouped into 62 industry categories and within these divided by order of the security code number for each company. An alphabetical index by company name is provided. Information for each company includes equipment or service provided, outlook, income, sales breakdown, stock prices, stock price chart, stocks, financial data, facility investments including R&D expenditures, references, date of establishment, and employee information. The address of the principal office and up to three overseas offices are given. A companion publication *Second Section Firms* provides similar information for companies listed on the second section of the stock exchange.

201. *Japan EBG [Japan Electronics Buyers Guide].* Dempa Publications Inc., 1-11-15 Higoshi-Gotanda, Shingawa-ku, Tokyo 141. (03) 445-6111. Annual. Vol. 1, Components, 379 p., $58.00; Vol. 2, Consumer Electronics, 294 p., $58.00; Vol. 3, Professional Equipment, 362 p., $58.00; Vol. 4, Office Electronics, 185 p., $54.00. ISBN 0-8002-4133-9. 4-vol. set. $185.00.

Manufacturers are listed by classified product listings. Over 2,000 items are covered for 1,540 manufacturers. A trading firm directory of 800 companies is also included. Each entry lists key personnel; address, telephone, and fax numbers; capital; annual sales; number of employees; export sales; trade names; overseas plants; and main products. Branches and agents, an alphabetical listing of trade names, and related organizations are also included.

202. *Japan Publishers Directory.* Japan Publications Guide Service, CPO Box 971, Tokyo, 100-91. (03) 661-8373. (03) 667-9646 Fax. Irregular. 1st ed. 1986. 198 p. ISBN 4-900178-05-5. $55.00.

The best listing of Japanese publishers and other organizations publishing wholly or partly in English. Entries include commercial publishers, academic organizations, associations, individuals, institutes, government agencies, and others. Data for each publisher include ISBN prefixes, complete mailing address, telephone and facsimile numbers, and a contact person. This directory complements another publication from the JPGS, *Japan English Publications in Print.* All information is taken from the JPGS database.

203. *Japan Trade and Investment Directory.* Asia-Pacific Communications Inc., 110 Sutter St., #708, San Francisco, CA 94104. (415) 989-8330. (415) 989-1816 Fax. Annual. 125 p. $195.00.

Contains comprehensive listings of U.S. and Japanese companies offering business support services and joint-venture activities in Japan. These include U.S.-Japan business consultants; market research firms; media contacts and organizations; pharmaceutical, medical, and biotechnology companies; language schools, translation services; Japan-U.S. business organizations; Japan-America societies; JETRO offices in the U.S.; and U.S. Department of Commerce and government resources. Includes names, address, telephone, telex, and fax numbers for both U.S. and Japan offices and a description of services offered. Field and company indexes are provided.

204. *Japan Trade Directory.* Japan External Trade Organization (JETRO), 2-2-5 Toranomon, Minato-ku, Tokyo 105. (03) 582-3518. (03) 587-2485 Fax. Distributed by Dodwell Marketing Consultants, Kowa No. 35 Bldg., 1-14-14 Akasaka, Minato-ku, Tokyo 107. (03) 589-0207. (03) 589-0516 Fax. Annual. 1,210 p. ISBN 4-8224-0438-9. $230.00.

Information is provided on 2,900 Japanese companies engaged in overseas trade. Over 18,000 products and services are covered. Part 1 "Products and Services," is arranged in two sequences, one alphabetical and one by product category. Entries indicate companies offering the product or service, countries or regions each company is interested in doing business with, and references to company entries contained in part 2. Part 2 "Prefecture and Companies," gives information on Japan's 47 prefectures including brief business and tourist information, main products, and industries. The company information provided here is more detailed than in standard trade directories. It includes names of personnel in charge of import/export, telephone numbers, language spoken, office hours, trade names, availability of catalogs. Further sections list trade and industrial associations and alphabetical company and trade name indexes. The final section contains advertising for products and services. An informative guide section is included on how to use and read the directory.

205. *Japanese Companies: Consolidated Data.* Nihon Keizai Shimbun, Inc., Japan Economic Journal, 1-9-5 Ohtemachi, Chiyoda-ku, Tokyo 100. (03) 270-0251. Annual. 527 p. ISSN 0911-7016. $116.00.

Provides data on 1,044 major public companies taken from the NEEDS (Nikkei Economic Electronic Databank System). Provides an overview of the parent company's activities, recent business results, strength of the group, and results of the latest major activities of the subsidiaries. Consolidated financials are included. There is an alphabetical index by company name. Companies are listed in order of stock code numbers within 19 industry categories. For each company, information provided includes name, address, primary banks, and shares issued.

206. *Japanese Firms and Representatives in Singapore '79/80.* Gray and Associates Pte. Ltd., #405, 4th Fl., Afro-Asia Bldg., 63 Robinson Rd., Singapore 0106. (65) 220-6889. 1979. 280 p. Singapore $30.00.

Listing of some 800 Japanese companies in Singapore. Published in association with the Japanese Embassy, Singapore; JETRO; and the Japanese Chamber of Commerce and Industry, Singapore. As well as Japanese companies, there are non-Japanese companies listed that represent Japanese business or market Japanese products. There are also noncommercial enterprises, academic institutions, and associations serving the Japanese community in Singapore. Arranged in five sections alphabetical listing of companies (gives name and address, main line of business, relationships to parent entity in Japan, and name of key personnel in Singapore); products and services listing by broad product categories; alphabetical listing of key personnel; alphabetical listing of local companies marketing Japanese products and services; and listing of products and services by broad product categories of local companies representing Japanese firms.

207. *Japanese Overseas Investment: A Complete Listing by Firms and Countries.* Toyo Keizai Shinposha Ltd., The Oriental Economist, 1-4 Nihonbashi Hongoku-cho, Chuo-ku, Tokyo 103. (03) 270-4111. Biannual. 369 p. $230.00.

Data were collected from a survey sent to leading Japanese companies, both listed and unlisted, on the stock exchange. Telephone interviews were also conducted. The unlisted companies are noted by italics. Arrangement is by country and within country, alphabetically by name of the Japanese company. Information provided includes names of Japanese investors; capital ratio; name of the companies; date of startup of operations; capital, in currency of country of investment; number of employees; major business or product lines; annual sales or production figures; names of any partner firms; investment objectives; business results; and location by city and state. Three tables are included that present overseas loans and investment, overseas production, and Japanese overseas investment by countries divided by region.

208. *JAPTA List: Japanese Drug Directory.* Pharmaceutical Traders Association, 1-23 Nishikicho Kanda, Chiyoda-ku, Tokyo 101. (03) 294-6533. Distributed by Taylor and Francis, 3 E. 44th St., New York, NY 10017. (800) 821-8312. Irregular. 3d ed. 1987. 668 p. ISBN 0-8002-4156-8. $350.00.

Information on 25,000 drugs in Japan and abroad, including manufacturers, drug composition, dosage, and trade names. Code numbers are provided for investigational drugs, as well as abbreviations for antimicrobial agents. A directory of manufacturers and members of the Pharmaceutical Traders Association is included.

209. *Major Companies of the Far East.* Carr, Jennifer L., ed. Graham and Trotman, Sterling House, 66 Wilton Rd., London, SW1V 1DE. (01) 821-1123. In the U.S., contact Kluwer Academic Publishers, PO Box 358, Accord Station, Hingham, MA 02018-0358. 5th ed. 1988. 817 p. (2 Vols.) ISBN 1-85333-046-9. ISSN 0267-226X. $193.00.

Volume 2 covers East Asia, including Japan (nearly 200 pages of major Japanese companies). The following information is provided: name and address; telephone number; president or CEO; senior management; principle activities; parent company; principle subsidiaries; number of employees; financial information; major share holders; and date of establishment. Indexing is as follows: alphabetical by name of company independent of location; by country; and by business activity.

210. *New Materials Developed in Japan, 1988.* Kamada, N., ed. Toray Research Center, Inc., 3-1-8 Nihonbashi-Muromachi, Chuo-ku, Tokyo 103. (03) 245-5895. (03) 245-5818 Fax. Annual. 677 p. $1,250.00.

Provides data on 209 new materials developed in Japan between January 1986 and March 1987. Earlier editions cover materials developed prior to this time period. Covers metals, ceramics, plastics, electronic materials, paints, adhesives, photographic materials, and medical materials. Data provided include material name, trade name, name of developing organization, composition of the material, method of manufacture, properties, applications, references, relevant patents, and company address. Keyword, trade name, and organizational indexes are included.

211. *Pharmcast Japan.* Technomic Information Service, Inc., CPO Box 882, Sun Bldg., 8-7 Tomizawacho Nihonbashi, Chuo-ku, Tokyo 103. (03) 666-2952. (03) 666-2730 Fax. Quarterly. $1,000.00.

Covers drugs originating in Japan. Eight hundred agents (1,200 products) currently under development by 120 manufacturers and research institutions are represented. Information includes chemical structure, animal/clinical data, stages of development, and worldwide marketing and licensing status. Data are compiled from published and unpublished sources including interviews with manufacturers.

212. *Pharmaceutical Manufacturers of Japan.* Yakugyo Jiho Co. Ltd., 2-36 Jimbocho Kanda, Chiyoda-ku, Tokyo 101. (03) 265-7751. (03) 234-6573 Fax. 1988/89. 309 p. ISBN 4-8407-1426-6. $136.00.

Directory of 350 of the largest drug manufacturers in Japan. Business performance, sales breakdown, manufacturing and research facilities, addresses, and phone numbers are given.

213. *Second Section Firms, Japan Company Handbook.* Toyo Keizai Shimposha, The Oriental Economist, 1-4 Nihonbashi Hongo-ku, Chuo-ku, Tokyo 103. (03) 270-4111. Quarterly. 1,008 p. $190.00.

A companion to the *Japan Company Handbook*, this publication covers companies listed on the second sections of the Tokyo, Osaka, and Nagoya stock exchanges.

214. *Specialty Chemicals Handbook.* Chemical Daily Co. Ltd., 3-16-8 Nihonbashi, Hama-cho, Chuo-ku, Tokyo 103. (03) 663-7932. (03) 663-2530 Fax. 3d ed. 1989. 406 p. $134.00 (inc airmail).

Covers the field of organic intermediaries. Part 1 lists the 650 major organic intermediaries. Information includes class reference number of existing chemical substances, CAS registry number, export/import statistics, market price, and Japanese manufacturers names. Part 2 is a buyer's guide listing 7,900 organic intermediaries and fine chemicals, together with names of Japanese manufacturers. Part 3 lists address of manufacturers listed in Parts 1 and 2 and distributors and trading companies. Data are collected primarily by surveys sent to the manufacturers and then edited by Japan Chemical Week staff.

215. *Specifications and Applications of Industrial Robots in Japan.* Japan Industrial Robot Association, #213, Kikaishinko Bldg., 3-5-8 Shibakoen, Minato-ku, Tokyo 105. (03) 434-2919. (03) 578-1404 Fax. 1990. Manufacturing Fields. 893 p. $150.00. 1990. Non-manufacturing Fields. 247 p. $75.00.

These are indexes to the specifications for industrial robots in Japan. For the manufacturing fields, 445 specifications and 223 applications are included. All are currently manufactured by member companies of the Japan Industrial Robot Association. For nonmanufacturing fields—mining, construction, electricity, gas, and service industries—123 specifications and 123 applications are covered. Detailed specifications follow which include drawings and technical data. There is an alphabetical index by company name and an index by type of application. Each application is then described together with drawings, in the following section.

216. *Standard Industrial Classification for Japan.* Statistical Standards Department, Statistical Bureau, Management and Coordination Agency, 19-1 Wakamatsu-cho, Shinjuku-ku, Tokyo 162. (03) 202-1111. 1987. 207 p. $36.00.

This directory is a useful tool for understanding the commodity classifications used in many business directories. This is a bilingual publication although the introduction and contents pages are only in Japanese. Part 1 lists the major groups with names in Japanese and English. Part 2 gives a detailed breakdown of each group.

217. *Standard Trade Index of Japan.* Japan Chamber of Commerce and Industry, #505, World Trade Center Bldg., 2-4-1 Hamamatsu-cho, Minato-ku, Tokyo 105. (03) 435-4785. Annual. 1,445 p. ISSN 0585-0444. ISBN 0-8002-4244-0. $250.00.

Begun in 1957, this is a general buyer's guide covering 8,000 manufacturers, businesses, and trading firms. To be included, companies must have products being exported or have potential for export. They must be capable of conducting foreign trade, have capital over 1,000,000 yen, or have significant overseas trade already established. Companies may be Japanese or foreign companies located in Japan. Section 1 is an alphabetical index to 28,000 products and services. Under each product is a reference to the company producing it. Section 2 is an alphabetical index to trade names, and Section 3 is an alphabetical index to companies, giving address and major products. Section 4 provides an advertisement section arranged into 12 industry categories. Section 5 includes names and addresses of government agencies, trade and industrial organizations, and other relevant organizations.

218. *Top 1,500 Japanese Companies.* Japan Times Ltd., 4-5-4 Shibaura, Minato-ku, Tokyo 108. (03) 453-5311. (03) 453-5265 Fax. Annual. 91 p. ISBN 4-7890-0415-5. $10.00.

Originally published in Japanese, the data were supplied by the Teikoku Data Bank Ltd. The top rankings were determined by taxable earnings as determined by the taxation offices. Company data are listed in tabular format beginning with the first Japanese company which holds the most U.S. patents. Information gives current ranking; previous year's ranking; company name; industry category; income; percentage growth; sales; capital; net worth; and a telephone number. An alphabetical index by company name is provided.

219. *2000 Importers of Japan.* Japan External Trade Organization (JETRO), 2-2-5 Toranomon, Minato-ku, Tokyo 105. (03) 582-3518. (03) 587-2485 Fax. 1984. 320 p. ISBN 4-8224-8894-0. $65.00.

A guide to who wants what in Japan, published by the Japan External Trade Organization to promote export to Japan. Contains 2,000 company entries arranged by 100 product categories. There is also a guide to the Soga Shosha—the general trading companies of Japan.

220. *World Source Book for State Owned Enterprises.* Aristarchus Group, PO Box 12625, Tucson, AZ 85732. (602) 620-1240. Annual. 168 p. $155.00.

Reference guide to public Asian corporate organizations, including subsidiaries and joint ventures worldwide. Includes name changes, ownership, and hierarchical relationships among groups of companies.

TRADE AND SERVICE ORGANIZATIONS, TRADE HANDBOOKS

221. *Access Nippon.* Access Nippon, Inc., Yamaguchi Bldg., 2-8-5 Uchikanda, Chiyoda-ku, Tokyo 101. (03) 5256-1541 (03) 258-1487 Fax. Annual. 474 p. ISSN 0915-4841. $50.00.

A general guide for foreigners wishing to enter the Japanese market. Information includes general data on the Japanese market, government purchasing procedures, comprehensive trading firms, maps of major Japanese cities, and Japanese transportation facilities and costs and a directory of 1,000 companies giving address, telephone and fax numbers, capital, number of employees, annual sales figures, import and export activities, and names of contacts able to answer inquiries in foreign languages related to export/import matters. The directory section lists 250 government departments and organizations.

222. *A Compendium of Japan-Related Trade, Business, Labor and Media Organizations (Private and Governmental).* Victoria, Brian A. Prepared for the Office of International Trade, Department of Economic and Business Development, Business and Transportation Agency, Sacramento, CA 95801. 1977. 81 p.

This older directory has been included because it is useful to locate smaller organizations not listed elsewhere. Alphabetically arranged by organization's English title, this work gives English abbreviations, if any, and Japanese title, generally in abbreviated form. If there is an alternative English title, this is also noted. Provides an address and telephone number. Description gives purpose, structure, leadership, and other comments useful for understanding the organization. All indexes are at the front of the main work. Organizations are divided into those in California and those in Japan. An index giving romanized Japanese title is also provided to help locate an organization if only the Japanese title is known. An index of acronyms is also included.

223. *Directory of Business Support Organizations in Japan.* U.S. and Foreign Commercial Service, U.S. Embassy/Tokyo, 1-10-5 Akasaka, Minato-ku, Tokyo 107. (03) 583-7141. (03) 589-4235 Fax. In U.S., contact U.S. and Foreign Commercial Service, Japanese Market Section, FCS, American Embassy/Tokyo, Box 204, APO San Francisco, CA 96503. 1988. 101 p. (Japan Market Information Report No. 1). Supplement April 1988. 29 p. $25.00.

Lists private sector sources available to help with market entry and selling in Japan for U.S. businesses. Sections include Market Research and Business Consulting Firms in Japan; Advertising and Public Relations Firms in Japan; Executive Search Firms, Temporary Staff Services, and Placement Agencies in Japan; Testing Services Firms or Associations; Selected Lawyers and Patent Attorneys; Accounting Firms; Banks; Insurance Companies; Shipping Companies; U.S. State, Region and Port Representatives; Japan-U.S. Business Organizations; and Cooperators with U.S. Department of Agriculture Foreign Agricultural Service. There are a number of appendixes listing other useful U.S. and Japanese organizations for U.S. businesspersons and their services. Suggested readings are also given. Supplement lists additional firms in above categories as well as a new section on translation and interpreting services. Note: Many cities have regional offices of the US & FCS. Contacting them directly is the easiest way to obtain US & FCS publications.

224. *Directory of Service-Sector Organizations for U.S. Business Representatives in Japan.* U.S. and Foreign Commercial Service, Japanese Market Section, FCS, American Embassy/Tokyo, 1-10-5 Akasuka, Minato-ku, Tokyo 107. (03) 583-7141. (03) 589-4235 Fax. In U.S., contact U.S. and Foreign Commercial Service, Japanese Market Section, FCS, American Embassy/Tokyo, Box 204, APO San Francisco, CA 96503. July 1984. 21 p. (Japan Market Information Report Series). Gratis.

Addendum updates main work as of April 25, 1985. Listed organizations are those who responded to inquiry from the embassy, but this does not imply endorsement by embassy of these organizations. Sections include U.S. Accounting Firms in Japan; U.S. Banks in Japan; U.S. Insurance Companies in Japan; U.S. Shipping Companies in Japan; Law Firms in Japan; Patent Attorneys in Japan; U.S. State, Region, and Port Representatives in Japan; Japan-U.S. Trade Promotion Organizations; and Cooperators in Foreign Agricultural Service of U.S. Department of Agriculture in Japan. Name, address, phone, fax, cable, telex numbers are listed. Note: Many cities have regional offices of the US & FCS. Contacting them directly is the quickest way to obtain US & FCS publications.

225. *Directory of Sources of Information and Business Services.* Japan External Trade Organization (JETRO), 2-2-5 Toranomon, Minato-ku, Tokyo 105. (03) 582-3518. (03) 587-2485 Fax. In U.S., contact OCS America, Inc., #1186, National Press Bldg., 14th and F St., NW, Washington, DC 20045. (202) 347-4233. (202) 639-8673 Fax. or JETRO Regional Offices. (See Appendix C for details). 1989. 86 p. $35.00.

Divided into 19 sections, each dealing with a different source. Very useful for anyone interested in doing business with Japan. Covers English-language publications in areas such as market information, immigration procedures, employment of staff, etc. Gives list of importers and business services such as law firms and consultants.

226. *Distribution Systems in Japan.* Business Intercommunications, Inc. (BII), CPO Box 587, Tokyo 100-91. (03) 423-3971. (03) 423-3996 Fax. 1985. 464 p. $280.00.

Handbook setting out the complex distribution system in Japan which can be confusing for foreigners trying to distribute to customers in Japan. Covers commercial practices such as contracts, returns, and discounts. Transportation, settlement procedures, and sales promotion are detailed. Role of general trading companies, the new trends in rebate systems, and the connectivity between Japanese industries are also discussed. Industries covered include energy, materials, machinery, chemicals, biotechnology, pharmaceuticals, etc. Provides manufacturers and dealers pricing mechanisms, roles of the various parties involved, trading conditions, distribution means, industry organizations, and market data for each product discussed. Arranged by industry and then by product within each industry category. Charts and tables as well as an alphabetical index of products are included.

227. *Doing Business in Japan.* Gakaseisha Pub. Co., 3-27-14 Shikahama, Adachiku, Tokyo 123. (03) 857-3031. (03) 857-3037 Fax. 1984. 276 p. $15.00.

A compilation of three previously published booklets from JETRO (*Doing Business in Japan, Sales Promotion in the Japanese Market*, and *Japanese Corporate Decision Making*). Trilingual (Japanese, English, French), it is designed for the Japanese as well as for the foreign businessperson. Part 1 covers basic requirements for successful business negotiations. Cultural differences are explained clearly. Part 2 repeats much of the information covered in the decision-making section in Part 1. Part 3 provides practical guidelines on retailing, distribution, and advertising. Facts and figures are provided for such areas as margins, rebates, and advertising costs.

228. *Doing Business in Japan.* Price, Waterhouse Center for Transnational Taxation, 530 Fifth Ave., New York, NY 10036. (212) 944-9750. 1983. Supplement 1986. 159 p., 30 p.

A brief guide to assist those wishing to enter the Japanese market. For detailed advice, the guide cautions the need to consult Japanese laws, regulations, and decisions and to obtain professional accounting and legal advice. The guide addresses the following areas: Business Climate in Japan, Accounting, and Taxation.

229. *Economic and Industrial Organizations in Japan.* Tokyo Chamber of Commerce and Industry, 3-2-2 Marunouchi, Chiyoda-ku, Tokyo 100. (03) 382-7600. (03) 216-6497 Fax. Distributed by Maruzen Co. Ltd., 2-3-10 Nihon Beishi, Chuo-ku, Tokyo 103. (03) 272-2458. (03) 278-9784 Fax. Annual. 280 p. $25.00.

This bilingual publication provides a useful directory of economic, commercial, trade, and industrial organizations. Covers large number of specialized trade associations. Gives full name and address in English and Japanese.

230. *Executive Search Firms in Japan.* U.S. and Foreign Commercial Service, Japanese Market Section, FCS, U.S. Export Information Center, American Embassy/Tokyo, 1-10-5 Akasaka, Minato-ku, Tokyo 107. (03) 583-7141. (03) 583-4235 Fax. In U.S., contact U.S. and Foreign Commercial Service, American Embassy/Tokyo, Box 204, APO San Francisco, CA 96503. May 1984. 14 p. (Japan Market Information Report Series). Gratis.

This directory includes four categories: Executive Search Firms, Temporary Staff Services, Placement Agencies, and Dependent Employment/Cultural Organization. Note: Many cities have district offices of the US & FCS. Contacting them directly is the fastest way to obtain US & FCS publications

231. *Exporting to Japan.* JETRO, Information Service Department, 2-2-5 Toranomon, Minato-ku, Tokyo 105. (03) 582-3518. (03) 587-2485 Fax. Annual. 186 p. ISBN 4-8224-0154-5 (1982 ed.). $30.00.

Guide for overseas companies interested in exporting to Japan. Arranged in two sections, the first lists products in which Japanese companies are interested, and the second provides company information on those Japanese companies interested in importing foreign goods. Information is gathered from a survey distributed by JETRO.

232. *Exporting to Japan: A Practical Guide.* Bush, Richard. International Trade and Investment Division, Washington State Department of Commerce and Economic Development, 312 First Ave., N, Seattle, WA 98109. (206) 464-6282. 1983. 35 p. Gratis.

Originally published by American Chamber of Commerce in Japan and the U.S. Foreign Commercial Service, 1981, this is a practical guide to successfully exporting to Japan. Written by an American living in Tokyo, who has 20 years of experience in importing and exporting products to and from Japan.

233. *International Directory of Market Research Organizations.* Market Research Society, 15 Belgrave Sq., London, SW1X 8PF; and British Overseas Trade Board (BOTB), Department of Trade and Industry, 1 Victoria St., London, SW1H OET. Irregular. 7th ed., 1985. 662 p. ISBN 0-906616-0402. 26 pounds.

Alphabetical product index provides the initial lookup point. Provides a listing of market research studies in table format. This is the main body of the work. Coverage is worldwide, and each entry gives title, countries covered, products and services covered, date, source, and price. The source codes refer to a source index listing names and addresses.

234. *Japan Marketing Handbook.* Hallstrom, Conje. Euromonitor, Distributed in the U.S. by Gale Research, Inc., Book Tower, Detroit, MI 48277-0748. (313) 961-2242. (313) 961-6083 Fax. 1st ed., 1988. 160 p. ISBN 0-86338-213-4. $160.00.

Presents an analysis of Japan's economic situation, consumer markets, and growth industries. Contains practical advice on gaining access to the Japanese market. The book is arranged in six chapters, each dealing with a specific aspect of the Japanese market and economy. Statistics are presented at the end of the text in the appendixes. There is a directory of addresses.

235. *Japanese Market: A Compendium of Information for the Prospective Exporter.* Japan External Trade Organization (JETRO), 2-2-5 Toranomon, Minato-ku, Tokyo 105. (03) 582-3518. (03) 587-2485 Fax. 2d ed. 1987. 276 p.

A practical handbook designed to help foreign business persons exporting to Japan. Arrangement is designed to help with the steps and procedures that need to be followed. The nine chapters cover Overview of the Market; Japanese Consumer; Business Practices; Distribution System; Import System and Settlements; Customs Clearance; Legal Procedures; Product Standards; and Government Support. Key addresses are listed in the appendix.

236. *Market Research and Business Consulting Firms in Japan.* U.S. and Foreign Commercial Service, American Embassy/Tokyo, 1-10-5 Akasaka, Minato-ku, Tokyo 107. (03) 583-7141. (03) 589-4235 Fax. In U.S., contact U.S. and Foreign Commercial Service, Japanese Market Section, FCS, American Embassy/Tokyo, Box 204, APO San Francisco, CA 95603. 1983. $5.00.

Provides name, address, size of company, and name of managing director. Type of consultancy offered including any specialties are listed for 43 companies. The information was obtained by questionnaire. Note: Many cities have regional offices of the US&FCS. Contacting them directly is the easiest way to obtain US&FCS publications.

237. *MITI Handbook.* Japan Trade and Industry Publicity, Inc., Toranomon Kotohira Kaikan, 1-2-8 Toranomon, Minato-ku, Tokyo 105. (03) 503-4051. Overseas Public Affairs Office, Ministry of International Trade and Industry, 3-1-1 Kasumigaseki, Chiyoda-ku, Tokyo 100. (03) 501-1654. Biannual. 288 p. $50.00.

Published every other year since 1984, this handbook edited by the Information Office of MITI, is a comprehensive guide to the Ministry of International Trade and Industry, its external bureaus, and attached organizations. Explains duties of the major MITI divisions. Includes lists of all central government agencies and MITI-related trade associations in Japan and overseas.

238. *Organization of the Government of Japan.* Institute of Administrative Management, PO Box 1106, Sunshine 60, 3-1-1 Higashi-Ikebukuro, Toshima-ku, Tokyo 170. (03) 981-0441. Contact Government Publications Service Center, Osaka Gohdo Chohsha #3 Bldg., Ohtemaenomachi, Higashi-ku, Osaka 540. (06) 942-1681. Annual. 144 p. $27.00.

Edited by the Administrative Management Bureau, Management and Coordination Agency, Prime Minister's Office, this publication provides organization charts and narrative descriptions of the functions of Japanese government agencies. A series of appendixes provide important background information on the structure of government in Japan.

239. *Selling to Japan from A to Z.* Japan External Trade Organization (JETRO), 2-2-5 Toranomon, Minato-ku, Tokyo 105. (03) 582-3518. (03) 587-2485 Fax. 1985. 32 p. Gratis.

Edited by the Ministry of International Trade and Industry, this is a promotional, glossy booklet offering general information for the foreign businessperson wishing to enter the Japanese market.

240. *Trade Associations and Their Activities in Japan's High-Tech Industries: A Guide for Technological Cooperation with Japan.* Japan External Trade Organization (JETRO), 2-2-5 Toranomon, Minato-ku, Tokyo 105. (03) 582-3518. (03) 587-2485 Fax. In U.S., contact O.C.S. America, Inc., #1186, National Press Bldg., 14th and F St., NW, Washington, DC 20045. (202) 347-4233. (202) 639-8673 Fax. or JETRO Regional Offices, New York (212) 997-0400, Los Angeles (213) 626-5700, San Francisco (415) 922-0234, Chicago (312) 726-4340/2, Houston (713) 759-9595/7, Dallas (214) 651-0839. 1986 (out of stock—new edition due but no expected date of publication).

List of trade associations and other nonbusiness organizations involved in Japanese high-tech industries. Focus is on associations involved in technical exchange with overseas partners. Each listing gives organization name, purpose, address and telephone/fax numbers, details of membership, main products of its member companies, contact person for technical exchanges, and related organizations. Publications of these organizations are also listed. Any conferences or exhibits that the organization sponsors are also included. Forthcoming events are listed where known.

TRADE FAIRS

241. *Exhibitions and Events in Japan.* Japan Convention Bureau (JNTO), 2-10-1 Yurakucho, Chiyoda-ku, Tokyo 100. (03) 216-1901. (03) 214-7680 Fax. Biannual January, July. 18 p. Vol. 40 (Jan 1989-Feb 1993). Gratis.

Calendar of trade shows and cultural and sporting events in Japan. Gives contacts for the various events and availability for foreign participation. Copies available at JNTO offices in the U.S.

242. *Foreign Participation in International Fairs and Exhibitions in Japan.* Manufactured Imports Promotion Organization (MIPRO), 2000 L St., NW, #616, Washington, DC 20036. (202) 659-3729. Annual. 120 p. Gratis.

This bilingual English and Japanese publication from MIPRO lists exhibitions that will accept foreign participation. MIPRO was established in 1978 to help industrially advanced countries expand their exports to Japan. It lists some 200 exhibitions. Index is by broad business category, e.g., electric, electronic, machines, instruments, medical, and hospital equipment. Main body of work gives details of each exhibition: city, venue, organizer, dates, frequency, exhibition area in square meters, products displayed. There is an alphabetical title index and an appendix that gives tips on successful exhibiting in Japan. Other data include rental fee per booth, category of attendees, application deadline, availability of an English-language guidebook, languages spoken by contact organizer, and past attendance size and breakdown.

243. *List of Trade Fairs in Japan, 1989–90.* Japan External Trade Organization (JETRO), 2-2-5 Toranomon, Minato-ku, Tokyo 105. (03) 582-3518. (03) 587-2485 Fax. In U.S., contact JETRO, 1221 Avenue of the Americas, 44th Fl., New York, NY 10020-1060. (212) 997-0400; or JETRO Regional Offices, Los Angeles (213) 626-5700, San Francisco (415) 922-0234, Chicago (312) 726-4340/2, Houston (713) 759-9595/7, Dallas (214) 651-0839. 1989. 108 p. Gratis.

Lists 317 trade fairs over a two-year span. Gives locations, organizer's name and address, and contact number. Does not include fees, application deadlines, description of exhibit space available, or availability of overseas publicity. For this information, see *Trade Fairs in Japan*, also published by JETRO. Section 1 lists trade fairs by industry classification; section 2 is a tabular listing of trade fairs, again by industry classification but only includes those being held during period covered in the directory. Gives details such as name of fair, dates, frequency held, site and name, address, and phone number of the organizing agency. Indexes provided are alphabetical by English name of trade fair; alphabetical by Japanese name; chronologically by date of fair; and by locations and sites.

244. *Trade Fairs in Japan.* Japan External Trade Organization (JETRO), 2-2-5 Toranomon, Minato-ku, Tokyo 105. (03) 582-3518. (03) 587-2485 Fax. 1987–88. 312 p. $80.00.

Published in English and Japanese, this publication is distributed by JETRO to promote international imports. Directory for foreign companies wanting to exhibit at Japan's trade fairs. Information organized to provide information for specific products and industries. Information provided includes application deadlines, overseas publicity, and descriptions of exhibit space, etc.

BIOGRAPHICAL

245. *American Chamber of Commerce in Japan: Directory of Members.* American Chamber of Commerce in Japan, Fukide Bldg. No. 2, 7th Fl., 4-1-21 Toranomon, Minato-ku, Tokyo 105. (03) 433-5381. (03) 436-1446 Fax. Annual. 391 p. $65.00.

A listing of members, member firms, and supporting associations of the American Chamber of Commerce in Japan.

246. *Directory of Japan Specialists and Japanese Studies Institutions in the United States and Canada.* Japan Foundation, Publications Department, Park Bldg., 3-6 Kio-cho, Chiyoda-ku, Tokyo 102. (03) 263-4494. Distributed by Association for Asian Studies, One Lane Hall, University of Michigan, Ann Arbor, MI 48109. (313) 665-2490. 1989. 651 p. ISBN 0-924304-02-2 (Set). 2 Vols. ISBN 0-924304-00-6 (Vol. 1). ISBN 0-924304-01-4 (Vol. 2). $35.00.

Very up-to-date, comprehensive source of information on Japan specialists and Japanese studies institutions. Canadian data have also been included. Much of this information was taken from an earlier publication *Japan Studies in Canada*, 1987. Volume 1 contains main listing for the 1,420 Japan specialists, in alphabetical order. For each entry, the following information is included: name, occupation, sex, birthdate and place, current title and occupation, affiliation, languages, periods of research or study in Japan, and disciplines. A brief statement of the specialist's research interests, specializations in periods of Japanese history, subject matter, and geographic areas within Japan are listed. Academic credentials, professional experience, fellowships and grants, and up to six major publications are also included. Address and telephone number is the final entry. A brief alphabetical listing of 441 doctoral candidates in Japanese studies is also given. Entry includes name, department, university, and dissertation topic, if known. Volume 2 contains institutional listings and the indexes. This two-volume work forms part 2 of *Japanese Studies in the United States.*

247. *Directory of Japan Specialists in Australia.* Japan Foundation, Publications Department, Park Bldg., 3-6 Kioi-cho, Chiyoda-ku, Tokyo 102. (03) 263-4494. 1986 rev. ed. 61 p. (Directory Series, vol. 8). Unpriced.

Revision of the 1983 edition, information again was collected by survey conducted by the Japan Foundation, Canberra Office. Arrangement is by institution in three categories: universities, colleges of advanced education, and other organizations. Information provides specialist's position, academic degree, academic fields confined to professional interests related to Japan, and publications on Japan. Indexes by subject area and personal name are included. For a more recent directory covering Japanese studies in Australia, see *Japanese Studies in Australia.*

248. *Directory of Japan Specialists in Thailand.* Japan Foundation, Publications Department, Park Bldg., 3-6 Kioi-cho, Chiyoda-ku, Tokyo 102. (03) 263-4505. 1983. 62 p. (Directory Series, vol. 5). Unpriced.

Data compiled from a 1980 survey conducted by the Bangkok office of the Japan Foundation. First half of the directory provides a narrative description of Japanese studies in Thailand by broad subject discipline. Alphabetical listing of Japan specialists in Thailand follows. Their position, academic qualifications, academic interests related to Japan, and publications in Japanese studies are listed. An index by subject specialty is included.

249. *Directory of University Professors and Researchers in Japan 1982: Engineering.* Japan Society for the Promotion of Science, 5-3-1, Kojimachi, Chiyoda-ku, Tokyo 102. (03) 263-1721. (03) 237-8238 Fax. Distributed by Maruzen Co. 1984. 874 p. ISBN 4-8181-8259-1. $150.00.

Each researcher is listed alphabetically by romanized name within subject categories, e.g., Applied Physics, Mechanical Engineering, Electrical Engineering, Naval Architecture, Civil Engineering, Architecture, Mining, Metallurgical Engineering, and Applied Chemistry. All researchers listed are from institutions under the direction of the Ministry of Education (Monbusho). These institutions are universities, interuniversity research institutes (national research institutes); and Monbusho research institutes. Details provided include name, year of birth, current position, education level, academic degree, membership in three scientific societies, three subjects of current research interest, and name of publication or journal title, volume, and year. Although there are a number of other subject sections published in Japanese, only the engineering section has been translated into English. This directory was translated, published, and edited by the Japan Society for the Promotion of Science. No other sections are currently planned for English translation.

250. *Japanese Studies in Australia.* Japan Foundation, Park Bldg., 3-6 Kioi-cho, Chiyoda-ku, Tokyo 102. (03) 263-4494. 1989. 235 p. ISBN 0-7316-6673-9. (Japanese Studies Series No. 21). Unpriced.

This directory offers a comprehensive guide to Japanese studies in tertiary institutions in Australia. Information was gathered by survey carried out between April 1988 and June 1989 by the Australia-Japan Research Centre, Research School of Pacific Studies, Australian National University. The directory is included under the biographical directories section because a major section of the work is devoted to a directory listing of Japan specialists in Australian tertiary institutions. Specialists are listed alphabetically. Information includes current position, institution name, education, broad subject area, regional specialization, current research projects, research conducted in the last three years, Japan-related courses, recent Japan-related lectures and seminars, graduate supervision, and selected major publications. Part 1 of the directory contains commentaries describing the Japanese studies programs in Australian tertiary institutions. Part 2 is a directory of the institutions in Australia that offer Japanese studies programs. It includes details of the current courses, research, and publications programs.

251. *List of Members (International House of Japan).* International House of Japan, Inc., 5-11-16 Roppongi, Minato-ku, Tokyo 105. (03) 470-4611. (03) 479-1738 Fax. 1986. 440 p. $23.00.

Alphabetical listing of regular and supporting members of the International House of Japan. It gives the name, position or field of interest, residential or business address, and telephone. Information about the International House of Japan is contained in the appendixes. There is no index to the subject specialties of the members.

252. *Roster of Members of the Japanese National Diet.* Japan Times Ltd., 4-5-4 Shibaura, Minato-ku, Tokyo 108. (03) 453-2013. (03) 453-5265 Fax. 1988. 186 p. ISBN 4-7890-0402-3. $15.00.

Contains a wealth of information on representatives of the Diet and the Japanese political parties. Organizational charts help lay out the Japanese political system. There is a clear explanation of the arrangement of the information contained therein. Contents include main addresses and telephone numbers for the Diet followed by organizational charts for the Diet and the political parties. The next section includes biographical information, including photographs for the House of Representatives, the House of Councillors, Administrative Organs, and their managing staffs. There is an index of Diet members, arranged alphabetically by family name.

253. *Who's Who in Japan 1987–88.* International Culture Institute, OAG House #407, 7-5-56 Akasaka, Minato-ku, Tokyo 107. (03) 505-2296. (03) 584-0108 Fax. In U.S., contact Gale Research, Inc., Book Tower, Detroit, MI 48277-0748. (313) 961-2242. 2d ed. 1,083 p. ISBN 962-7191-01-9. $210.00.

Signifying Japan's growing international outlook, this national who's who for Japan provides 42,000 biographical sketches on leading figures in Japan today from government, medicine, journalism, visual and performing arts, religion, and culture among others. Each entry provides individual's name, degree or license, position, education, birthdate, career, honors, memberships, hobbies, address, and telephone number.

254. *Who's Who in Japanese Government 1988.* International Culture Association, Japan Co., Ltd., OAG House #407, 7-5-56 Akasaka, Minato-ku, Tokyo 107. (03) 505-2296. (03) 584-0108 Fax. Biennial. 408 p. ISBN 4-8002-4222-X. $76.00.

Provides details of numbers, names, and background of Japanese government officials. Complete directory of every member of upper and lower houses of the Diet. Brief career summary, party function, and committee membership. Breakdown of government agencies responsible for specific business, industrial, and trade matters. Full list of government-sponsored committees, task forces, and associations. Tables list Chamber of Commerce and Trade Associations from outside Japan, Law Offices, Accountants, Trade Federations, and Special Interests.

TELEPHONE DIRECTORIES

255. *City Source: English Telephone Directory.* Japan Telecommunications Welfare Association, Tokyo Office, 5-14-9 Sendagaya, Shinbuya-ku, Tokyo 150. (03) 350-7005. Annual. 564 p. $15.00.

Similar arrangement to yellow pages, ie., by type of business. Includes zip codes, index by type of business, alphabetical arrangement within each classification. Compiled for foreigners in Japan.

256. *Japan Times Directory; Foreign Residents, Business Firms, Organizations.* Japan Times Ltd., 4-5-4 Shibaura, Minato-ku, Tokyo 108. (03) 453-5311. Annual. 38th ed., 1985. 773 p. $72.00.

Telephone directory, yellow pages, this is an alphabetical listing of companies, both Japanese and foreign, and foreign residents. Subtitle may vary slightly.

257. *Telephone Directories.* Regent Book Co., Inc. 101A U.S. Hwy 46, Saddle Brook, NJ 07662. (201) 368-2208.

A variety of these directories are available:

Aichi Nagoya City (2 vols.), white pages	$145.00
Aichi Nagoya City (2 vols.), yellow pages	$245.00
Hyogo Kobe City (2 vols.)	$425.00
Kanagawa Kawasaki City, yellow pages	$185.00
Kanagawa Yokohama City, white pages	$115.00
Kanagawa Yokohama City, yellow pages	$225.00
Kyoto City, white pages	$115.00
Kyoto City, yellow pages	$575.00
Okinawa (Mainland), yellow pages	$205.00

Osaka City (3 vols.), white pages	$875.00
Osaka City (3 vols.), yellow pages	$575.00
Tokyo Izu-Ogasawara, yellow pages	$85.00
Tokyo Tama District East, white pages	$175.00
Tokyo Tama District East, yellow pages	$375.00
Tokyo Tama District South, white pages	$115.00
Tokyo Tama District South, yellow pages	$325.00
Tokyo Tama District West, white pages	$135.00
Tokyo Tama District West, yellow pages	$285.00
Tokyo City, white pages	$1,125.00
Tokyo City (3 vols.), yellow pages	$475.00

258. *Yellow Pages—Japan Telephone Book.* Japan Yellow Pages Ltd., ST Bldg., 4-6-9 Iidabashi, Chiyoda-ku, Tokyo 102. (03) 239-3501. (03) 237-8948 Fax. In the U.S., contact Croner Publications, Inc., 211-05 Jamaica Ave., Queens Village, NY 11428. (718) 464-0866; or Kinokuniya Bookstores (See Appendix C for details). Semiannual. 605 p. $175.00.

Classified directory in English with table of contents in English and Japanese. Listing of over 25,000 businesses in Japan listed under 800 categories. Similar to U.S. classified telephone directory, but focus is on companies of interest to foreigners. Subdivided by major cities, also gives postal codes, postage rates, international telephone calling lines, government organizations, calendar of trade fairs and exhibitions, calendar of international conferences. Contains quick reference index. Title varies, *Japan Yellow Pages.*

259. *Yellow Pages Japan in USA: Directory of Japanese Firms and Business Covering the 10 Metropolitan Areas of New York, New Jersey, Atlanta, Houston, Chicago, Seattle, San Francisco, Los Angeles, San Diego, Honolulu and Japan.* Apcon International, Inc. (YPJ Department). 420 Boyd St., #502, Los Angeles, CA 90013. (213) 680-9101. (213) 680-1459 Fax. Annual. $23.50.

Covers listing of Japanese firms, organizations, restaurants, retail stores, hotels, airlines, and U.S. firms and professionals doing business with Japan and the Japanese in 10 major cities in the U.S.

Chapter 7
Yearbooks

This section contains annual publications, generally of a statistical nature. Every effort was made to include as many publications dealing with specific high technology industries as possible. Many of the entries included are general statistical compilations, but some of these contain sections dealing with high-tech industries of Japan.

Much of the information contained in these works is repetitive, but it can be useful to take statistics from a number of different sources to arrive at a comprehensive viewpoint. Also, by offering a variety of titles, there is a greater chance that at least one will be easily obtainable from local sources.

260. *Analysts' Guide.* Daiwa Securities Research Institute. 1-2-1 Kyobashi, Chuo-ku, Tokyo 104. (03) 243-5771. Annual. 1,347 p. $150.00.

Published in English and Japanese, this guide provides a tabular analysis of industry groups and individual companies for investors and research firms. Statistical tables cover data for the preceding five years.

261. *Budget in Brief, Japan.* Budget Bureau, Ministry of Finance, 3-1-1 Kasumigaseki, Chiyoda-ku, Tokyo 100. (03) 581-4111. Annual. 106 p. Gratis.

Part 1 is a full translation of the budget speech by the Minister of Finance. Part 2 contains a discussion of the current status of government finance, including problem areas. Part 3 outlines the full budget, and part 4 is a narrative discussion of the budget by program functions, e.g., social security, public works, education, and science, etc. Part 5 explains the budget system and the budget process, whereas part 6 outlines the Fiscal Investment and Loan Program (FILIP)—a program closely related to the budget although not a part of it. Detailed summaries are provided in a series of tables at the back of the publication. Ample tables, charts, and graphs are also used throughout the text.

262. *Computer White Paper.* Japan Information Processing Development Center, 3-5-8 Shibakoen, Minato-ku, Tokyo 105. (03) 434-8211. (03) 432-9379 Fax. Annual. 63 p. $33.00.

This is an English summary of the highlights from the original Japanese white paper. It reviews the Japanese computer industry and provides commentary on the state-of-the-art. It covers government policy, market penetration, online databases systems, the information industry, and future trends.

263. *Concise Reference to the Japanese Economy and Industry.* Japan External Trade Organization (JETRO), 2-2-5 Toranomon, Minato-ku, Tokyo 105. (03) 582-3518. (03) 587-2485 Fax. 1987. 50 p. Gratis.
Covers aspects of Japan's trade and economy using a graphical and tabular presentation. Characteristics and recent trends provided for major industries.

264. *Economic Statistics Annual.* Bank of Japan, Research and Statistics Department, 2-2-1 Hongoku-cho, Nihonbashi, Chuo-ku, Tokyo 103. (03) 279-1111. (03) 279-5801 Fax. Annual. 310 p. $20.00.
Published in English and Japanese, this report contains statistical tables. These include standard Japanese economic statistics—key economic indicators, money and banking, public finance, industry, foreign trade, foreign exchange, balance of payments, prices, household economy, labor, population, national wealth, national income, interindustry relations table, and economic prospects. For more timely information, see *Economic Statistics Monthly* (each issue approximately 220 pages; yearly subscription costs $99.00).

265. *Economic Survey of Japan.* Ministry of Finance, Publications, 3-1-1 Kasumigaseki, Chiyoda-ku, Tokyo 100. (03) 581-4111. (03) 586-3210 Fax. Annual. 327 p. ISBN 4-17-566388-6. $85.00.
This is an abridged translation of the *White Paper on the Japanese Economy* published by the Economic Planning Agency of the Prime Minister's Office each fiscal year. It provides a wealth of economic statistics covering the Japanese economy for the previous fiscal year. Areas covered include an overview of the economy, Japan's position in the global economy, new developments with Japan's industries, future issues facing Japan's economy, and strategies for the future.

266. *Electronics in Japan.* Electronics Industries Association of Japan, 5F, Tokyo Chamber of Commerce and Industry Bldg., 3-2-2 Marunouchi, Chiyoda-ku, Tokyo 100. (03) 211-2765. (03) 287-1712 Fax. Annual. 150 p. $20.00.
A detailed overview of the electronics industry in Japan, including trends and future outlook for the industry, R&D, and international cooperation. Major companies that are members of the Electronics Industries Association of Japan are listed. Their addresses and major product lines are provided, and some special reports are included. Section headings are practical application of electronics; electronics industry; and R&D in electronics, including a general overview as well as current work in national and public research laboratories, international cooperation, and universities.

267. *Export Statistical Schedule Japan.* Japan Tariff Association, No. 2 Jibiki Bldg., 4-7-8 Kojimachi, Chiyoda-ku, Tokyo 102. (03) 263-7221. (03) 263-7345 Fax. Annual. 426 p. $136.00.
Edited by the Customs and Tariff Bureau of the Ministry of Finance, this publication gives annual statistics on exports from Japan. Commodity classification based on Customs Co-operation Council Nomenclature (CCCN).

268. *Facts and Figures—On the Japanese Electronics Industry.* Overseas Public Affairs Office, Electronics Industries Association of Japan, 3-2-2 Marunouchi, Chiyoda-ku, Tokyo 100. (03) 213-1070. (03) 213-1078 Fax. In U.S., contact Baron/Canning and Co., Inc., New York, NY 10022. (212) 751-7100. (212) 593-4906 Fax. Annual. 132 p. $50.00.

Formerly *Trends in Japan's Electronic Industry,* this is a pocket guide to production and export/import statistics. All information is given in tables and graphs. Executive summary is the only narrative section. Other sections include overview of the industry worldwide; electronics industry in Japan—facts and figures; overview of the Japanese electronics industry; consumer electronic equipment; industrial electronic equipment; and electronic components and devices. There is no index, but the contents listing is very detailed. This is an invaluable source of facts and figures for electronics in Japan.

269. *Foreign Economic Trends (FET).* Superintendent of Documents, U.S. Government Printing Office, Washington, DC 20402. (202) 275-2951. Single copies available from Publication Sales Branch, #1617, U.S. Department of Commerce, Washington, DC 20230. Irregular. 10 p. $1.00.

The *Foreign Economic Trends* are prepared for a number of countries, Japan among them. They include key economic indicators, a brief summary of the state of the economy of the subject country, current situation and economic trends, industrial and agricultural report, foreign trade situation, living costs, monetary situation, and implications for the U.S.

270. *Indicators of Science and Technology.* Ministry of Finance, Printing Bureau, 2-2-4 Toranomon, Minato-ku, Tokyo 105. (03) 582-4411. (03) 586-3210 Fax. Annual (June). 242 p. $36.00.

Edited by the Planning Bureau, Science and Technology Agency, this publication provides information and statistics on scientific and technological developments in Japan. Data on R&D, scientific and technical progress and expenditure, number of scientists and researchers, colleges, universities, and research institutions are included. Patent applications in Japan are also covered. Comparative data for Japan and other industrialized countries are given. This is a bilingual publication in Japanese with English translation. Latest edition is 1987, but an English translation has not been published.

271. *Industrial Statistics Monthly.* Research Institute of International Trade and Industry, 2-8-9 Ginza, Chuo-ku, Tokyo 104. (03) 535-4881. Monthly. 200 p. $238.00/year.

Edited by the Research and Statistics Department of the Ministry of International Trade and Industry, this publication provides a detailed statistical overview of Japan's industrial production and shipments, producer's and dealer's inventories, raw materials inventories and consumption, and wholesale and retail sales. Figures are taken from MITI compilations.

272. *Japan: An International Comparison.* Keizai Koho Center (Japan Institute for Social and Economic Affairs), Ohtemachi Bldg., 1-6-1 Ohtemachi, Chiyoda-ku, Tokyo 100. (03) 201-1404. (03) 201-1418 Fax. Annual (October). 100 p. ISBN 4-87605-017-X. ISSN 0389-3502. $7.00.

This is a statistical handbook intended for businesspersons with most of the information in tabular form. Gives population, area, national income, foreign trade, overseas investment, wages, and productivity figures. Shows a comparison with the U.S. and other developed nations.

273. *Japan Annual Reviews in Electronics, Computers and Telecommunications (JARECT).* Copublished by Ohmsha Ltd., 3-1 Nishiki-cho Kanda, Chiyoda-ku, Tokyo 101. (03) 233-0641. (03) 293-2824 Fax; and Elsevier Science Publishers B.V. (North-Holland), PO Box 1991, 1000 BZ Amsterdam. In the U.S., contact Elsevier Science Publishing Co., Inc., PO Box 1663, Grand Central Station, NY 10163. (212) 989-5800. Irregular. ISSN 0167-5036. $95.00/vol.

Begun in 1981, this is a series within a series: Semiconductor Technologies (vol. 1, 1981; vol. 8, 1983; vol. 13, 1984; vol. 19, 1986), Amorphous Semiconductor Technologies and Devices (vol. 2, 1981; vol. 6, 1983; vol. 16, 1984; vol. 22, 1987), Optical Devices and Fibers (vol. 3, 1982; vol. 5, 1983; vol. 7, 1984; vol. 17, 1985), Computer Science and Technologies (vol. 4, 1982; vol. 7, 1983; vol. 12, 1984; vol. 18, 1987), and Recent Magnetics for Electronics (vol. 10, 1983; vol. 15, 1984; vol. 21, 1986). Annual review of the previous year's work. Comprises articles by leading experts in the field.

274. *Japan Drug Industry Review.* Yakugyo Jiho Co., Ltd., 2-36 Jimbocho Kanda, Chiyoda-ku, Tokyo 101. (03) 265-7751. (03) 234-6573 Fax. Annual. 116 p. $88.00.

Covers problems facing the Japanese pharmaceutical industry, trends in drug production, business activities, health spending, and statistical data presented in tabular form.

275. *Japan Economic Almanac.* Nihon Keizai Shimbun, Inc. (Japan Economic Journal), 1-9-5 Ohtemachi, Chiyoda-ku, Tokyo 100. (03) 270-0251. Annual (June). ISSN 0910-830. ISBN 4-532-05589-X. 304 p. $75.00.

Continuing *Industrial Review of Japan*, this comprehsive review of the previous year's Japanese business and economic activity provides industry-specific reports, which contain a detailed analysis for the previous year together with future trends, of 70 industries. Production figures and import and export statistics are listed and a directory of over 300 prominent Japanese businesspersons is included. Since the *Industrial Review of Japan* was published, various sections have been expanded including the statistics and basic data on national finances, banking, international trade and finance, industrial activities, government ministries and organizations, and profits. A chronology of the previous year's major news events and a directory of government agencies, political parties, private business, and labor organizations are included.

276. *Japan Electronics Almanac.* Dempa Publications, Inc., 1-11-15 Higashigotanda, Shinagawa-ku, Tokyo 141. (03) 445-6111. (03) 444-7515 Fax. In U.S., contact Dempa Publications, Inc., 380 Madison Ave., New York, NY 10017. (212) 752-3003. (212) 752-3289 Fax. Annual (April). 334 p. ISBN 0-8002-4134-7. $35.00.

Continuing *Japan Fact Book*, this almanac lists the leading Japanese electronic firms, showing their present status and future prospects. Part 1 is a detailed review of the Japanese electronics industry by sector. Gives profiles of companies as well as forecasts of anticipated performance. Provides a great deal of statistical and tabular information. Narrative information is provided on the industry rather than on individual companies. The top 100 electronics companies are listed in rank order by sales value. Part 2 profiles Japanese electronics companies. The companies in this section are advertisers. No consistency of information other than in the brief profile, i.e., address, company president, date company established, capital stock, number of employees. This section is not extensive.

277. *Japan Marketing/Advertising Yearbook.* Dentsu, Inc., 1-11-10 Tsukiji, Chuo-ku, Tokyo 104. (03) 544-5585. (03) 545-1227 Fax. In Europe, contact Duncan Pub. Co., 3 Colin Gardens, Hendon, London NW9 6EL. (01) 205-4186. Annual. ISBN A-88553-861-4. 350 p. $40.00.

Formerly *Dentsu Japan Marketing/Advertising*, this is a thorough guide to the Japanese advertizing marketplace providing a general overview of marketing in Japan followed by specific chapters detailing advice and data on the industrial buyer; economics of marketing in Japan; advertizing costs and volume; advertizing by sector; newspapers, magazines and books; and television, radio, and the news media. Statistical data and a calendar of marketing opportunities are provided. Directory sections include advertizing agencies and PR firms; market research organizations; publishing details for newspapers and magazines, including their advertizing rates; and listing of television and radio stations, including their advertizing rates.

278. *Japan Science and Technology Outlook.* Fuji Corp., Han-ei Dai-2 Bldg., 1-10-1 Shinjuku, Shinjuku-ku, Tokyo 160. (03) 350-8701. Annual. 300 p. $65.00.

This is a summary of the white paper published annually by the Science and Technology Agency. It analyzes progress made in various scientific and technical fields.

279. *Japan Statistical Yearbook.* Japan Statistical Association (Mainichi Shimbun-shu), 19-1 Wakamatsu-cho, Shinjuku-ku, Tokyo 162. (03) 202-1589. Annual. 38th ed., 1988. 836 p. ISSN 0389-9004. ISBN 0-8002-4241-6. $200.00.

Edited by Statistics Bureau, Management and Coordination Agency of the Prime Minister's Office, this is a comprehensive compilation of economic and social statistics. Covers land, population, economy, business, finance, living standards, and cultural statistical data in Japanese with English translation. Unfortunately the appendix—Guide to Sources—is in Japanese only, as is the index, but a detailed table of contents is adequate because the work is arranged logically within broad categories. This is the official statistical yearbook for basic statistics in all fields.

280. *Japan's Financial Markets.* Foundation for Advanced Information and Research (FAIR), Tokyo. Distributed by Look Japan International Ltd., 712-713 Jardine House, 1 Connaught Pl., Central Hong Kong. (852) 525-8015. (852) 810-0670 Fax. 1986–87. ISSN 0912-9812. (FAIR Fact Series). $135.00.

Edited by the Financial Fact Series Committee of the Foundation for Advanced Information and Research (FAIR), this is a series of 40 booklets in looseleaf format. It provides a guide to the changing Japanese financial market in a historical and international context. Each booklet discusses a single topic and is complete in itself. They are written by experts in the area and provide a range of differing perspectives.

281. *Japan's Iron and Steel Industry.* Kawata Publicity, Inc., Hatori Bldg., 5-5-6 Koishikawa, Bunkyo-ku, Tokyo 112; CPO Box 1157, Tokyo 100-91. (03) 945-3878. (03) 945-4870 Fax. Annual. 218 p. ISBN 4-905615-0301. $42.00 (includes airmail).

Provides a good overview of the iron and steel industry. Part 1 offers the steel industry at a glance, including tables. Part 2 is an annual review, and Part 3 discusses trade in steel. Part 4 predicts the future of Japan's steel industry. Part 5 details research in new steel-making technology. Part 6 discusses new steel products; Part 7, management strategies; Part 8, buyer's guide; and Part 9, steel statistics.

282. *JIS Yearbook.* Japanese Standards Association, 4-1-24 Akasaka, Minato-ku, Tokyo 107. (03) 583-8001. (03) 586-2014 Fax. In the U.S., contact Information Handling Services, 15 Inverness Way, E, Englewood, CO 80110. (303) 790-0600 or (800) 241-7824. (303) 790-0617 Fax. Annual. 191 p. $20.00.

A listing of Japanese industrial standards together with prices. JIS has also published a number of industry-specific, English-language compilations of Japanese standards. Some of these are Electronics, Ferrous Materials and Metallurgy, NonFerrous Metals and Metallurgy, Electrical Installation and Apparatus, Piping, Ceramics, Fasteners and Screw Threads, Plastics, Concrete Practice, Machine Elements, and Welding. A monthly publication, *Standardization Journal,* also published by the Japanese Standards Association, lists new and revised standards. The sales agent for Japanese standards in the U.S. is the American National Standards Institute (ANSI), New York.

283. *Nippon: A Chartered Survey of Japan.* Kokusei-Sha Corp., Daiichi-Seimei Bldg., 2-19-3 Nishi-Gotunda, Shinagawa-ku, Tokyo 141. (03) 492-5878. Distributed in the U.S. by Maruzen Co. Annual. 360 p. ISBN 0-8002-4245-9. $60.00.

Edited by the Tsuneta Yano Memorial Society, this monograph provides accurate statistical data on Japan. It features over 300 tables and 100 charts and statistics arranged by prefectures. Contents include geography in brief; people; political aspects; climate; population; economy—labor, national income, foreign trade, commodity prices; industries—agriculture, manufacturing, textiles, rubber, chemicals, banking, insurance, communications; social life; and trends.

284. *Nippon Business Facts and Figures.* Japan External Trade Organization (JETRO), 1221 Avenue of the Americas, New York, NY 10020. (212) 997-0400. Annual (June). 160 p. $20.00.

A bilingual publication in Japanese and English, this monograph presents a wide range of statistical information covering the economy, business, and industry. Information is selected on the basis that it is useful to the foreign businessperson. Special sections include analysis of the Japanese new materials market, R&D expenditures, effects of the yen appreciation, and the increasing internationalization of Japan's economy.

285. *A Perspective on the Japanese Electronics Industry.* Electronics Industries Association of Japan, Tokyo Chamber of Commerce and Industry Bldg., 3-2-2 Marunouchi, Chiyoda-ku, Tokyo 100. (03) 211-2765. (03) 287-1712 Fax. In U.S., contact Japan Electronics Bureau (JEB), #1533, One Penn Plaza, 250 W. 34th St., New York, NY 10119. (212) 489-6270. (212) 279-6130 Fax. Annual. 16 p. Gratis.

A small pamphlet which outlines trends in the Japanese electronics industry through a series of tables, charts, and graphs. Useful as a freely available source of current statistics for the Japanese electronics industry.

286. *Pharma Japan Yearbook.* Yakugyo Jiho Co., Ltd., 2-36 Jimbocho Kanda, Chiyoda-ku, Tokyo 101. (03) 265-7751. (03) 234-6573 Fax. Annual. 124 p. $70.00.

Covers background information and future trends in the Japanese pharmaceutical industry. Includes new products, R&D activity, and government policy. Yakugyo Jiho Co. Ltd. also publishes the weekly *Pharma Japan Journal.*

287. *Practical Handbook of Productivity and Labour Statistics.* Japan Productivity Center, Overseas Technical Cooperation Department, 3-1-1 Shibuya, Shibuya-ku, Tokyo 150. (03) 409-1111. (03) 409-1986 Fax. Biannual. 157 p. $30.00.

Handbook covers macro- and micro-performance, trends, levels of productivity, wages, prices, and other data relating to labor management practices. International comparisons are provided. Data are presented in tabular format. The Japanese-language edition is published annually. Since 1985, an English-language edition is published every other year.

288. *Price Indexes Annual.* Bank of Japan, Research and Statistics Department, 2-2-1 Hongoku-cho, Nihonbashi, Chuo-ku, Tokyo 103. (03) 279-1111. (03) 279-5801 Fax. Annual. 487 p. $25.00.

Contains a breakdown by sector of wholesale (domestic wholesale, export, import, and overall wholesale) price indexes and input-output price indexes for the manufacturing industry. Data are presented in tabular format. In Japanese with English translation. Monthly price indexes are also available, *Price Indexes Monthly.*

289. *Report on the Survey of Research and Development.* Statistics Bureau, Management and Coordination Agency, 19-1 Wakama-suchu, Shinjukuku, Tokyo 162. (03) 202-1111. Annual. 241 p. ISBN 4-8223-1030-2. $30.00.

Bilingual reports on the annual *Survey of Research and Development* which has been published annually since 1959. Object of the survey is to report on current status of research and development in Japan. Originally, the survey only covered universities and research institutions. In 1960, it was expanded to cover private firms and special corporations.

290. *Science Council of Japan Annual Report.* Science Council of Japan, 7-22-34 Roppongi, Minato-ku, Tokyo 106. (03) 403-6291. Annual. 71 p.

The Science Council of Japan, founded in 1949, represents Japanese scientists both in Japan and internationally. It is concerned with the development of science in Japan and the international exchange of science. It also recommends science policy to the government, arranges international visits for Japanese scientists, and sponsors international conferences. The annual report outlines activities of the various divisions and committees for the preceding fiscal year.

291. *Statistical Handbook of Japan.* Japan Statistical Association, 19-1 Wakamatsu-cho, Shinjuku-ku, Tokyo 162. (03) 202-1589. Annual (May). 158 p. ISSN 0081-4792. $23.00.

Compiled by the Statistics Bureau of the Management and Coordination Agency, this is a pocket-sized handbook for foreigners. It covers the major statistics for Japan—political, economic, social, and cultural—through tables, charts, colored photographs, and short textual notes. Data are taken from major statistical publications, both governmental and private.

292. *Statistical Survey of Japan's Economy.* Sekai-No-Ugoki-sha, 1-6-14 Nishishimbashi, Minato-ku, Tokyo 105. (03) 504-1655. Annual (November). 84 p. $28.00.

Continues *Statistical Survey of Economy of Japan*, published for the Economic and Foreign Affairs Research Institute. This publication presents historical and comparative data on the Japanese economy by means of charts, tables, and graphs.

293. *Statistics on Japanese Industries.* Ministry of International Trade and Industry, Statistics Association, Kobikikan Ginza Bldg., 2-8-9 Ginza, Chuo-ku, Tokyo 104. (03) 561-2974. Annual (March). 196 p. $30.00.

Published for the Research and Statistics Department of the Ministry of International Trade and Industry (MITI), this annual provides production figures (actual and indices) and the census of manufacturers and commerce. It contains sections on national accounts; indexed statistics; manufacturing; commerce; current production in selected industries; foreign transactions; finance and banking; employment; and prices. Statistics are compiled by MITI with supplementary materials from other agencies for the previous five years. For more detailed monthly statistics, see *Industrial Statistics Monthly.* Fourteen sections cover the following: indices of industrial activities; current production statistics; manufacturing; commerce; index of tertiary industries' activity; energy; public utilities; construction; business operation; industrial technology, patents; foreign transactions; national accounts; money, prices; and population, employment.

294. *Steel Industry of Japan.* Japan Iron and Steel Federation, 1-9-4 Otemachi, Chiyoda-ku, Tokyo 100. (03) 279-3611. Annual. 33 p. $5.00.

Largely a promotional type of publication setting out the previous year's activities in the Japanese steel industry. Charts are used to portray factual information. Contents include a general overview of the industry, production, the domestic market, the steel trade, energy, raw materials, equipment and technology, industrial relations, plant management and computerization, and international markets.

295. *White Paper on International Trade.* Japan External Trade Organization (JETRO), Publications Department, 2-2-5 Toranomon, Minato-ku, Tokyo 105. (03) 582-3518. (03) 587-2485 Fax. Annual. 430 p. ISBN 4-8224-0424-2. $75.00.

This is a partial English translation of MITI's *White Paper on International Trade.* Only the "General Section" and "Japan's Trade Statistics" sections are translated from the Japanese white paper.

296. *White Paper on Japanese Economy.* Business Intercommunications, Inc. (BII), CPO Box 587, Tokyo 100-91. (03) 423-3971. (03) 423-3996 Fax. Annual. 112 p. ISBN 4-89377-003-9. $86.00 (including airmail).

Edited by the Economic Planning Agency, this is an annual translation and abridgement of the Japanese-language white paper on the Japanese economy prepared by the Economic Planning Agency. Contains major points from the original Japanese report.

297. *White Papers of Japan: Annual Abstract of Official Reports and Statistics of the Japanese Government.* Japan Institute of International Affairs, 19th Mori Bldg., 1-2-20 Toranomon, Minato-ku, Tokyo 105. (03) 503-7261. (03) 595-1755 Fax. Annual. 1971–. 214 p.

Subtitled "annual abstracts of official reports and statistics of the Japanese government," this publication provides a brief abstract of white papers and reports from Japan that are available in English translation. There is a useful list of the white papers providing title, date of publication, and the ministry that published the paper. Part 1 contains the extensive translated abstracts of the white papers. Numerous tables and figures are reproduced throughout the text. Part 2 includes translated versions of policy speeches from the Prime Minister and the Foreign Minister. The appendix provides basic statistical data on Japan.

298. *Yearbook of World Electronics Data 1990. Vol. 2: America, Japan and Asia-Pacific.* Elsevier Advanced Technology, Mayfield House, 256 Banbury Rd., Oxford, OX2 7DH. (0865) 51-2242. (0865) 31-0981 Fax. 7th ed. 1990. ISBN 0-948577-43-6. $890.00.

Provides market data for 1988–93 and production data for 1987–90. Summary import-export values are provided. Four major sections cover introduction and statistical interpretation, summary data, country data, and appendixes. The following categories are handled in depth: electronic data processing, office equipment, control and instrumentation, medical and industrial communications, and military, telecommunications, consumer and components. The appendixes include exchange rate summaries, translations of product headings in French, German, and Italian, and guides to International Statistical Classifications and definitions of electronic product headings. The extensive statistical information from the yearbook is also available on Lotus 1-2-3 compatible diskettes.

Chapter 8
Newsletters and Magazines

The titles listed in this chapter are grouped together under the heading newsletters because most of them are short (under 10 pages), frequently published works whose function is to keep the reader abreast of current developments in Japan. These are most prevalent in the scientific and technological areas, but some also relate to business.

The publications represented in this group are among the most volatile of all Japanese information sources. Because they are typically expensive and aimed at a narrow market, the offerings of new titles are frequent, but their demise is also highly probable. For this reason, the reader should be aware that, although the titles were extant at this writing, they may already have ceased publication by the time one attempts to place a subscription.

Because the cost tends to be high, sample copies can usually be requested from the publisher. This will enable the prospective subscriber to review the contents for relevancy. If possible, request a couple of issues to avoid disappointment when subsequent issues fail to meet the expectations set by perusing the contents of a single issue.

Along with the true newsletter publications, a few magazines or more substantial publications have been included because their content is essentially similar, i.e., they represent current awareness-types of services. No attempt has been made to include specialty journals covering specific areas of science and technology or business, because this is outside the scope of this reference work. By referring to the bibliographies listed in the chapter on bibliographies, one can obtain titles of primary journals in specific subject areas.

299. *Advanced Technology Series.* Newmedia International Japan, Avenida Infanta Carlota, 74, 5° 1ª, 08029 Barcelona, Spain. (93) 410-7034. Monthly. 21 p. Three titles. $275.00 (each title/year).

Special rate for subscribers to all three titles in the series: Magnetic Materials, Film Technologies and Applications, and Laser Technologies and Applications. Provides extensive abstracts with some more detailed reports for some entries. Provides information on new products, technologies, and processes. The name and address of the relevant company is included for each entry. Sources for the information are not given.

300. *Biotechnology in Japan News Service.* Japan Pacific Associates, 467 Hamilton Ave., #2, Palo Alto, CA 94301. (415) 322-8441. Monthly. 7–8 p. $450.00.

Begun in 1982, this service covers developments in biotechnology in Japan for readers outside of Japan. Material on current biotechnology developments in Japan is selected, translated, and reviewed by a panel of experts.

301. *Business Japan.* Nihon Kogyo Shimbun, 1-28-5 Kanda Jinbocho 1-chome, Chiyoda-ku, Tokyo 100. (03) 292-6131. Monthly. $96.00.

Intended for the businessperson, this publication covers international operations of Japanese companies and developments in industrial technology. Economic and political news is included.

302. *Business Tokyo.* Keizaikai U.S.A., Inc., 1270 Avenue of the Americas, New York, NY 10020. (212) 757-2135. Monthly. $60.00.

General interest magazine that publishes news and commentary on Japanese business.

303. *CITEC Newsletter.* Japan External Trade Organization (JETRO), 1221 Avenue of the Americas, New York, NY 10020. (212) 997-0400. Quarterly. 4 p. Gratis.

A newsletter of the events of the Centers for Industrial and Technological Cooperation (CITEC), of which there are seven in the U.S. located within the JETRO offices. There are also five centers in European cities. CITEC was established in 1983 to foster capital investment and technology transfer between Japan and Japanese companies and foreign countries.

304. *Comline Daily News.* Comline International Corp., Shugetsu Bldg., 3-12-7, Kita-Aoyama, Minato-ku, Tokyo 107. (03) 486-0696. (03) 400-7704 Fax. In U.S., contact InfoCorp., 20370 Town Center Ln. #137, Cupertino, CA 95014. (408) 257-9956. (408) 257-0695 Fax. Weeklies. $2,376.00/year. Monthlies. $650.00/year.

Offers a series of printed newsletters which provide very timely information directly from Tokyo. Information is compiled by the Comline staff from mass media publications, television broadcasts, trade and business publications, and government publications. The same information is also offered electronically via the G.E. Mark III Network. All information can be downloaded into personalized databases using proprietary TRBase software which is provided along with the subscription. There are eight weekly services covering the following areas: electronics; computers; telecommunications; chemicals; biotechnology; industrial automation; transportation; and financial markets. There are 28 monthly publications that represent subsets taken from the above broad categories for those who require a more limited subject area, at a lower cost. These subsets are aerospace; agricultural technology; artificial intelligence; biotechnology equipment; CAD/CAM and FA; ceramic materials; communications equipment; composite materials; electronic materials; genetic engineering; IC technology; image processing; machine tools; magnetic optical storage; medical instrumentation; measuring equipment; metallurgy; microcomputers and peripherals; optoelectronics; pharmaceuticals; plastics, resins, and fibers; robots; sensors; software; super, mainframe, and minicomputers; superconductors; and wafer fabrication. The company also provides a customized monthly service if none of the above categories are suitable or if one prefers to pay only for relevant citations. This service is priced at $11.00 per month and $0.89 per article retrieved. For more details on the Comline service offered by the online vendor, DIALOG (see Chapter 11, Online Databases).

305. *Dempa Digest.* Dempa Publications, Inc., Dempa Shimbu-sha, 1-11-15 Higashi-Gotanda, Shinagawa-ku, Tokyo 141. (03) 445-6111. (03) 444-7515 Fax. In the U.S., contact Dempa Publications, Inc., 400 Madison Ave., New York, NY 10017. (212) 752-3003. (212) 752-3289 Fax. Weekly (50 issues/year). 12 p. ISSN 0288-6103. $300.00.

Subtitled "a weekly survey from Japan's largest electronics publisher," the digest provides brief reviews of new developments and the current status of all aspects of the electronics industry in Japan—people, processes, procurement, patents, profits, and production. It covers audio, video, semiconductors, ICs, and company news. It reprints articles from Japan's largest daily electronics newspaper (*Dempa Shimbun*). Compiled and edited from *Dempa Shimbun,* it is prepared in English and distributed by air mail from Tokyo.

306. *Digitized Information.* Akatsutsumi 3-4-2-202, Setagaya-ku, Tokyo 156. (03) 325-4660. (03) 325-7540 Fax. In U.S., contact Tech Search International, Inc., 9430 Research Blvd., Bldg. 4, #400, Austin, TX 78759. (512) 343-4508. (512) 345-2924 Fax. Daily report. $1,800/year. Weekly report. $1,800/year. Industry-specific weeklies. $750.00 each/year; $375.00 to subscribers of the daily/weekly service. Company-specific weeklies. $550.00 each/year; $275.00 to subscribers of the daily/weekly service.

A daily newspaper abstracting service that monitors the Japanese press covering the Japanese electronics industry. It covers Japan's six most influential industrial, financial, and electronics dailies. It is delivered by telefacsimile or electronic mail by 10:00 a.m. each morning. A print option is available. A weekly service is also offered. The weekly service is a compilation of the week's five daily reports. There are five industry-specific weeklies covering Telecommunications, Semiconductors, Data Processing, Microcomputers, and Optoelectronics. The following organizations are covered: Fujitsu, Hitachi, IBM Japan, Japanese Government, Matsushita, Mitsubishi, NEC, NTT, and Toshiba.

307. *DJIT—Digest of Japanese Industry and Technology.* Japan Trade and Industry Publicity, Inc., Teranomon Kotohira Kaikan, 1-2-8 Toranomon, Minato-ku, Tokyo 105. (03) 503-4051. (03) 501-4615 Fax. Bimonthly. 64 p. $90.00.

This publication is aimed at foreigners interested in importing Japanese products. It includes articles on Japan's international trade relations from both the economic and political aspects. It also provides information on current technology and on specific industries and products for export.

308. *EGIS Sector Specific Newsletters.* EGIS, Inc., 22-1 Ichibancho, Chiyoda-ku, Tokyo. (03) 264-1060. (03) 265-2260 Fax. In U.S., contact EGIS, Inc., 220 W. Mercer St., Seattle, WA 98119. (206) 282-6001. (206) 283-4938 Fax.

Industry-specific newsletters that monitor Japanese technology. They contain approximately 15–20 articles covering important recent events, forming a representative perspective of technical and industrial developments in Japanese high technology areas. They are transmitted directly from Tokyo in printed format, generally six pages in length. Front page provides a brief editorial analysis written by EGIS staff members and a list of headlines of the articles contained within the report for rapid scanning. Diagrams and small format photos occasionally accompany the text. Some overlap of coverage exists between the newsletters. Sectors covered are Telecommunications, Optoelectronics, Microelectronics, Mechatronics, Information Technology, Automotive Technology, and Biotechnology. EGIS also publishes industry surveys. (See Chapter 9, Industry Reports.)

309. *EIAJ Newsletter.* Electronics Industries Association of Japan, Nihon Denshi Kikai Kogyokai, Tosho Bldg., 3-2-2 Marunouchi, Chiyoda-ku, Tokyo 100. (03) 213-1071. (03) 213-1078 Fax. In U.S., contact Baron/Canning Co., Inc., 555 Madison Ave., New York, NY 10022. (212) 751-7100. (212) 593-4906 Fax. Quarterly. 8 p. Gratis.

Newsletter for the electronics industry. Also provides news of the association and statistics of production and exports and imports for the Japanese electronics industry.

310. *EIU Country Reporting Service. Japan.* Economist Intelligence Unit, Economist Publications Ltd., 40 Duke St., London W1A 1DW. (01) 493-6711. In U.S., contact Economist Publications, 10 Rockefeller Plaza, 12th Fl., New York, NY 10020. (212) 541-5730. $110.00.

Consists of two components: *Country Report*, quarterly, providing an analysis of economic and political developments; and *Country Profile*, annual, detailing the political and economic structure within the country and how it functions. This service is also available for 164 other countries.

311. *Electro Data Net.* Marcom International, Inc., #805, Akasaka Omotemachi Bldg., 4-8-19 Akasaka, Minato-ku, Tokyo 107. (03) 403-8515. Monthly. $500.00.

Provides news on the semiconductor industry in the Pacific Rim region, it identifies trends and new applications for existing technology. Subscribers to the newsletter are entitled to a retrieval-consultation service for additional information on articles appearing in *Electro Data Net.* There is a limit of two inquiries per month for this consultation service.

312. *Focus Japan.* Japan External Trade Organization (JETRO), Overseas Public Relations Department, 2-2-5 Toranomon, Minato-ku, Tokyo 105. (03) 582-5511. (03) 582-0656 Fax. Distributed in U.S. by JETRO, 1221 Avenue of the Americas, New York, NY 10020. (212) 997-0400. Also distributed through Japan Trade Center offices in New York, Chicago, Los Angeles, San Francisco, and Houston. Monthly. 10 p. $28.00.

Covers economic and business developments in Japan. A general interest newsletter, it includes short articles on Japanese business, labor, technological developments, life styles, and culture. Business news, MITI news, and government news is included. Format is glossy with many photographs, more a public relations tool for JETRO. It includes advertising.

313. *Focus on Japan.* Council on Superconductivity for American Competitiveness, 1050 Thomas Jefferson St., NW, 6th Fl., Washington, DC 20007. (202) 965-4070. Monthly. 4 p. $125.00 (free to members).

Reports on Japanese developments in superconductivity. Information is taken from Japanese trade and technical publications, then translated. Begun in

1988, the council has published 11 issues to date; however, translation costs are causing problems. Indications are that the council will continue to publish information for subscribers in some form, but new subscribers are not being accepted at this time.

314. *Forward Technology Series.* Newmedia International Japan, Avenida Infanta Carlota, 74, 5° 1ª, 08029 Barcelona, Spain. (93) 410-7034. Monthly. 21 p. 2 titles. $275.00 each title/year.

The two titles comprising this monthly, Photo-Active Materials and Advanced Materials, Processes and Equipment, provide an extensive abstract with some more detailed reports for some entries. Provides information on new products, technologies, and processes. Name and address of the relevant company included for each entry, sources for information not provided.

315. *Headline News.* Evision Enterprises, 65 Ashey Rd., Ryde, Isle of Wight, P033 2UZ U.K. Monthly. $240.00/year.

Various subject-specific bulletins are offered: Magnetic Recording Discs and Drives, Magnetic Tape Recording, Magnetic Tape Media, Magnetic Recording Heads, Video Recording, Optical Recording, Electronic Components, and Electronic Circuit Technology. Provides information on new products, applications, business developments and company news, improvements in production designs, materials, equipment, techniques, testing, specifications, reliability, and R&D. Information is taken from current publications of manufacturers/suppliers, technical journals, reports and books, reviews of conferences and exhibitions, and patents and patent applications. Although not limited to Japan, much of the information contained therein originates in Japan, particularly patent activity. Unfortunately, some of the bibliographic information is incomplete.

316. *Industrial and Commercial Applications of Japanese New Materials (IACA Series).* Newmedia International Japan, Avenida Infanta Carlota, 74, 5° 1ª, 08029 Barcelona, Spain. (93) 410-7034. Monthly. Four titles. 21 p./monthly issue. $275.00 each title/year. Special rate offered to subscribers to all four titles in the series.

1. *High Performance Ceramics* — covers industry applications, new processes, new technologies, new products, composites, fibers, powders, structural materials, porous materials, machinable materials, electronic materials, and new test and measuring equipment.
2. *Electronic Materials* — covers electronic ceramics, quartz, bioelectronics, semiconductors, metallic materials, inorganic materials, high-purity chemicals and gases, recording materials, insulating materials, magnetic materials, rare earth materials, synthetic metals, superconducting materials.
3. *Advanced Plastics* — covers coatings, films, paints, adhesives, membranes, fibers, shape-memory plastics, resins, composites, super engineering plastics, and electrical and electronic related materials.
4. *Advanced Alloys and Metals* — covers electrical, electronic, automobile, aircraft, aerospace, optical, audiovisual, office automation, telecommunications, information, general engineering, precision engineering, construction, general machinery, nuclear engineering, chemical, petrochemical, energy, and medical.

There is no overlap in coverage, i.e., no report is contained in more than one newsletter. Included are addresses of companies and associations referred to in the articles, which is useful for obtaining more detailed information.

317. *International Information Report: The International Industry Dossier.* Washington Researchers Pub. Co., 2612 P St., NW, Washington, DC 20007. (202) 333-3533. Monthly. 8 p. $120.00/year.

Global information covering foreign competition, political risk, demographic changes, export markets, investment opportunities, and supply forecasts. Covers the world, but some very useful information on Japan appears regularly.

318. *J-TIES Evaluation Reports.* Japan Technical Information and Evaluation Service (J-TIES Inc.), 312 Nagatani Hill Plaza, 7-3-8 Roppongi, Minato-ku, Tokyo 106. (03) 423-2400. (03) 470-4141 Fax. In U.S., contact J-TIES, USA Office, c/o Prof. Jeffrey Frey, University of Maryland, College Park, MD 20742. (301) 454-1608. (301) 454-1917 Fax. Monthly. $15,000; $8,000 for each additional field; $50,000 for all eight fields.

Monitors Japanese-language conferences, seminars, and technical meetings of professional societies. The best papers are selected for evaluation. A panel of technical experts composed of Japanese university faculty and industrial researchers further evaluate the selected papers and prepare brief summary evaluation sheets. These are then compiled by the J-TIES staff and distributed to subscribers. The evaluation sheets are generally sent within three weeks of the paper being presented at the conference or meeting. *J-TIES Reports* are available in the following areas: Semiconductor Electronics I (Silicon-based), Semiconductor Electronics II (Compounds), Integrated Electronics, New Ceramics and Superconductors, Artificial Intelligence, Computers and Communication, and Image Processing and Databases. J-TIES evaluates approximately 5,400 papers in the above fields per year. For an extra fee, translations of abstracts or full papers are available.

319. *Japan Bioindustry Letters.* BioIndustry Development Center (BIDEC), 5-10-5 Shimbashi, Minato-ku, Tokyo 105. (03) 433-3545. (03) 459-1440 Fax. Quarterly. 20 p. Gratis to nonprofit organizations.

BIDEC is a nonprofit organization that promotes the industrialization of the Japanese biotechnology industry. Formed in 1983 under an initiative proposed by MITI, it promotes cooperation among industry, academia, and government. Newsletter provides an introductory section that reports at some length on recent meetings or conferences. Feature sections include Topics—brief entries taken from Japanese newspapers and trade literature—and News—brief entries on newsworthy items of interest to the bioindustry taken from Japanese newspapers.

320. *Japan Chemical Week.* Chemical Daily Co. Ltd., 3-16-8 Nihonbashi, Hama-cho, Chuo-ku, Tokyo 103. (03) 663-7932. (03) 663-2530 Fax. Weekly. 8 p. ISSN 0047-1755. $312.00.

Published since 1960, this weekly newsletter covers news and statistical data on the Japanese chemical market. Coverage includes petrochemicals, plastics, organic and inorganic chemicals, agrochemicals, synthetic fibers and rubbers, pharmaceuticals, dyestuffs, surfactants, paints and varnishes, biochemicals as well as market information. Specialty chemicals, biotechnology, and electronics, materials and chemicals-related industries are also covered.

321. *Japan Compunews.* McWord Center, Inc. (subsidiary of Mitsubishi Corp.), 1-1, Ichigaya Honmura-cho, Shinjuku-ku, Tokyo 162. (03) 269-5959. (03) 269-5967 Fax. Biweekly (25 issues). 12 p. ISSN 0914-1448. $995.00.

Available in print or electronic format, this newsletter provides information on Japan's computer and communications industry. Coverage includes current industry trends, analysis, market projections; new product developments in mainframes, PCs, peripherals, electronics, software, telecommunications, networks, artificial intelligence; corporate strategies for domestic and export business by Japanese computer companies; Japanese government positions on computer and communications issues; and summaries of research conducted by Japanese computer and information associations.

322. *Japan Computer Quarterly.* Japan Information Processing Development Center (JIPDEC), Kikai Shinko Kaikan Bldg., 5-8 Shibakoen 3-chome, Minato-ku, Tokyo 105. (03) 434-8211. (03) 432-9379 Fax. Order from Fuji Corp., Han-ei, No. 2, Bldg. 6F, 1-10-1 Shinjuku, Shinjuku-ku, Tokyo 160. (03) 350-8701. (03) 350-8708 Fax. Quarterly (Mar, June, Sep, Dec). ISSN 0910-6707. $85.00/year; $22.00/single issue.

Formerly *JIPDEC Report*, each issue published is complete in itself. Coverage includes data on the use and sales of computer hardware and software, information on the impact of new technology, and news briefs.

323. *Japan Daily Hi-Tech Letter (JDHL).* EGIS, Inc., 22-1 Ichibancho, Chiyuda-ku, Tokyo. (03) 264-1060. (03) 265-2260 Fax. In U.S., contact EGIS, Inc., 220 W. Mercer St., Seattle, WA 98119. (206) 282-6001. (206) 283-4938 Fax. Daily. $265.00/month.

EGIS staff scan the trade and industrial press to identify commercial- and technology-related events of interest to the electronics industry. Each news item consists of a 10-line synopsis. Information is sent via electronic mail or facsimile. More detailed information on each report is available from EGIS.

324. *Japan Economic Survey.* Japan Economic Institute (JEI), 1000 Connecticut Ave., NW, Washington, DC 20036. (202) 296-5633. Monthly. 16 p. ISSN 0888-5710. Gratis.

Provides a review of U.S.-Japan economic relations. Contains some in-depth articles on the economy and industry-specific issues. Regular sections include "Month in Review" and "Issue Briefs."

325. *Japan Electronics Today News (JET News).* Benn Electronics Publications Ltd., P.O. Box 28, Luton, LU1 2NT. (0582) 41-7438. Bimonthly (24 issues). ISSN 0261-3506. $495.00.

Benn publishes several publications on the Japanese electronics industry. This newsletter covers new developments in electronics—products, technology, companies, and markets. The coverage of the electronics industry is broad based: consumer electronics, components, transport, computers/office equipment, communications/telecommunications, production equipment, materials and associated components, industrial and medical equipment, control and instrumentation, industrial news, statistics.

326. *Japan High Tech Review.* The Mead Ventures, Inc., PO Box 44952, Phoenix, AZ 85064. Or from Oryx Press, 4041 N. Central Ave., Phoenix, AZ 85012. (602) 234-0044. (602) 234-0076 Fax. Monthly. 12-16 p. ISSN 0743-4871. $295.00.

Published by a U.S. firm monitoring high-tech areas in Japan. It is nontechnical in scope, aimed at the market-research community for the computer and communications industry. Its tone is provocative, gossipy. Mead reads Japanese publications, travels to Japan, and maintains sources throughout industry and government here and in Japan. Articles on high-tech developments in Japan cover one to two pages. A "Notes" section gives a page of short three to four line items on company and product news or other items of interest to Japan watchers such as Japanese vs U.S. production statistics in electronics. Final section is the "Editor's Corner," an editorial section.

327. *Japan M&A Reporter.* Ulmer Brothers, Inc., 80 Maiden Ln., 22nd Fl., New York, NY 10038. (212) 344-4411. (212) 344-8074 Fax. Monthly. 8 p. $575.00 (inc. *Pacific M&A Reporter*, bimonthly 4 p., and *Japan/Europe M&A Reporter*, bimonthly 4 p.).

Tracks mergers, acquisitions, investments, and real estate deals between U.S. and Japanese companies. First few pages of narrative are journalistic in style. Brief two to three line reports follow covering recent deals and acquisitions. The last three pages consist of a chart listing recent M&A activity between Japanese and U.S. companies.

328. *Japan Medical Review.* Japan Publications Inc., Kyodo (Akasuka) Bldg., 4-3-1 Akasuka, Minato-ku, Tokyo 107. (03) 589-3627. (03) 505-0376 Fax. In U.S., contact Japan Publications Inc., 150 Post St., #500, San Francisco, CA 94108. (415) 772-5555. (415) 772-5659 Fax. Monthly. 20 p. Semiannual index. $450.00.

Covers Ministry of Health news, manufacturer and distributor news, Japanese market segment analysis, R&D, and manufacturer/distributor profiles. Also joint venture/licensing news; who's who in Japanese healthcare industry; calendar of forthcoming Japanese medical conventions; stock market trends; and management news, e.g., new appointments are included. Many charts, statistics, and graphical material included.

329. *Japan Report: Science and Technology.* Foreign Broadcast Information Service (FBIS), Joint Publications Research Service (JPRS). Available from U.S. Department of Commerce, National Technical Information Service (NTIS), 5285 Port Royal Rd., Springfield, VA 22161. (703) 487-4650. (703) 321-8199 Fax. 3/week. $5.00/issue.

Full text English translations of articles selected from 250 Japanese scientific and technical journals. Occasionally, the complete proceedings will be included from important conferences. Covers the following areas: advanced materials, aerospace, civil aviation, automotive industry, defense industries, energy, lasers, sensors, optics, and telecommunications.

330. *Japan Report Series.* Newmedia International Japan, Avenida Infanta Carlota, 74, 5º 1ª, 08029 Barcelona, Spain. (93) 410-7134. Monthly. 21 p. 6 titles. Special rates apply for combined subscriptions. Biotechnology, $425.00; Medical Technology, $425.00; Telecommunications, $345.00; Information Technology, $345.00; Software, $425.00; Product Opportunities, $475.00.

Provides information on new products, technologies, and processes. The name and address of companies mentioned in each article is included. Sources for the information are not included.

331. *Japan Robot News.* Survey Japan, 61, No. 6 Kojimachi Bldg., 4-5 Kojimachi, Chiyoda-ku, Tokyo 102. (03) 262-7476. (03) 262-7453 Fax. Quarterly. 10 p. $380.00.

Consists primarily of brief new items, with two to three more in-depth articles in each issue. It covers the robotics and automation industry in Japan. Major developments, new products, R&D, government policies, and market trends are covered.

332. *Japan Technology Bulletin.* Three "I" Publications Ltd., 1-5-16 Uchikanda, Chiyoda-ku, Tokyo 101. (03) 256-3100. (03) 256-3160 Fax. Monthly. $300.00 (including airmail).

Arranged in three sections. General Information covers government reports, high tech trends, business trends. Techno-Reports covers mechatronics, computers and electronics, new materials, energy and resources, chemicals and biochemicals. There are brief summaries of approximately 300 words. New Products and Technologies Index is arranged by the same five broad subject areas used in the other two sections. Brief three to four line summaries are provided. Listed under company. Brief information about latest products and technologies from various companies.

333. *Japan-U.S. Business Report.* Japan Economic Institute (JEI), 1000 Connecticut Ave., NW, Washington, DC 20036. (202) 296-5633. Monthly. ISSN 0888-5702. $125.00.

See also *JEI REPORT* published by JEI (special combined rate of $150.00 for this and *JEI REPORT*, $130.00 for academic institutions). Activities of U.S. companies in Japan and Japanese companies in the U.S. with an index of company names. Gives details of marketing plans, investment strategies, mergers, and joint-venture agreements between Japanese and U.S. companies. Provides information by company name and geographic location on what U.S. companies are doing in Japan and what Japanese companies are doing in the U.S. Information taken from Japanese- and English-language trade journals, bank publications, newspapers, and government trading and investment sources.

334. *JAPANSCAN Food Industry Bulletin.* Mitaka, 3-5 Tavistock St., Leamington, Spa CV3 5PF. (0926) 31-1126. (0926) 32-990 Fax. Monthly. 34 p. ISSN 0264-3812. 265 pounds (including airmail).

A series of monthly current awareness reports that provide an English-language summary of developments that occurred over the last four to five weeks in the Japanese food industry. Information is taken from Japanese newspapers, journals, and other resources. Section 1 discusses latest news on new products, R&D including new machinery and equipment, and company news and government activity such as new laws, tariff policy changes, etc. Section 2 covers company profiles of leading companies, and Section 3, Market Report, provides statistical information. Section 4 lists patent applications in food technology and biotechnology. A subject and company name index is included. Further information on any of the items contained in the bulletin can be obtained through the publisher, Mitaka, as can translations, company information, product samples, and other information services.

335. *Japanese Economic Indicators.* Ministry of Finance, Printing Bureau, 2-2-4 Toranomon, Minato-ku, Tokyo 105. (03) 582-4411. (03) 586-3210 Fax. Monthly. 126 p. $13.84.

Edited by the Economic Planning Agency, this covers general macroeconomic and financial statistics for Japan. Charts, tables, graphs on national income, international trade, finance, financial statements of incorporated businesses, industrial production, new orders for machinery and construction work, household economy, labor and wages, prices, and diffusion indexes are covered. Publication is in Japanese and English.

336. *Japanese Economic Service.* DRI/McGraw Hill, 24 Hartwell Ave., Lexington, MA 02173. (617) 863-5100. Quarterly. $7,000.00/year.

An electronic newsletter service that provides information on and analyses of Japanese business and financial conditions. Uses surveys and forecasting to provide a macroeconomic overview of the Japanese economy. The service consists of the following: *Japanese Review*, quarterly, contains forecast tables, graphs, and a comprehensive analysis of the Japanese economy as well as special studies; *Japanese Preprint*, quarterly, analyzes recent important events and gives DRI forecasts; *GNP Statistics Announcement*, quarterly, details of the recently released GNP statistics. Also 10-year forecasts are published biannually; five- to six-year forecasts are published biannually. The service is provided via DRI's mainframe computer in Tokyo from which subscribers can download the information. Alternatively, the information can be provided on diskettes.

337. *Japanese High Technology Monitor.* Sumika Technical Information Service, Inc., 6th Fl., Sumitomo Bldg., 5-15 Kitahama, Higashiku, Osaka, 541. (06) 220-3364. (06) 220-3345 Fax. Semimonthly (24 issues). ISSN 0912-4772. $998.00/year (including airmail).

This publication places particular emphasis on new technologies, new products, R&D activities, etc., of Japanese companies reported in the following Japanese newspapers: *Chemical Daily*, *Dempa Publications*, *Industrial Daily News*, *Nihon Kogyo Shimbun*, etc. More complete information is available as a followup to each item for an additional cost. Newsletter is arranged as follows: section A, New Technology and R&D; section B, New Materials and Products, brief one- to two-line reports; section C Marketing, brief one- to two-line reports; section D, Technology Overview, detailed reports, focusing on a particular technology; and section E, Company Profile, detailed reports, focusing on a particular technology.

338. *Japan's High Technology Industries.* Japan Long Term Credit Bank, 1-2-4 Ohtemachi, Chiyoda-ku, Tokyo 100. (03) 211-5111. Irregular. ISSN 0287-2424. Gratis.

Reports on specific high-tech industries showing new developments and trends. Some examples are Volume 1, May 1983, industrial robots, ICs, office automation, new industrial materials, optoelectronics; Volume 2, Feb 1984, new ceramics, bioindustry, venture capital; and Volume 5, Feb 1986, ocean development in Japan.

339. *JEI Report.* Japan Economic Institute, 1000 Connecticut Ave., NW, Washington, DC 20036. (202) 296-5633. Weekly. ISSN 0744-6489. Issued in 2 parts (A & B). $40.00, $20.00 for academic institutions (Special combined rate of $130.00 for academic institutions includes *Japan-U.S. Business Reports*).

JEI Report A covers a specific topic in some depth each issue. *JEI Report* B provides highlights of Japan-U.S. developments during the previous week. Information is taken from Japanese and English news sources. Covers various trade, economic, and political issues in Japan which affect U.S. companies. The Japan Economic Institute is a research organization supported by the Japanese Ministry of Foreign Affairs. Note: JEI publishes a quarterly report, *Japan-U.S. Business Reports* (see under separate entry).

340. *JETRO Monitor.* Japan External Trade Organization (JETRO), 1221 Avenue of the Americas, New York, NY 10020. (212) 997-0400. Bimonthly. 4 p. Gratis.

A newsletter on Japanese economic and trade issues, published by the Japan External Trade Organization (JETRO). Contains informative, short articles on the Japanese economy. The last page gives short news briefs on Japanese-owned companies in Japan and the U.S., particularly joint ventures. Occasionally, special supplements are issued on topics of current interest. These are longer reports of 10–12 pages.

341. *Keidanren Review on Japanese Economy.* Keidanren (Federation of Economic Organizations), Public Affairs Department, 1-9-4 Ohtemachi, Chiyoda-ku, Tokyo 100. (03) 279-1411. (03) 246-0574 Fax. Bimonthly. 10–15 p. ISSN 0022-9695. Gratis.

Keidanren is a private, nonprofit economic organization which attempts to solve economic problems and contribute to the economic development of Japan with other countries. The bimonthly newsletter reports on various activities of the Keidanren, including foreign investigative missions, international policy, and local issues.

342. *Monthly Report—Foreign Capital Affiliated Enterprises.* Business Intercommunications, Inc. for International Labor Office, CPO Box 587, Tokyo, 100-91. (03) 423-3971. (03) 423-3996 Fax. Monthly. $144.00/year.

Monthly report on newly established foreign capital affiliated enterprises. See also *Directory of Foreign Capital Affiliated Enterprises in Japan.*

343. *New Materials Japan.* Elsevier Advanced Technology, Mayfield House, 256 Banbury Rd., Oxford 0X2 7D4. (0865) 51-2242. Monthly. 16 p. ISSN 0265-3443. $335.00.

Covers the following areas: Metals and Alloys; Ceramics; Composites; Plastics; Films and Coating; Electronic Materials; Optics; Optoelectronics; Textiles; Energy; Wood and Paper; Equipment and Testing. A calendar section on forthcoming meetings is included. Brief reports discuss new materials and processes. Contact name, address, and telephone and/or fax number are provided at the end of each article for further information.

344. *New Technology Japan.* Three "I" Publications Ltd., 1-5-16 Uchikanda, Chiyoda-ku, Tokyo 101. (03) 291-3761. (03) 291-3764 Fax. Monthly. 40 p. ISSN 0385-6542. $143.50/year (including airmail).

Formerly *Japan Industrial and Technological Bulletin*, this glossy magazine published for JETRO describes new products, systems, and news on current R&D projects. In-depth articles are included on selected topics. The aim is to promote the international exchange of technology by introducing new technologies from Japan to possible trade partners outside Japan. Photographs are included as well as details of each manufacturer's address and a contact person for further information. Coverage includes robotics and precision machines, materials, electronics and computers, biotechnology and medical equipment, energy, transportation and construction, mechanical engineering and processing. Japanese national and industrial technology policies and advances are also included.

345. *News from MITI.* Ministry of International Trade and Industry (MITI), Overseas Public Affairs Office, 1-3-1 Kasumigaseki, Chiyoda-ku, Tokyo 100. (03) 501-1657. (03) 501-2081 Fax. Irregular. 2–10 p. Gratis.

In 1986, 16 issues of this photocopied report were published with limited distribution. Summarizes articles and statistics to present Japanese government views on Japan's economy and international trade to non-Japanese-language readers. Some of the latest issues covered the following topics: Trends in Japanese International Trade for 86/87; Japan's Direct Overseas Investments in FY 1986; Trade Imbalance Problem—speech by Minister Tamara; Trends in Japanese International Trade, 1986; Policy Speech to the Diet by Minister of International Trade and Industry, Tamara; and Outline of Direct Investment measures. Includes listings of new imported goods, and summaries of white papers on trade issues are frequently included.

346. *Nikkei High Tech Report.* Nikkei International Ltd., Nikkei Bldg., 1-9-5 Ohtemachi, Chiyoda-ku, Tokyo 100. (03) 293-2796. (03) 293-2759 Fax. In U.S., contact Nikkei High Tech Report, 245 S. Norton Ave., Los Angeles, CA 90004. (213) 939-9315. (213) 933-9460 Fax. Bimonthly. 16 p. $580.00/year.

A current awareness newsletter that monitors and researches technical developments of high-tech corporate activity in Japan and Southeast Asia. Covers marketing, research, and planning for high-tech products. Data are taken from the Nikkei Telecom Japan News Retrieval online service. Covers electronics, data processing, telecommunications, biotechnology, new materials, robotics, and new energy sources. Thirty key technology areas are covered. The newsletter is aimed at a U.S. audience because it reports on events as they affect U.S.-Japan relations. Despite this, it is still useful to a European audience. Written for management, marketing, research, and planning personnel, as well as for the engineer, this newsletter contains original reporting, not rewrites of published reports. Nikkei, in business for 110 years with an excellent reputation, utilizes a vast network of researchers throughout the world to produce this high quality report.

347. *Optoelectronics Japan.* High Tech Group, 101 S. Pearl St., Albany, NY 12207. (518) 472-1533. Monthly. 20 p. $150.00 (30 percent discount for educational institutions).

Covers electrooptical, optical, and optoelectronic industries in Japan. Extensive coverage of advanced technologies and new developments; industry trends and activities; government policies and activities; company news;

industrial associations' programs and activities; research activities of industries, government, scientific societies, and universities; foreign corporations in Japan; Japanese corporations overseas; conferences and slide shows; and market analysis. Sources for information include newspapers, journals, seminars and conferences, shows and exhibits, research reports, and news releases, both governmental and industrial.

348. *Pharma Japan.* Yakugyo Jiho Co. Ltd., 2-36 Kanda Jimbo-cho, Chiyoda-ku, Tokyo 101. (03) 261-8527. (03) 234-6573 Fax. In U.S., contact F-D-C Reports, Inc., 5550 Friendship Blvd., #1, Chevy Chase, MD 20815. (301) 657-9830. (301) 656-3094 Fax. Weekly. 20 p. ISSN 0285-4937. $970.00 (including postage; prepayment required).

Covers the Japanese drug industry. Covers new products, technology, drug regulations, government policy, business news, and R&D information. A table of contents is provided. Many entries provide quite a detailed synopsis.

349. *RLJ Roskill's Letter from Japan.* Roskill Information Services, Ltd., 2 Clapham Rd., London SW9 0JA. (01) 582-5155. Monthly. $250.00/year.

Subtitled "Events and Trends in Japan—as Seen in Japan," this newsletter provides news items and statistics on the Japanese metals and minerals industry. Material is drawn entirely from Japanese sources.

350. *Science and Technology in Japan.* Three "I" Publications, Yamaguchi Bldg., 2-8-5 Uchikanda, Chiyoda-ku, Tokyo 101. (03) 256-3100. (03) 256-3160 Fax. In U.S., contact Japan Pacific Associates, 467 Hamilton Ave., #2, Palo Alto, CA 94301. (415) 322-8441. Quarterly. 70 p. ISSN 0286-0406. $50.00/year (including airmail).

This publication is partially funded by the Japanese Prime Minister's Office, Science and Technology Agency. Gives the latest developments in Japanese science and technology. It includes a who's who column. Each issue contains a feature story, R&D highlights, research institute news, and an interview with a prominent industry leader. Biotechnology, new materials, and electronics, in both the public and private sector, are covered.

351. *Scientific Information Bulletin.* Director, Office of Naval Research, Liaison Office Far East, APO San Francisco, CA 96503-0007. Quarterly. Gratis.

Published for the Office of Scientific Research, Far East, and U.S. Army Research Office, Far East, the title varies: ONR Far East Scientific Bulletin and ONR Tokyo Scientific Bulletin. These are declassified reports from the Office of Scientific Research, Far East, and the U.S. Army Research Office, Far East, on recent developments in Far Eastern (particularly Japanese) scientific research.

352. *Techno Japan.* Fuji Marketing Research Co. Ltd., 7F Dai-ni Bunsei Bldg., 1-11-7 Toranomon, Minato-ku, Tokyo 105. (03) 508-0051. (03) 592-0648 Fax. Monthly. 120 p. $160.00/year.

Formerly *Technocrat*, this work is aimed at the generalist. A glossy publication providing an overview of a broad range of topics, its stated purpose is to report on current status and new developments in technology, but it has been criticized for sometimes inaccurate information, probably a result of the nontechnical editorial staff.

353. *Tokyo Business Today.* Toyo Keizai Shinposha, 1-2-1 Nihonbashi Hongoku-cho, Chuo-ku, Tokyo 103. (03) 246-5655. (03) 242-7436 Fax. Monthly. 56 p. ISSN 0911-7008. $95.00 (including airmail).

Formerly *Oriental Economist,* despite the title, coverage includes the whole of Japan for business and finance information. Glossy, colorful format similar to *Business Week.* Contains feature stories and regular columns.

354. *Tokyo Insider.* Insider, Inc., Token Bldg., 2-6-6 Misaki-cho, Chiyoda-ku, Tokyo 101. (03) 234-6821. In U.S., contact Tokyo Insider, 110 Sutter St., San Francisco, CA 94104. (415) 989-8330. (415) 989-1816 Fax. Monthly. $240.00/year (offers a special combined rate with *Venture Japan,* $200.00/year).

This is the English version of the Japanese newsletter *Insider.* Provides insights on Asia-Pacific affairs from a Tokyo viewpoint and major events in Japan. It presents political analyses of issues concerning Japan, the Pacific Rim, and the international community. Discusses emerging trends in Japan and Asia. Published in Japan, it is written by two political journalists based in Tokyo.

355. *Venture Japan.* Asia Pacific Communications, Inc., 110 Sutter St., #708, San Francisco, CA 94104. (415) 989-8330. (415) 989-1816 Fax. Quarterly. 86 p. $72.00/year.

Subtitled *The Journal of Global Opportunity,* this quarterly magazine, which began publication in 1988, deals with U.S.-Japan trade issues. It is designed to assist U.S. companies wanting to enter the Japanese market or better the communication flow for those already involved in marketing to Japan. Covers investment issues such as joint ventures, mergers and acquisitions, licensing, legal and tax issues, and sources of venture capital.

Chapter 9
Industry Reports

The reports listed in this section are by no means exhaustive. There are numerous reports published covering all areas of Japanese industry that tend to be expensive and are, therefore, not usually found in public library collections. The exception is the fairly large collection held by the Science Reference Library of the British Library, located in London. Material in industry or market reports is of a timely nature, thereby characteristically reducing their importance within a year or two after their issuance. When used to provide an industry overview, however, the older reports serve a valuable purpose. Because of their emphasis on currency, many publishers of market reports are willing to sell older reports at significant discounts. To determine whether a particular report is of sufficient interest to warrant purchase, it may be useful to request a detailed table of contents before commiting to purchase.

For some researchers, the value in perusing this listing of market reports may be purely for the information it provides on consulting companies that publish reports covering a particular industry of interest. One should consider calling or writing to relevant companies to inquire about the existence of any reports or to determine whether they are in the process of producing a report.

In contrast to the very expensive surveys published by private consulting companies, the small pamphlets published by JETRO and distributed free, or those published by U.S. government agencies, may be sufficient for some needs. Of course, custom reports, or even multiclient reports, can be negotiated with most of the consulting firms working in market research.

Some government reports have been included in this chapter because they provide an overview of a particular market segment or industry.

356. *Advanced Engineering Ceramics Technology in Japan.* DIA Research Institute, Inc., Daini-Ryoka Bldg., 4-2-12 Sendagaya, Shibuya-ku, Tokyo 151. (03) 478-8131. (03) 478-8137 Fax. In U.S., contact Technology Catalysts, Inc., 6073 Arlington Blvd., Falls Church, VA 22044. (703) 237-9600. (703) 237-7967 Fax. July 1987. 422 p. Price on application.

Although dated, this study is still useful for background information on the engineering ceramics field in Japan. Was originally published in Japanese for the home market and then translated in full into English. The report focuses on recent developments in engineering ceramics in Japan by analyzing the patent activity of 1,200 Japanese patent applications covering 1981–86. Presents an overview of trends in research and development; covers technical problems related to engineering ceramics; and looks at future trends.

357. *Applied Artificial Intelligence in Japan: Current Status, Key Research and Industrial Performers—Strategic Focus.* Rubinger, Bruce. Hemisphere Pub. Corp., 79 Madison Ave., #110, New York, NY 10016. (212) 725-1999. 1988. 256 p. ISBN 0-89116-744-7. $300.00.

Acts as a reference source to artificial intelligence in Japan. Chapter 1 provides an introduction to the Japanese Artificial Intelligence (AI) market; and Chapter 2 lists major meetings and professional organizations covering applied AI. Also lists major publications for AI information, although the majority are Japanese-language publications. Chapter 3 is an alphabetical listing of the major companies involved in AI. Each of the 26 companies gives (1) address, narrative description of the company's background, corporate data including date of establishment, capital, president's name, number of employees, and sales figures; (2) major segment devoted to the R&D efforts of the company, providing narrative description of company's R&D followed by details of individual research labs; and (3) list of applied AI projects in progress, with a narrative description. A final section suggests publications, meetings, and a contact person/department for more information.

358. *Assessment of the Japanese Artificial Intelligence Market: Trends, Developments and Market Opportunities for U.S. Products.* U.S. Department of Commerce, National Technical Information Service (NTIS), 5285 Port Royal Rd., Springfield, VA 22161. (703) 487-4650. (703) 321-8199 Fax. 1989. 80 p. NTIS Order #PB89-188684. $495.00.

Report of a study commissioned by U.S. Department of Commerce on the Japanese market for artificial intelligence products from the U.S. Aimed as a guide to U.S. business wanting to export to Japan, the study gives an overview of the Japanese industry, identifies market opportunities, and suggests possible strategies for successful marketing in Japan. The report suggests that Japan is a promising market for U.S. AI products. Chapters include U.S. AI Market, Japanese AI Market, The Competition—The AI Industry in Japan, Future Trends, and Entering the Japanese AI Market.

359. *Basic Research in Superconductor, Ceramic, and Semiconductor Sciences at Selected Japanese Laboratories.* Gottschall, Robert J. U.S. Department of Commerce, National Technical Information Service (NTIS), 5285 Port Royal Rd., Springfield, VA 22161. (703) 487-4650. (703) 321-8199 Fax. 1989. 215 p. NTIS Order No. PB89-172464. $28.95.

Report describes current research projects at 14 major Japanese R&D organizations. On-site visits by Gottschall to the International Superconductivity Technical Center, Japan Fine Ceramics Center, Government Industrial Research Institute at Nagoya, NGK Insulators Ltd., etc. This report describes research projects being undertaken in 14 major Japanese R&D organizations in high-temperature superconductivity, structural mechanics, semiconductor materials and devices, and related areas. The specific subjects covered include high T_c superconductivity; diamond films; cubic boron nitride; synchrotron radiation applications; beam lithography; semiconductor science; fine ceramics properties, processing, and component fabrication (including ceramic engine applications); ceramic-matrix composites; carbon materials; metal matrix composites; and advanced instruments and facilities.

360. *Biotechnology in Japan.* Fujimura, Robert. International Trade Administration, Biotechnology Program, and U.S. and Foreign Commercial Service. Available from U.S. Department of Commerce, National Technical Information Service (NTIS), 5285 Port Royal Rd., Springfield, VA 22161. (703) 487-4650. (703) 321-8199 Fax. 1988. 181 p. NTIS Order No. PB89-141147. $21.95.

The report covers basic research in the biological sciences, R&D conducted by government and private companies, and guidelines and regulations covering products and processes. Focuses on cooperative programs designed to move biotechnology research ahead more quickly. These programs are mission-oriented basic research. There was an earlier report, June 1984, NTIS Order No. PB85-169464. (See also the related report *Research and Development in Biotechnology-Related Industries in Japan, 1989*, entry 409.)

361. *Biotechnology in Japan.* Alex and Associates Ltd., Villa Serena 204, 2-33-18, Jingumae, Shibuya-ku, Tokyo 150. (03) 479-8257. (03) 479-8253 Fax. Annual. 100 p. $130.00.

Comprehensive report on current developments and advances in biotechnology and medicine in Japan covering the previous 12 months.

362. *Biotechnology Industry in Japan 1986.* Yano Research Institute, Ltd., 3-9-19 Higashi Pola Ebisu Bldg., Shibuya-ku, Tokyo 150. (03) 5485-4618. (03) 5485-4681 Fax. In U.S. contact Yano Research Institute (USA) Ltd., Empire State Bldg., #6920, 350 Fifth Ave., New York, NY 10118. (212) 947-6120. (212) 736-1381 Fax. November 1985. 279 p. $750.00.

Analysis of current status of biotechnology industry in Japan, chapters include market trends of major products and future potential; current status of technological joint ventures and joint research program with foreign manufacturers; study of 15 major manufacturers, giving information on research history, research facilities, number of patents held, and corporate strategy; and company profiles of an additional 105 manufacturers. Covers pharmaceutical, chemical, foodstuffs, textiles, paper, and pulp industries.

363. *Cards in Japan: New Developments and Applications.* EGIS Inc., 22-1 Ichibancho, Chiyoda-ku, Tokyo 102. (03) 264-1060. (03) 265-2260 Fax. In U.S., contact EGIS Inc., 220 W. Mercer St., #509, Seattle, WA 98119. (206) 282-6001. (206) 283-4938 Fax. 1989. 233 p. $1,995.00.

A study of applications for integrated circuit (IC) cards. Evaluates cards in Japan focusing on IC smart cards, IC memory cards, prepaid magnetic cards, and optical cards. Covers electronics, manufacturing and printing technologies, costs, pricing, and market trends. Includes a directory of major industries and services within the IC card industry.

364. *Computer Industry in Japan: Today and Tomorrow.* Horiguchi, Tetsuo, comp. Survey Japan, 61, Nob Kojimachi Bldg., 4-5, Kojimachi, Chiyoda-ku, Tokyo 102. (03) 262-7476. (03) 262-7453 Fax. 1986. 300 p. $790.00.

Survey of the current status of Japan's computer industry and an analysis of future trends. Appendixes provide directories of computer companies, trading companies, related organizations, and showrooms. Also provides a list of related technical journals.

365. *Computer Peripherals Market in Japan.* Yano Research Institute, Ltd., 3-9-19 Higashi Pola Ebisu Bldg., Shibuya-ku, Tokyo 150. (03) 5485-4618. (03) 5485-4681 Fax. In U.S. contact Yano Research Institute (USA) Ltd., Empire State Bldg., #6920, 350 Fifth Ave., New York, NY 10118. (212) 947-6120. (212) 736-1381 Fax. Vol. 1. March 1986. 324 p. $500.00. Vol. 2. March 1986. 180 p. $500.00.

Revised edition of an earlier single volume published in 1984. Volume 1 covers auxiliary storage devices—floppy disk drives, hard disk drives—and display devices—cathode ray tube (CRT), graphic, and character displays. Volume 2 discusses plotters, printers, optical character readers, and other input devices. Data on major manufacturers included.

366. *Dirass Reports.* DIA Research Institute, Inc., Ryoka Bldg., 1-21-30 Shiba, Minato-ku, Tokyo 105. (03) 798-2611. (03) 798-1224 Fax. 20 reports each year. 100 p. each. 16 company and four technical reports per year. $8,500.00.

These reports present a detailed and comprehensive assessment of Japan's leading chemical and pharmaceutical companies. Each company report covers the following: executive summary; current topics—covering business activities such as strategic plans, production, sales and finance, and new businesses; technical trends—based on an analysis of the company's unexamined and open patent applications; and data section—current information on company administration, personnel, production, sales, and finance. Reference sources are listed. Dirass reports use trade sources, interviews, and examination of the patent activity of each company. As well as the 16 company reports each year, there are four technical reviews per year. Each one is complete in itself and focuses on a strategic area of advanced chemical or material technology. The reports cover background on the technology, and the various applications and identifies the leading Japanese companies in that area together with their research and development trends.

367. *Direct Marketing in Japan.* Dodwell Marketing Consultants, Kowa No. 35 Bldg., 1-14-14 Akasaka, Minato-ku, Tokyo 107. (03) 589-0207. (03) 589-0516 Fax. 1990. 150 p. $200.00 (including airmail).

Part 1 provides a general overview of direct marketing in Japan including a brief historical perspective and cultural and demographic factors. Part 2 discusses the characteristics of the direct marketing industry in Japan. Part 3 gives case histories of direct marketing companies operating in Japan. Part 4 is a directory of direct marketing companies.

368. *Electro-Optics Millimeter/Microwave Technology in Japan.* MacCallum, John M. U.S. Department of Defense, Office of the Under Secretary of Defense for Research and Engineering, Washington, DC 20301-1400. (202) 693-2978. 1987. 52 p. Gratis.

A classified version of this report from the DOD Technology Team is available to defense contractors, and an unclassified version is available to all others. This report is the outcome of visits by experts sent by the Department of Defense to observe progress in this area by Japanese companies.

369. *Factory Automation in Japan: Key Trends and Innovations.* Rubinger, Bruce, and Monden, Akihiko. Global Competitiveness Council, One Devonshire Pl., #1011, Boston, MA 02109. (617) 723-4947. (617) 723-4961 Fax. 1988. 158 p. NTIS Order No. PB88-245956. $23.00.

Available from NTIS and sponsored by the Department of Commerce, this report examines factory automation in Japan, in particular recent technological innovations and key trends. Seven case studies are provided.

370. *Findings of the U.S. Department of Defense Technology Assessment Team on Japanese Manufacturing Technology.* U.S. Department of Defense, Office of the Under Secretary of Defense for Research and Engineering, Washington, DC 20301-1900. (202) 693-2978. 1989. xxxviii, 212 p. Report No. CSDL-R-2161. Gratis.

This is the final report of the Technology Assessment Team (TAT) which was formed to "identify the principles underlying Japanese manufacturing excellence and to recommend practices that could be adopted by the Defense Industrial Base." The 84-page executive summary assesses Japanese management methods and manufacturing technologies, identifies suitable areas for transfer to the U.S., and makes recommendations for action to improve U.S. manufacturing performance. Detailed trip reports are included for the 1987 and 1988 visits to consumer electronics manufacturers, machine tool producers, automotive assembly plants, steel mills, steel production facilities, research laboratories, and various government and nongovernment agencies and technical organizations.

371. *Fundamental and Long-Term Iron and Steel-Making Research in Japan.* U.S. Department of Commerce, National Technical Information Service (NTIS), 5285 Port Royal Rd., Springfield, VA 22161. (703) 487-4650. (703) 321-8199 Fax. 1989. 33 p. NTIS Order No. PB90-107616. $16.95.

This report is based on visits to Nippon; NKK; Kawasaki and Kobe steel companies; the universities of Tokyo, Osaka, Tohoku, Kyoto, and Nagoya; and the Tokyo Institute of Technology. The report covers research in progress at these sites.

372. *Future of the Japanese Electronics Industry.* Fuji Corp., Han-ei Dai-2 Bldg., 1-10-1 Shinjuku, Shinjuku-ku, Tokyo 160. (03) 350-8701. Available from Japan Publications Trading Corp. 4th ed., 1985/86. 528 p. $500.00.

Researched by the Japan Electronics Industry Development Association (JEIDA) in the form of a survey conducted every five years. It provides an analysis and forecast of trends in the Japanese electronics industry. Chapter 1 is a general discussion, whereas chapter 2 covers current status and future outlook for the electronics industry. Chapter 3 forecasts an outlook for electronic technology, and chapter 4 provides a demand forecast of the electronics industry.

373. *Future Technology in Japan: Forecast to the Year 2015.* Institute for Future Technology, Science Museum, 2-1 Kitanomaru, Koen, Chiyoda-ku, Tokyo 102. 1988. 258 p. ISBN 944008-01-5. $45.00.

English translation of significant portions of a report published in 1987 "Nihon no Gijutsu, 1987-2015," the report contains the results of a survey conducted from 1985 to 1987 by the Science and Technology Agency to study future technological developments. Three thousand specialists from Japan were invited to participate in the survey which contained 1,071 questions about long-term developments in science and technology. The complete text for all questions is included as well as the processed answers. An outline, summary, and observations by field are provided.

374. *High Technology Ceramics in Japan.* National Materials Advisory Board, Research and Evaluation Division, 2101 Constitution Ave., NW, #HA 262, Washington, DC 20418. (202) 334-3505. 1984. 69 p. Report No. NMAB-418. $10.00. Xerox copy. Also available from NTIS $15.95.

This report was prepared by the Committee on the Status of High-Technology in Japan, a committee of the National Materials Advisory Board, National Research Council. The group was formed to assess the situation in Japan and the possible effect on this industry in the U.S.

375. *High Technology Report.* Yano Research Institute, Ltd., 3-9-19 Higashi Pola Ebisu Bldg., Shibuya-ku, Tokyo 150. (03) 5485-4618. (03) 5485-4681 Fax. In U.S., contact Yano Research Institute (USA) Ltd., Empire State Bldg., #6920, 350 Fifth Ave., New York, NY 10118. (212) 947-6120. (212) 736-1381 Fax. May 1984. 102 p. $400.00.

The report covers 101 fields within five broad subject groupings: energy, electronics, new materials, bioengineering, and pharmaceuticals. A brief overview of the five groups is given. The major portion of the report is devoted to one-page reports on each of the 101 fields. Gives development trends of manufacturers, companies in the market and those expected to enter the market, and prospects for market growth in 1982–86.

376. *Identifying Areas of Leading Edge Japanese Science and Technology.* Narin, Francis, and Olivastro, Dominic. CHI Research (Computer Horizons, Inc.), 10 White Horse Pike, Haddon Heights, NJ 08035. (609) 546-0600. (609) 546-9633 Fax. 1988. 174 p. $40.00.

This report, published for the National Science Foundation, discusses various indicators of Japanese scientific and technological performance, including the linkage between Japanese-invented technology and science. Used Science Citation Index to analyze Japanese-authored papers published between 1973 and 1984. Japanese-invented patents in the U.S. patent system between 1975 and 1986 were used to identify leading-edge technologies in Japan. Citations from Japanese-invented U.S. patents were used to link technological performance and scientific performance.

377. *Industrial Goods Distribution in Japan.* Dodwell Marketing Consultants, #35 Kowa Bldg., 1-14-14 Akasaka, Minato-ku, Tokyo 107. (03) 589-0207. (03) 589-0516 Fax. Nov 1987. 410 p. $550.00.

Analysis of the Japanese distribution systems for typical industrial goods. Describes the functions of the major trading companies. Areas discussed include an Economic Overview, Characteristics of the Distribution System, Overview of the Distribution Systems by Industry, Recommendations, Trade Associations, and Directory of the Major Sogo Shosha (trading companies)—over 500 companies indexed by industry.

378. *Industrial Groupings in Japan.* Dodwell Marketing Consultants, #35 Kowa Bldg., 1-14-14 Akasaka, Minato-ku, Tokyo 107. (03) 589-0207. (03) 589-0516 Fax. Biannual. 8th ed., 1988/89. 700 p. $620.00.

This extensive guide divides Japanese industry into 17 major groups and then analyzes each one. Provides financial data on leading corporations and banks in each group. A total of 3,500 companies are covered. Provides detailed analysis of the origins of the groups, their crossholding of shares, presidential councils, affiliations, joint ventures between major groups of companies, comparative analyses, and vital statistics. Also lists domestic and foreign subsidiaries.

379. *Industry Sector Analysis (ISA).* U.S. and Foreign Commercial Service, U.S. Embassy/Tokyo, 1-10-5 Akasaka, Minato-ku, Tokyo 107. (03) 583-7141. (03) 589-4235 Fax. In U.S., contact U.S. and Foreign Commercial Service, Japanese Market Section, FCS, American Embassy/Tokyo, Box 204, APO San Francisco, CA 96503. Annual. $15.00.

These annual reports by country are written on specific industries that offer good prospects for U.S. exports, e.g., Computer Industry (I.S.A. Industry Sector Analysis No. 407, June 1988, 11 p.). Covers both hardware—market assessment, competitive stance, and market access—and software—market demand, import market, and market access. Listing of useful computer-related publications is included. Note: Many cities have regional offices of the US & FCS. Contacting them directly is the quickest way to obtain US & FCS publications.

380. *Innovative Industrial Materials in Japan.* Yano Research Institute, Ltd., 3-9-19 Higashi Pola Ebisu Bldg., Shibuya-ku, Tokyo 150. (03) 5485-4618. (03) 5485-4681 Fax. In U.S., contact Yano Research Institute (USA) Ltd., Empire State Bldg., #6920, 350 Fifth Ave., New York, NY 10118. (212) 947-6120. (212) 736-1381 Fax. 1987. 160 p. $750.00.

Covers materials such as engineering plastics, fine ceramics, newly developed metals, functional paint, etc.

381. *JDB Research Report.* Japan Development Bank, International Department/Economic and Industrial Research Department, 1-9-1 Ohtemachi, Chiyoda-ku, Tokyo 100. (03) 270-3211. (03) 245-1938 Fax. In U.S., contact Japan Development Bank, 575 Fifth Ave., 28th Fl., New York, NY 10017. (212) 949-7551. (212) 949-7558 Fax. Irregular. Pages vary. Gratis.

The Japan Development Bank is a government financial institution that was created to promote industrial development in Japan through the supply of long-term funds to industry. These research reports cover a wide range of issues from macroeconomic issues to specific industries. Each report is complete, covering one specific issue. Recent titles include "Industrial and Trade Structures," "International Competitiveness of Asia's Newly Industrializing Economies," and "Impact of the EC Unification on Japan's Automobile and Electronics Industries."

382. *Japan Chemical Annual.* Chemical Daily Co., 3-16-8 Nihonbashi, Hama-cho, Chuo-ku, Tokyo 103. (03) 663-7932. (03) 663-2530 Fax. Annual. 182 p. ISSN 0075-319X. $90.00 (plus $12.00 airmail).

Covers trends in the chemical industry in Japan. Covers petrochemicals, fine chemicals, inorganic chemicals, biotechnology, and electronics. Analyzes trends in supply and demand for each product. An appendix "Japan's Chemical Industry Globalizing Fast" discusses the internationalization of chemical industries and the moves of foreign-capital enterprises in Japan.

383. *Japan Technology 50.* Venture Economics, Inc., 16 Laurel Ave., PO Box 81348, Wellesley Hills, MA 02181. (617) 449-2100. (617) 449-7660 Fax. 1988. 400 p. $995.00.

Highly specialized report covering the patent activity of Japan's top 50 high-tech companies in terms of number of patents held. This is a joint publication of Venture Economics and CHI Research. Report focuses on innovative Japanese companies active in the areas of electronics, computers, electrical engineering, heavy industry, transportation, photo-optical, chemicals, and materials. U.S. Patent activity is analyzed for the past 12 years to provide technology indicators. Patents are mapped to 42 product codes, analyzed by computer and commented on by industry experts. These 50 companies are compared by industry group to selected U.S. benchmark companies.

384. *Japanese Foreign Direct Investment in the United States, 1974–1987 Trends and Developments.* Jeffries and Associates, Inc., 17200 Hughes Rd., Poolesville, MD 20837. (301) 428-8204. 1988. 2 vols. 500 p. $110.00.

Volume 1, an executive summary, and volume 2, supporting information, provide data on 1,532 investment transactions completed by the Japanese between 1974 and 1986. Data for 1987 are used to indicate future trends. Provides investment figures, U.S. company names, Japanese investor names, investment by type, and investments by state, SIC, and industrial sector. Figures and tables are used extensively throughout the report.

385. *Japanese Market for Machinery Products.* Want Pub. Co., 1511 K St., NW, Washington, DC 20005. (202) 783-1887. 1988. 174 p. $198.50.

The machinery products marketed in Japan are subdivided into five areas. Important marketing requirements such as rules and standards, current technology, and the distribution systems are discussed for each market sector. Current market conditions and future needs are also discussed.

386. *Japanese New Materials Yearbook 1986/87.* Nuttal, Susan, Guy, Ian, and Nixon, Malcolm, eds. Elsevier International Bulletins, Mayfield House, 256 Banbury Rd., Oxford, OX2 7DH. (0865) 51-2242. 1987. 128 p. ISBN 0-94639-526-8. $240.00.

Complete survey of major Japanese developments in new materials for previous year. Sections—high performance ceramics, polymers, fibres, composites and alloys, integrated circuits, and semiconductors—cover materials with high performance applications in electronics, biotechnology, and construction. Each entry details a specific product, process, application, research project, production, or processing technique. Gives company address or research institute involved. Each section provides a brief introduction with a detailed analysis of the perceived state-of-the-art to mid-1987. Drawn from *New Materials/Japan* during 1986.

387. *Japanese R&D Monitor.* Sumitomo Corporation of America, 345 Park Ave., New York, NY 10154. (212) 207-0565. (212) 207-0813 Fax. Annual report, bimonthly updates, and special supplements. $10,000–$26,000, according to number of reports desired.

Scheduled to begin in 1990, this full-service subscription package provides a comprehensive report on patent applications in Japan and other technical trends. The service is made up of a number of components. *Data Book* (annual. 350 p.) is a catalog of all patent applications laid open in Japan in the year prior to application. This information is provided as a means of identifying important trends in the R&D operations of major Japanese companies. *Focus Report* (bimonthly, 30–50 p.) provides an update on technology strategies of leading Japanese companies. Each report provides background, analysis, and forecasts for development in specific technical areas. *Topics Reports* (bimonthly, 30–50 p.) cover three major high technology areas: advanced materials, life sciences and biotechnology, and electronics and telecommunications. Within each of these areas there are six reports per year. The reports analyze available patent literature for significant corporate and market trends. Each subscriber is also entitled to 10 hours of custom inquiry service and attendance at an annual seminar. Data for the service are provided by Diamond, Inc., Tokyo, utilizing their Management and Development Intelligence (MDI) System which analyzes patent data.

388. *Japanese Technology Assessment: Computer Science, Opto-and Microelectroniccs, Mechatronics, Biotechnology.* Albus, J., et al. Noyes Data Corp., Mill Rd. at Grand Ave., Park Ridge, NJ 07656. (201) 391-8484. 1986. 1 vol. 597 p. ISBN 0-81551-096-9. $62.00.

Taken from four JTECH Reports and repackaged: JTECH Panel Report on Computer Science in Japan, 1984; JTECH Panel Report on Opto and Microelectronics, 1985; JTECH Panel Report on Mechatronics in Japan, 1985; and JTECH Panel Report on Biotechnology in Japan, 1985. Table of contents serves as subject index, and there are no other indexes provided.

389. *Japanese Technology Reviews.* Ikoma, Toshiaki, ed. Gordon and Breach Science Publishers, PO Box 786, Cooper Station, New York, NY 10276. Irregular. 120–160 p. Price varies.

Irregularly published series of books that present state-of-the-art technology from Japan in the following five areas: electronics, computers and communications, manufacturing technology, new materials, and biotechnology. Each book presents current status and future prospects from the Japanese perspective. Authors are prominent scientists and engineers actively engaged in research and development.

390. *Japan's CAD/CAM Market.* Yano Research Institute, Ltd., 3-9-19 Higashi Pola Ebisu Bldg., Shibuya-ku, Tokyo 150. (03) 5485-4618. (03) 5485-4681 Fax. In U.S., contact Yano Research Institute (USA) Ltd., Empire State Bldg., #6920, 350 Fifth Ave., New York, NY 10118. (212) 947-6120. (212) 736-1381 Fax. 1984. 191 p. $470.00.

Data collected from interviewing key personnel at Tokyo Electron, IBM Japan, C-Itoh, Hitachi, NEC, Seiko, and Zuken. Part 1 surveys current CAD/CAM market in Japan, analyzes seven major domestic suppliers' manufacturing and marketing strategies, demand trends, and future prospects. Part 2 profiles 42 manufacturers, providing business specialty, sales volume, sales by model, suppliers of hardware or software, manufacturing strengths, maintenance and services offered, distribution channels, and marketing policies.

391. *Japan's Expanding U.S. Manufacturing Presence.* MacKnight, Susan. Japan Economic Institute (JEI), 1000 Connecticut Ave., NW, Washington, DC 20036. (202) 296-5633. 1988. 82 p. $50.00.

A study of Japanese investment in the United States manufacturing sector with an appendix listing the companies together with parent company, line of business, number of employees, and the town and state of the company in the U.S. Street addresses are not given.

392. *Japan's General Trading Companies.* International Business Information, Izumiya Bldg./IBI, Inc., 3-1-1 Kojimachi, Chiyoda-ku, Tokyo 102. (03) 230-2151. (03) 234-6167 Fax. 1988. 48 p. $1,500.00.

Report on the sogo shosha (trading companies) in Japan. Discusses strategies of the trading companies, current status, and future prospects.

393. *Japan's Innovative Industrial Materials.* Yano Research Institute, Ltd., 3-9-19 Higashi Pola Ebisu Bldg., Shibuya-ku, Tokyo 150. (03) 5485-4618. (03) 5485-4681 Fax. In U.S., contact Yano Research Institute (USA) Ltd., Empire State Bldg., #6920, 350 Fifth Ave., New York, NY 10118. (212) 947-6120. (212) 736-1381 Fax. Vol. 1, Jan 1984. 150 p. $450.00. Vol. 2, Feb 1984. 175 p. $450.00.

Volume 1 is an in-depth study of Japanese research into industrial materials such as engineering plastics, carbon fibers, amorphous metals, shape remembering alloys, and optical fibers. Looks at trends for each segment. Volume 2 focuses on fine ceramics for industrial machinery, bioceramics, engineering ceramics, etc. Gives market performance of 89 major manufacturers.

394. *Japan's Laser Market and Industry.* Yano Research Institute, Ltd., 3-9-19 Higashi Pola Ebisu Bldg., Shibuya-ku, Tokyo 150. (03) 5485-4618. (03) 5485-4681 Fax. In U.S., contact Yano Research Institute (USA) Ltd., Empire State Bldg., #6920, 350 Fifth Ave., New York, NY 10118. (212) 947-6120. (212) 736-1381 Fax. June 1984. 108 p. $470.00.

Based on field studies, the report covers laser oscillators—YAG, glass, ruby, He-Ne, Ar, carbon dioxide, excimer, He-Cd, and semiconductor. Also covers laser products—laser beam machines, laser printers, optical discs, compact discs, measuring instruments, medical lasers, color scanners, and point of sale scanners.

395. *Japan's Machinery Market.* Japan External Trade Organization (JETRO), 2-2-5 Toranomon, Minato-ku, Tokyo 105. (03) 582-3518. (03) 587-2485 Fax. 1988. 130 p. ISBN 4-8224-0412-9. $148.00.

Covers the following five types of machine products: biotechnology equipment, medical electronics, analytical instruments, machine tools, and packaging machinery. Discusses the standards and specifications pertinent to the above areas. Directory information includes names of leading importers of machines for each of the five areas listed.

396. *Japan's Small Business Today: A Closer Look at 100 Industrial Segments.* Keiei Joho Shuppan, 2-2-1 Sarugaku-cho, Chiyoda-ku, Tokyo 101. (03) 291-5791. 1988. 348 p. $280.00.

Edited by Japan Advertising, Inc., this report contains 204 tables, 35 diagrams, and 15 graphs. The original Japanese version covered 300 industrial segments as compared with the 100 covered by the English-language version. It is divided into 11 broad segments which are further subdivided for a total of 100 industrial segments. Many nontechnical areas are included although areas such as electrical measuring instruments, machine tools, medical equipment, VCR manufacturers, audio equipment, and semiconductors are covered. The market segment analyzes current situation, significant developments, structure, distribution system, and scale of companies. The management portion looks at sales and profit, financial position, payment and collection, and trends.

397. *JETRO Series.* Japan External Trade Organization (JETRO), 2-2-5 Toranomon, Minato-ku, Tokyo 105. (03) 582-3518. (03) 587-2485 Fax. Irregular. Gratis.

JETRO publishes a series of pamphlets designed to help those wishing to enter the Japanese market. Series titles are Access to Japan's Import Market Series, Business Information Series, Keys to Success Series, Marketing Series, and Your Market in Japan Series.

398. *J-TECH Reports (Japanese Technology Evaluation Program).* U.S. Department of Commerce, National Technical Information Service (NTIS), 5285 Port Royal Rd., Springfield, VA 22161. (703) 487-4650. (703) 321-8199 Fax.

Phase I:		
Computer Science in Japan	PB85-216760	$20.50
Opto- and Microelectronics	PB85-242402	$31.00
Mechatronics in Japan	PB85-249019	$15.50
Biotechnology in Japan	PB85-249241	$23.00
Phase II:		
Telecommunications Technology in Japan	PB86-202330	$25.50
Advanced Materials in Japan	PB86-229929	$25.50
Phase III:		
Advanced Computing in Japan	PB88-153572	$15.50
Japanese Exploratory Research for Advanced Technology (ERATO)	PB89-133946	$28.00
Computer Integrated Manufacturing (CIM) and Computer Assisted Design (CAD) for the Semi-Conductor Industry in Japan	PB89-138259	$23.00
Advanced Sensors in Japan	PB89-158760	$33.50

The Japan Technology Evaluation Program (JTECH) was begun in 1983 by the International Trade Administration, Department of Commerce, to provide technical assessments of strategic areas of Japanese technology. Assessments are performed by panels of experts chosen from universities, government laboratories, and industry. Japanese capabilities are compared with those of the U.S. Objectives of the JTECH program are to develop appropriate assessment methodology, evaluate sources of Japanese scientific and technical information, and provide technical assessments as references for staying abreast of Japanese developments. Phase 1 was supported by the International Trade Administration (ITA) and NSF; Phase 2 was supported by Defense Advanced Research Projects Agency (DARPA) and NSF; and Phase 3 is supported by DARPA, NSF, and the Department of Commerce, Office of Japanese Technical Literature Program.

399. *Market Analysis of Unix-Based Computers in Japan-Business Applications.* Fuji-Keizai U.S.A., Inc., 141 E. 55th St., #3F, New York, NY 10022. (212) 371-4773. (212) 758-9040 Fax. 1989. 65 p. $1,400.00.

Fuji-Keizai, a large Japanese marketing research company, publishes industry reports on the Japanese market. This survey discusses new trends and marketing opportunities as well as competitive strategies for this expanding segment of the computer market in Japan. Other recent market analyses of strategic Japanese market sectors published by Fuji-Keizai include *Survey of the Floppy, Hard, and Optical Disk Drive Market and Manufacturers,* 1990, 98 p., $1,200; *Information Equipment Market Size, Share and Forecast in Japan,* 1990, 260 p., $1,200; and *ISDN Market, Manufacturers, and Usage in Japan,* 1990, 102 p., $1,400.

400. *Market Share in Japan.* Yano Research Institute, Ltd., 3-9-19 Higashi Pola Ebisu Bldg., Shibuya-ku, Tokyo 150. (03) 5485-4618. (03) 5485-4681 Fax. In U.S., contact Yano Research Institute (USA) Ltd., Empire State Bldg., #6920, 350 Fifth Ave., New York, NY 10118. (212) 947-6120. (212) 736-1381 Fax. Annual (July). 470 p. $750.00.

The only published report giving market share for various product areas in Japan. Mostly tabular information. Covers large number of industrial and consumer products. Gives four- to five-year growth plans and production and market share for top five or six companies in 1,000 product areas. Covers machine tools, machinery, metals, electric and electronic machines, automobiles, precision machines, chemicals, food products, textiles, cosmetics, pharmaceuticals, etc.

401. *Mobile Communications in Japan.* EGIS, Inc., 22-1 Ichibancho, Chiyoda-ku, Tokyo 102. (03) 264-1060. (03) 265-2260 Fax. In the U.S., contact EGIS, Inc., 220 W. Mercer St., Seattle, WA 98119. (206) 282-6001. (206) 283-4938 Fax. 1989. 413 p. $2,695.00.

Covers cellular and noncellular phone communications and paging and transient communications. Compares the Japanese market with overseas markets; outlines new technologies; and assesses the impact on markets outside of Japan. Data are based on extensive interviews and documentary research. Areas covered by the report include market potential, standards, current networks and future expansion, competitive services and pricing, state-of-the-art features currently available, leading manufacturers, significant R&D, and applications, both existing and projected.

402. *New Media Market and Industry in Japan.* Yano Research Institute, Ltd., 3-9-19 Higashi Pola Ebisu Bldg., Shibuya-ku, Tokyo 150. (03) 5485-4618. (03) 5485-4681 Fax. In U.S., contact Yano Research Institute (USA) Ltd., Empire State Bldg., #6920, 350 Fifth Ave., New York, NY 10118. (212) 947-6120. (212) 736-1381 Fax. April 1984. 100 p. $390.00.

Covers prospective new media markets and industries which the survey expects will come to full emergence within 10 years. Includes executive summary, manufacturers' strategy, users' response, social impact of new media, and future prospects. Information gathered from field studies.

403. *NSF/Tokyo Report Memoranda.* National Science Foundation, Division of International Programs, Information/Analysis and Japan Programs Section, 1800 G St., NW, Washington DC 20550. (202) 357-9632. Back issues available from U.S. Department of Commerce, National Technical Information Service (NTIS), 5285 Port Royal Rd., Springfield, VA 22161. (703) 487-4650. (703) 321-8199 Fax. Irregular, approximately 25–30 each year. Price varies for back issues, current issues gratis.

These are high-quality reports covering significant Japanese scientific and technical developments. Included in the reports issued each year are an annual survey of R&D in Japan, science and technology policy in Japan, and reports on various Japanese research laboratories. A current list of memoranda published over the last few years is available at no cost from the National Science Foundation.

404. *Profile of Fine Ceramics Manufacturers in Japan.* Market Intelligence Corp., 4-7-12-302 Kosuge, Katsushika-ku, Tokyo 124. (03) 602-8629. 1987. 250 p. $380.00.

A comprehensive report covering 104 major Japanese manufacturers of fine ceramics. Data were collected from field surveys of each manufacturer, supplemented with official data and statistics. Manufacturers range from electronics, ceramics, cement, glass, chemical, textile, steel, metal, and machinery companies. Information in this report includes sales and production data, distribution, market share, procurement of materials, R&D trends, and foreign associates.

405. *Profile of Japanese Electronics Components Manufacturers—Updated.* Yano Research Institute, Ltd., 3-9-19 Higashi Pola Ebisu Bldg., Shibuya-ku, Tokyo 150. (03) 5485-4618. (03) 5485-4681 Fax. In U.S., contact Yano Research Institute (USA) Ltd., Empire State Bldg., #6920, 350 Fifth Ave., New York, NY 10118. (212) 947-6120. (212) 736-1381 Fax. Feb 1983. 226 p. $390.00.

Gives information on 212 larger components manufacturers in Japan. Covers location, financial activity of the company, sales for 1980–82, capital, subsidiary, exports, and suppliers for the components.

406. *R&D Activities of Major Japanese Chemical Companies.* Dodwell Marketing Consultants, #35 Kowa Bldg., 1-14-14 Akasaka, Minato-ku, Tokyo 107. (03) 589-0207. (03) 589-0516 Fax. 1990. 350 p. $550.00.

Describes current business strategies and research and development activities of 35 major Japanese chemical companies.

407. *Recent Activities in Ceramic and Semiconductor Sciences in Japan.* Gottschall, Robert J. U.S. Department of Commerce, Japanese Technical Literature Program (JTLP), #4817, H.C. Hoover Bldg., 14th & Constitution Ave., N.W., Washington, DC 20230. (202) 377-1288. (202) 377-4498 Fax. 1987. 49 p. NTIS Order No. PB88-122478. $13.00.

Prepared by the Japanese Scientific and Technical Literature Program as part of its mission to summarize current status of Japanese research and development in key high technology areas. Based on review of Japanese laboratories engaged in advanced ceramics R&D. Discusses the factors underlying Japanese long-term private sector and government funded research in structural and electronic ceramics and semiconductors. Management and funding of

Japanese materials research in government laboratories, universities and private companies, and mechanisms by which they cooperate are discussed.

408. *Recombinant DNA in Japan: Current Status and Future Prospects.* U.S. Department of Commerce National Technical Information Service (NTIS), 5285 Port Royal Rd., Springfield, VA 22161. (703) 487-4650. (703) 321-8199 Fax. 1989. 147 p. NTIS Order No. PB89-158752. $20.50.

Reports on the current status of recombinant DNA research in Japan. Suggestions are given for improving access to the Japanese literature in this field. An overview of the industry is presented by means of translated titles and abstracts of papers presented at Japanese conferences from November 1987 to November 1988. Report concludes that Japan and the U.S. are on a par in this field.

409. *Research and Development in Biotechnology-Related Industries in Japan, 1989.* Fujimura, Robert. U.S. Department of Commerce, National Technical Information Service (NTIS), 5285 Port Royal Rd., Springfield, VA 22161. (703) 487-4650. (703) 321-8199 Fax. 1989. 63 p. NTIS Order No. PB89-167936. $15.50.

An update of an earlier report *Biotechnology in Japan*, 1988, this account focuses more on industrial efforts in Japanese biotechnology.

410. *Retail Distribution in Japan.* Dodwell Marketing Consultants, #35 Kowa Bldg., 1-14-14 Akasaka, Minato-ku, Tokyo 107. (03) 589-0207. (03) 589-0516 Fax. 3d ed. 1988. 520 p. $540.00.

Divided into six parts, Distribution System in Japan; Retailers; Wholesalers; Who Supplies Whom; Directory of Major Retailers, Wholesalers, Importers; and List of Trade Associations, this comprehensive guide to the Japanese retail distribution system includes its characteristics, recent developments, and channels for imported goods. An alphabetical name index is provided.

411. *Science and Technology Resources of Japan: A Comparison with the United States.* National Science Foundation, 1800 G St., NW, Washington, DC 20550. (202) 357-3619. 1988. 69 p. NSF Special Report NSF 88-318. Gratis.

This report forms part of the NSF Division of Science Resources Studies which were initiated to obtain detailed current information on foreign science and technology capabilities. This report covers Japanese science and technology efforts since 1965 and compares them to U.S. activity. Research and development at the national level as well as for individual sectors are profiled, and science and technology outputs are discussed.

412. *Steel Industry in Japan, 1988.* Materials Information, American Society for Metals, Metals Park, OH 44073. (216) 338-5151. Annual. 94 p. $225.00.

Detailed analysis of technical and business-related developments in individual steel plants, supplier companies, universities, and research institutes. Covers as well as Japan, joint ventures of Japan with other countries. There are three sections: Tabular Displays of Company Activity, Outlines of Individual Projects, and References for the Preceding Year.

413. *Structure of the Japanese Auto Parts Industry.* Dodwell Marketing Consultants, #35 Kowa Bldg., 1-14-14 Akasaka, Minato-ku, Tokyo 107. (03) 589-0207. (03) 589-0516 Fax. 4th ed., 1990. 500 p. $830.00.

Designed as a comprehensive guide to the auto industry in Japan, it analyzes the structure of the parts industry. This report is divided into six in-depth sections: The Japanese Auto Parts Industry, Profiles of the 11 Automobile Manufacturers, Who Supplies Whom, Directory of Major Auto Parts Manufacturers, Overseas Investments by Japanese Automobile and Auto Parts Manufacturers, and Statistics.

414. *Structure of the Japanese Electronics Industry.* Dodwell Marketing Consultants, #35 Kowa Bldg., 1-14-14 Akasaka, Minato-ku, Tokyo 107. (03) 589-0207. (03) 589-0516 Fax. 1988. 610 p. $540.00.

Formerly, *Key Players in the Japanese Electronics Industry*, this comprehensive guide focuses on profiles of the major Japanese electronics conglomerates and the electronics industry overall. Part 1 discusses Japanese electronics industry, and Part 2 is a comparative analysis of 64 major electronics companies. Part 3 profiles the top 45 electronics companies, Part 4 looks at market trends and market share analysis by major electronics products, and Part 5 is a directory of 400 major companies. This section gives company outline, financials, major shareholders, major products, major suppliers and customers, major manufacturing subsidiaries and affiliated companies, foreign associations, and technology import/export and overseas operations. Sections on trade associations and statistics conclude this guide.

415. *A Study of the Japanese Computer Industry.* Yamaguchi, R., and Hegedus, Michael J. U.S. and Foreign Commercial Service, U.S. Embassy/Tokyo, 1-10-5 Akasaka, Minato-ku, Tokyo 107. (03) 583-7141. (03) 589-4235 Fax. In U.S., contact U.S. and Foreign Commercial Service, Japanese Market Section, FCS, American Embassy/Tokyo, Box 204, APO San Francisco, CA 96503. May 1986. 51 p. Post Market Research Report No. 602. $50.00.

This overview of the Japanese computer industry includes a number of comparative tables and discusses various categories of computers. There is a section on computer software. The guide lists target areas for development by end of 1990. Names and addresses are listed for computer-related organizations—government organizations, public organizations, and industry organizations. Also gives names and addresses of companies working in the information industry in Japan. Finally, a ranked list of the top 100 companies in Japan in the information processing industry is given. Note: Many cities have regional offices of the US & FCS. Direct contact is the fastest way of obtaining US & FCS publications.

416. *Yano Market Surveys.* Yano Research Institute, Ltd., 3-9-19 Higashi Pola Ebisu Bldg., Shibuya-ku, Tokyo 150. (03) 5485-4618. (03) 5485-4681 Fax. In U.S., contact Yano Research Institute (USA) Ltd., Empire State Bldg., #6920, 350 Fifth Ave., New York, NY 10118. (212) 947-6120. (212) 736-1381 Fax.

ASIC's, Its Future Market	1986	$650.00
Electronic Display Devices Market in Japan	1982	$560.00
Japanese Electronic Components Industry and Its Perspectives	1983	$575.00
Optoelectronic Industry in Japan	1983	$575.00

Study of the Antibiotics and Anticancer Agents Market in Japan	1984	$320.00
Measuring Instruments Market in Japan	1984	$490.00
High Technology Robot Market in Japan	1985	$650.00
Biotechnology Industry in Japan	1985	$750.00
Micro-Computer Market in Japan	1986	$550.00
Japanese Semiconductor and IC Industry	1988	$550.00
Report on Semiconductor User Industries in Japan	1986	$495.00
Telecommunications Equipment Industry in Japan	1986	$550.00
Personal Computer Systems Market in Japan	1986	$550.00
Biotechnology-Related Equipment Market in Japan	1986	$675.00
Sogo-Shosha in Electronics	1985	$470.00
OEM Business in Japan's Electronics Industries	1985	$440.00
Automotive Electronics Market in Japan	1987	$600.00
Diagnostic Reagent and Test Equipment Market in Japan	1987	$700.00
Medical Device Market in Japan	1988	$550.00
Midterm Prospects for Japanese Semiconductor Market	1989	$1,200.00

Yano is a major publisher of market research reports in Japan. A selection of some titles relevant to the scope of this work are listed above. Other major Yano reports have been included in this section with a detailed description under individual titles.

Chapter 10
Newspapers

Although most of the major English-language newspapers from Japan are general interest, rather than trade-specific newspapers, they have been included because they represent excellent sources of information for anyone wishing to stay abreast of current Japanese affairs. Some news of science and technology is contained in all newspapers, but the coverage is brief and somewhat superficial for the serious researcher.

417. *Asahi Evening News.* Asahi Evening News K.K., 7-8-5 Tsukiji, Chuo-ku, Tokyo 104. (03) 543-3321. (03) 543-1660 Fax. Daily except Sunday. 10–14 p. ISSN 0025-2816. $40.00/month (surface mail).

Only English-language evening newspaper, its format is similar to U.S. evening newspapers. Covers international news, local, business, finance, sports, and entertainment news. Articles on new technology are included. The editorial section contains translations of Japanese views on current events taken from the companion Japanese newspaper *Asahi Shimbun.* International wire service news is well represented in this newspaper, particularly news from the U.S.

418. *Asian Wall Street Journal.* Dow Jones and Co., Inc. PO Box 300, Princeton, NJ 08543-0300. (800) 622-2742. Daily. $225.00.

Only business daily for Asia. Provides good coverage of Japanese business news along with other Asian countries—South Korea, Taiwan, Hong Kong, Philippines, Malaysia, Singapore, Australia, and New Zealand. Covers news, markets trends, and politics.

419. *Japan Economic Journal.* Nihon Keizai Shimbun America, Inc., #1515, 725 S. Figueroa St., Los Angeles, CA 90017. (213) 955-7470. (213) 955-7479 Fax. Weekly. 51 issues. $102.50/year.

Weekly English version of Japan's leading daily financial newspaper—*Nihon Keizai Shimbun*, the Japanese equivalent to the *Wall Street Journal* and the *Nikkei Sangyo Shimbun.* It is printed simultaneously in Tokyo, San Francisco, and New York. Provides information on Japanese business developments and weekly review of Tokyo's stocks, bonds, and financial markets. Covers company news, especially people in the news both in Japan and overseas. Some coverage of developments in Japanese science and technology and new products is provided.

420. *Japan Times.* Japan Times Ltd., 4-5-4 Shibaura, Minato-ku, Tokyo 108. (03) 453-5311. (03) 453-5265 Fax. Daily. 18 p. ISSN 0447-5763. $52.98–91.70/month (subscription for overseas airmail depending on region).

This is the largest circulation English-language daily. It is the only English-language newspaper not affiliated with a vernacular daily. International, domestic, political, social, and business and financial news are covered, along with sports, entertainment, and editorials. Begun in 1897, it is the oldest of the English-language papers. There is a large classified section. Daily airmail edition is available.

421. *Japan Times Weekly International Edition.* Japan Times Weekly International Edition, 5750 Wilshire Blvd., #287, Los Angeles, CA 90036. (800) 446-0200. (213) 937-3067. Weekly (Saturday). 24 p. ISSN 0447-5763. $95.00.

This is the weekly airmail edition of the *Japan Times* daily. It contains the week's top national news, editorials, and columns from the *Japan Times*, plus a number of features, frequently on Japanese society and culture. The publication is useful for foreigners not living in Japan who want to keep up with events in Japan and a Japanese view of recent world events. There is also a monthly bound volume published complete with an alphabetical index which is useful for libraries.

422. *Mainichi Daily News.* Mainichi Shimbunsha, 1-1-1 Hitotsubashi, Chiyoda-ku, Tokyo 100. (03) 212-0321. (03) 216-2574 Fax. Daily. 12 p. $50.70/month (overseas surface).

This English-language newspaper carries mostly international news. Coverage also includes national business, financial, entertainment and sporting news. The back page carries exclusively Japanese news, similar to the vernaculars. It includes more detailed information, particularly on Japanese politics, than the other English-language papers. It is widely held in U.S. libraries.

423. *Yomiuri.* Yomiuri Shimbunsha, 1-7-1 Ohtemachi, Chiyoda-ku, Tokyo 100. (03) 242-1111. Daily. 12 p. $11.00/month.

This is an English-language daily newspaper. Its coverage includes international, national, business and financial news, sports, and feature articles. The most important political and economic stories and local news stories are translated from *Yomiuri Shimbun* for inclusion in *Yomiuri*. It is noted for its English-language page and features on Japan.

Chapter 11
Online Databases

The databases listed in this chapter are either international in scope and include a significant amount of Japanese information or are English-language databases originating in Japan with most of the information being Japanese. Only brief outlines are provided. The database creator should be contacted for more complete information on content and for rates and access methods. Some databases contain bibliographic information and an abstract, whereas others include the full text of articles.

There are many Japanese-language databases available, most of which are unavailable outside of Japan. This is an area where we can expect to see changes over the next five years as Japan attempts to internationalize its information industry. High costs associated with translation into English and an uncertain demand have kept many of the Japanese database producers from marketing their databases outside of Japan.

Addresses of vendors for each database listed are in Appendix D.

PRINTED GUIDES

424. *Database in Japan.* Database Promotion Center, Japan, 7th Fl., World Trade Center Bldg., 2-4-1 Hamamatsu-cho, Minato-ku, Tokyo 105. (03) 459-8581. (03) 432-7558 Fax. Annual. 102 p. ISSN 0915-5686. Gratis.

Provides an annual overview of the database industry in Japan. Covers a broad range of topics including usage of both foreign and domestic databases in Japan and problems in the industry. Many useful tables are provided with much of the data taken from recent surveys conducted in Japan.

425. *Directory of Japanese Databases in 1989.* Database Promotion Center, Japan, 7th Fl., World Trade Center Bldg., 2-4-1 Hamamatsu-cho, Minato-ku, Tokyo 105. (03) 459-8581. (03) 432-7558 Fax. 1989. 236 p. Gratis.

Published to advise foreigners of Japanese databases, it contains details of 528 databases produced in Japan irrespective of whether they can be accessed outside of Japan. Information is taken from the *Directory of Databases Usable in Japan*, published in Japanese by the Database Promotion Center. This directly lists some 1,964 databases of which only 528 are of Japanese origin. The directory lists Japanese databases alphabetically and in a separate listing

Japanese database agents, again listed alphabetically. Indexes to Japanese databases by keywords and by producer are included. Unfortunately there is no index to databases that are in English or to those available outside of Japan.

426. *Directory of Japanese Databases—1990.* U.S. Department of Commerce, Japanese Technical Literature Program, National Technical Information Service (NTIS), 5285 Port Royal Rd., Springfield, VA 22161. (703) 487-4650. (703) 321-8199 Fax. 1990. ISBN 0-934213-28-3. 98 p. NTIS Order No. PB90-163080. $35.00.

A directory of forty-three Japanese databases that are accessible from the United States. The majority of these are in the Japanese language. The first half of the publication contains a report by Tom Satoh which was commisioned in 1988 by the Office of Japanese Technical Literature to identify and assess the availability of Japanese databases outside of Japan.

427. *Electronic Databases in Japan.* Sigurdson, Jon, and Greatrex, Roger. Research Policy Institute, Lund University, Box 2017, S-220 02 Lund, Sweden. 1986. 143 p. ISBN 91-86002-59-7. 16.70 pounds.

Subtitled "an information resource to be reached on-line," this is a report of a 1986 project carried out at the Research Policy Institute of Lund University to access Japanese-language databases on line. Although the project is directly concerned with the technical and linguistic problems associated with accessing Japanese-language databases via telephone in Sweden, the authors also hope to increase the awareness of Japanese databases by those outside of Japan. With the increasing pressure on the Japanese to internationalize their information and the steady progress in machine-translation systems, the authors predict greater access to Japanese databases for non-Japanese-speaking users within the next few years.

ONLINE DATABASES

428. ABI/Inform. Data Courier, Inc., 620 S. Fifth St., Louisville, KY 40202. (800) 626-2823. (502) 582-4111.

Updated weekly, this database covers all aspects of business management and administration for many types of businesses and industries. Product and industry information is covered, but this is not a primary focus. Covering 680 business and related journals, it can be a useful source for business information about Japan. Vendors: BRS, DIALOG, ESA-IRS, Maxwell Online, and Mead Data Central.

429. Aerospace Database. American Institute of Aeronautics and Astronautics, Technical Information Service, 555 W. 57th St., New York, NY 10019. (212) 582-4901.

Updated on a bimonthly schedule, coverage includes key scientific and technical documents, books, reports, and conferences for aerospace research and development in 40 countries including Japan. Japanese items account for 5 percent of the database. Japanese sources include the National Aerospace Laboratory and the National Space Development Agency (NASDA), other government agencies, and laboratories and the universities active in space science and applications research. Vendors: DIALOG.

430. Asahi News Service. Asahi Shimbun, New York Times Syndication Sales Corp., 130 Fifth Ave., New York, NY 10011.

Daily full-text coverage of economic, financial, political, and technological news focusing on Japan and Southeast Asia. Usually available within two days after publication. Vendors: Mead Data Central.

431. Asia Pacific Database. Aristarchus Group, Inc., PO Box 12625, Tucson, AZ 85732. (602) 620-1240.

Covers information from 150 journals, newspapers, government documents, newsletters, conference proceedings, annual reports, press releases, and books. Covers company, product, and market research in the business economics of Asia and the Pacific, including insider trading cases and regulatory changes; corporate diversifications; acquisitions and mergers; expert control regulations affecting high-tech products between specific countries; rate of emerging technologies and materials research; and the tracking of global operations and the subsidiaries of transnational and multinational corporations. Vendors: DIALOG.

432. CA Search (Chemical Abstracts). Chemical Abstracts Service, 2540 Olentangy River Rd., PO Box 3012, Columbus, OH 43210-0012. (614) 447-3600. (614) 447-3709 Fax.

Worldwide coverage of chemical literature including patents. The Japan Association for International Chemical Information (JAICI) provides bibliographic entries and Japanese chemical information extracted from Japanese journals. Japanese patent information is also provided to CAS by JAICI. In 1988, 12.7 percent of the publications abstracted were in Japanese; 11.5 percent of the journals abstracted were from Japan, and 53.8 percent of the basic patents were from Japan. Vendors: BRS, CISTI, Data-Star, DIALOG, ESA-IRS, Maxwell Online, and STN.

433. Comline News Service. Comline International Corp., Shugetsu Bldg., 3-12-7 Kita Aoyama, Minato-ku, Tokyo 107. (03) 486-0696. (03) 486-7704 Fax. In U.S., contact InfoCorp, 20370 Town Center Ln., Cupertino, CA 95014-2107. (408) 257-9956. (408) 257-0695.

English-language information service monitoring economic and high-tech developments in Japan. Full text and abstracts available daily or weekly. Covers 130 Japanese-language sources. After a 30-day embargo period, the Comline records are merged into the PTS Promt database. Vendors: COM-NET (Comline), and DIALOG (as PTS Promt file).

434. Compendex Plus. Engineering Information, Inc., 345 E. 47th St., New York, NY 10017. (800) 221-1044. (212) 705-7635.

Worldwide coverage of engineering and technological literature. In addition to 4,500 journals, government reports and books, there are records for significant published proceedings of engineering and technical conferences. Approximately 150 Japanese journals are included in this database. Vendors: BRS, CISTI, Data-Star, DIALOG, ESA-IRS, STN, and Maxwell Online.

435. D&B—International Dun's Market Identifiers. Dun's Marketing Services, Three Sylvan Way, Parsippany, NJ 07054. (800) 223-1026. (201) 605-6000, ext. 6439.

This is a directory database containing names, addresses, SIC codes, annual sales, number of employees, type of company, D-U-N-S numbers, and parent company information. Some 500,000 non-U.S. companies are listed from 133 countries including Japan. Both public and private companies are included. Vendors: DIALOG.

436. Fairbase. Fairbase Database Ltd., Deisterstrasse 13, Postfach 91 04 46, 3000 Hannover 91, Federal Republic of Germany. (511) 44-3330. (511) 44-2770 Fax.

References to trade fairs, exhibitions, conferences, and meetings in 100 countries, including Japan. Provides name and address of sponsoring organization, dates, location, exhibitors, registration cost, and some information on attendees, exhibitors, and exhibition space. Covers meetings held since 1986, as well as meetings scheduled up to 10 years in advance. Vendors: BRS and Data-Star.

437. Foreign Trade and Economic Abstracts. Netherlands Foreign Trade Agency, Bezuidenhoutseweg 151, 2594 AG, The Hague, Netherlands. (070) 79-7221.

Covers worldwide literature on markets, industries, country-specific economic data, and research in economic science and management. Some 1,800 journals, books, directories, and reports are covered to produce this database. Information on specific industries including investment climate data, import regulations, distribution channels, and the economic structure of worldwide markets is included. Vendors: Data-Star and DIALOG.

438. HINET. Heiwa Information Center Co., Ltd., 3-9-2 Nishi-Shinjuku, Shinjuku-ku, Tokyo 160. (03) 374-8673.

Although this database is in Japanese, it has been included here because Heiwa is currently investigating the possibility of translating the database into English and marketing it in the U.S. HINET comprises two databases. Title Search information is taken from 850 journal publications. Coverage is science and technology with an emphasis on applied papers. Included are technical magazines, company publications, and university publications. Timeliness is an important factor in this database. Articles are generally online within 15 days of publication. Only titles, no abstracts, are provided. Techno-Search covers five major technical newspapers: *Kagaku Kogyo Nippon* (Chemical Industry Daily), *Nihon Kogyo Shimbun* (Japan Industrial Newspaper), *Dempa Sangyo Shimbun* (Electronics Newspaper), *Goho Sangyo Shimbun* (Data Industry Newspaper), and *Nikkan Kogyo Shimbun* (Daily Industrial Newspaper). Database is technical rather than economically focused, and the delay is about one month from publication to online availability. It is hoped to decrease this time delay to approximately one week. Vendors: direct access via Tymnet.

439. Infomat International Business. Predicasts, 11001 Cedar Ave., Cleveland, OH 44016. (216) 795-3000. (800) 321-6388.

Updated weekly, this database covers business articles from 425 business publications worldwide. Coverage includes new products, technology, economics, and management. Journal titles covered from Japan include *Asian Wall Street Journal, Japan Chemical Week, Japan Economic Journal, Japanscan, Japan Times, Japanese Industry Newsletter.* Vendors: Data-Star and DIALOG.

440. INPADOC. International Patent Documentation Center, Mollwaldplatz 4, 1040 Vienna, Austria. (0222) 65-8784.

Covers patents worldwide. Accession numbers for the Japanese patent database, JAPIO, are provided to aid in crossfile searching. For details, see under chapter on patents. Vendors: DIALOG, Maxwell Online, and STN.

441. INSPEC. Institution of Electrical Engineers, IEEE Service Center, 445 Hoes Ln., PO Box 1331, Piscataway, NJ 08855-1331. (201) 981-0060, ext. 380. (201) 981-0027 Fax.

Updated monthly, INSPEC is the largest English-language database covering physics, electrotechnology, computers, and control and information technology, worldwide. Covers over 600 Japanese journals. Non-English-language material is included with an English-language abstract and indexing. The INSPEC list of serials indicates whether journals are indexed cover to cover or selectively. Vendors: BRS, CISTI, Data-Star, DIALOG, ESA-IRS, FIZ-Technik, Maxwell Online, and STN.

442. Investext. Thomson Financial Networks, 12 Farnsworth St., 4th Fl., Boston, MA 02210. (617) 330-7878. (800) 662-7878. (617) 350-5011 Fax.

Updated weekly, this database provides full-text coverage of financial and market reports for 8,000 companies from 27 leading investment banking firms in the U.S., Canada, Europe, and Japan. For Japan, coverage from Nomura Securities, Yamaichi Securities, Sanyo Securities, and Salomon Brothers, Tokyo is included. Many U.S. firms also provide reports of Japanese companies that are involved in technological areas competitive with the U.S. The research reports contain sales and earnings forecasts, market share projections, research and development expenditures, and related data. Vendors: BRS, Data-Star, DIALOG, Dow Jones News/Retrieval, and NewsNet.

443. JANET (Japan Network). United Data Telecom Corp., Tiger Bldg., 1F, 3-5-22 Shiba Koen, Minato-ku, Tokyo 105. (03) 431-6891. (03) 437-6769 Fax.

Information for living and doing business in Japan. Information can be downloaded via computer or provided via fax. Vendors: United Data Telecom.

444. Japan Automation Review. Kokusai Information Services Co., Ltd., 9th Fl., Shibuya Sumitomo Shintaku Bldg., 1-22-3 Jinnan, Shibuya-ku, Tokyo 150. (03) 463-7181. (03) 770-1865 Fax.

Translated from Japanese, this full-text newsletter covers technology developments, products, applications, and industry trends for robotics and advanced manufacturing technology. Vendors: NewsNet.

445. Japan Computer Industry Scan. Kyodo News International, Inc., 2-2-5 Toranomon, Minato-ku, Tokyo 105. (03) 584-4111. (03) 584-6334 Fax.

Full-text weekly newsletter of feature articles and industry statistics for the Japanese computer market. Contains news on major breakthroughs, research and development, Japanese marketing techniques, and feature articles on the computer market. Vendors: Data-Star (as part of PTS Newsletter Database), DIALOG (as part of PTS Newsletter Database), and NewsNet.

446. Japan Consumer Electronics Scan. Kyodo News International, Inc., 2-2-5 Toranomon, Minato-ku, Tokyo 105. (03) 584-4111. (03) 584-6334 Fax.

Provides weekly coverage of the consumer electronics and electrical appliance industry in Japan. Trade statistics, overseas production, manufacturing, and new products are covered. Vendors: Data-Star (as part of PTS Newsletter Database), DIALOG (as part of PTS Newsletter Database), and NewsNet.

447. Japan Energy Scan. Kyodo News International, Inc., 2-2-5 Toranomon, Minato-ku, Tokyo 105. (03) 584-4111. (03) 584-6334 Fax.

Updated weekly, this database covers the Japanese oil industry, nuclear energy applications, utilities usage, geothermal energy techniques, and alternate fuels. Industry groups, government ministries, and agencies provide source material for this database. Vendors: Data-Star (as part of PTS Newsletter Database), DIALOG (as part of PTS Newsletter Database), and NewsNet.

448. Japan Free Press. C.T. Whipple Co. USA, PO Box 6713, Mesa, AZ 85216. (602) 380-0932.

Weekly synopsis of important issues, opinions, and analyses of Japan and the world, interpreted by the Japanese. Vendors: NewsNet.

449. Japan High Tech Review. Mead Ventures, Inc, PO Box 44952, Phoenix, AZ 85064. (602) 234-0044. (602) 234-0076 Fax.

Monthly online version of a printed newsletter of the same name. For details of coverage see *Japan High Tech Review* in Chapter 8, Newsletters and Magazines. Vendors: NewsNet.

450. Japan News & Retrieval. Nihon Keizai Shimbun, Inc. (Nikkei), 1-9-5 Ohtemachi, Chiyoda-ku, Tokyo 100. (03) 270-0251, ext. 3481. (03) 246-1871 Fax. In U.S., contact Mitsui and Co. (USA), Inc., 200 Park Ave., New York, NY 10166-0130. (212) 878-4000.

Available in the U.S. since fall 1986, this English-language database consists of part of the NEEDS (Nihon Electronic Economic Data Service) database. Nikkei Telecom is the information services arm of Nihon Keizai Shimbun Inc., the largest business publisher in Japan. The segments available in English include Nikkei News Flash; Nikkei Major News; Japan Economic Journal; Stock Market Analysis; Nikkei Newsletter on Bonds and Money; Nikkei Newsletter on Commodities; Nikkei High Tech Report; and Newsletters from Bank of Tokyo, Industrial Bank of Japan, JETRO, Finance Ministry, etc. Vendors: Direct access via Telenet, Tymnet or NEEDS-NET in New York, Los Angeles, Washington, DC, and Toronto.

451. Japan Policy and Politics. Kyodo News International, Inc., 2-2-5 Toranomon, Minato-ku, Tokyo 105. (03) 584-4111. (03) 584-6334 Fax.

Updated weekly, this database covers policy-making decisions, new political appointees, and news of the various political parties in Japan. Includes legal decisions of the Ministry of Justice, Tokyo Supreme Court, and city courts. Vendors: Data-Star (as part of PTS Newsletter Database), DIALOG (as part of PTS Newsletter Database), and NewsNet.

452. Japan Report: Biotechnology. Business Information and Solutions Ltd., Japan Report Division, Kirkman House, 12-14 Whitfield St., London, W1P 4RD. (01) 435-4050. (01) 436-8451 Fax.

Full text of a monthly print newsletter of the same name. Covers research and applied work in agriculture, brewing, food processing, and pharmaceuticals. Vendors: Data-Star (as part of PTS Newsletter Database) and DIALOG (as part of PTS Newsletter Database).

453. Japan Report: Information Technology. Business Information and Solutions, Inc., Japan Report Division, Kirkman House, 12-14 Whitfield St., London, W1P 4RD. (01) 435-4050. (01) 436-8451 Fax.

Full-text coverage of a monthly print newsletter on the Japanese computer industry. Covers computers, integrated circuits, optical disks, peripheral devices, voice systems, workstations, and software. Vendors: Data-Star (as part of PTS Newsletter Database) and DIALOG (as part of PTS Newsletter Database).

454. Japan Report: Medical Technology. Business Information and Solutions, Ltd., Japan Report Division, Kirkman House, 12-14 Whitfield St., London, W1P 4RD. (01) 435-4050. (01) 436-8451 Fax.

Contains the full text of a monthly print newsletter on the technology and production of medical diagnostic equipment and materials, therapeutic products, and prosthetic devices. Vendors: Data-Star (as part of PTS Newsletter Database) and DIALOG (as part of PTS Newsletter Database).

455. Japan Report: Product Opportunities. Business Information and Solutions Ltd., Japan Report Division, Kirkman House, 12-14 Whitfield St., London, W1P 4RD. (01) 435-4050. (01) 436-8451 Fax.

Contains full text of a monthly print report on business and product opportunities available outside of Japan for licensing and distribution. Vendors: Data-Star (as part of PTS Newsletter Database) and DIALOG (as part of PTS Newsletter Database).

456. Japan Report: Telecommunications. Business Information and Solutions Ltd., Japan Report Division, Kirkman House, 12-14 Whitfield St., London, W1P 4RD. (01) 435-4050. (01) 436-8451 Fax.

Full text of a monthly print newsletter that covers company news, product information, and technology of the telecommunications industry in Japan. Vendors: Data-Star (as part of PTS Newsletter Database) and DIALOG (as part of PTS Newsletter Database).

457. Japan Science Scan. Kyodo News International, Inc., 2-2-5 Toranomon, Minato-ku, Tokyo 105. (03) 584-4111. (03) 584-6334 Fax.

Weekly coverage of newsworthy developments in physics, chemistry, pharmaceuticals, and environmental issues. Vendors: Data-Star (as part of PTS Newsletter Database), DIALOG (as part of PTS Newsletter Database), and NewsNet.

458. Japan Semiconductor Scan. Electronics Industries Association of Japan, 3-2-2 Maranouchi, Chiyoda-ku, Tokyo 100. (03) 211-2765. (03) 287-1712 Fax.

Updated weekly, the focus for this database is the Japanese semiconductor market, particularly the competitive market situation with the U.S. Vendors:

Data-Star (as part of PTS Newsletter Database), DIALOG (as part of PTS Newsletter Database), and NewsNet.

459. Japan Telecommunications Scan (formerly NTT Topics). Kyodo News International, Inc., 2-2-5 Toranomon, Minato-ku, Tokyo 105. (03) 584-4111. (03) 584-6334 Fax.

Weekly coverage of Nippon Telegraph and Telephone corporation news. Latest technological developments and marketing in telecommunications and electronics is discussed, along with NTT's role in the telecommunications industry in Japan. Vendors: Data-Star (as part of PTS Newsletter Database), DIALOG (as part of PTS Newsletter Database), and NewsNet.

460. Japan Transportation Scan. Kyodo News International, 2-2-5 Toranomon, Minato-ku, Tokyo 105. (03) 584-4111. (03) 584-6334 Fax.

Weekly coverage of air, land, and sea transportation in Japan. Manufacturing, import/export statistics, earnings, contracts, and government regulation announcements are included. Vendors: Data-Star (as part of PTS Newsletter Database), DIALOG (as part of PTS Newsletter Database), and NewsNet.

461. Japan Weekly Monitor. Kyodo News International, Inc., 50 Rockefeller Plaza, #832, New York, NY 10020. (212) 586-0152.

News of the week's financial and industry news. It recaps daily activity on the Tokyo stock exchange as well as macroeconomic statistics on the state of the economy. News of U.S.-Japan trade developments in industry and government are also included. Vendors: Data-Star (as part of PTS Newsletter Database), DIALOG (as part of PTS Newsletter Database), and NewsNet.

462. Japanese Aviation News: Wing. Wing Aviation Press. 1-14-5 Ginza, Chuo-ku, Tokyo 104. (03) 561-8305. (03) 561-8309 Fax.

This electronic version of Japan's major weekly publication covering aeronautics is distributed via Kyodo News International. Coverage includes air transport, industry, space, defense, commercial aviation, traffic statistics, industrial news, and research and development. Japan's defense industry and aviation news from other Asian countries are also covered. Vendors: Data-Star (as part of PTS Newsletter Database), DIALOG (as part of PTS Newsletter Database), and NewsNet.

463. Japanese Economic Service. Data Resources, Inc./McGraw Hill, 24 Hartwell Ave., Lexington, MA 02173. (617) 860-6670.

Economic, financial, industrial, and energy data and analysis. Provides archival as well as forecast data. For more details see *Japanese Economic Service* in the Newsletters and Magazines chapter.

464. Japanese Government Weekly. Digitized Information, 5-26-301 Yoyogi, Shibuya-ku, Tokyo 151. (03) 466-0141. (03) 468-9229 Fax.

Full text of the *Japanese Government Weekly*, a newsletter of Japanese government regulatory action. It covers import policy, standards, and relations between the government and the private sector. Vendors: Data-Star (as part of the PTS Newsletter Database) and DIALOG (as part of the PTS Newsletter Database).

465. JAPIO. Japan Patent Information Organization (JAPIO), Bansei Bldg., 1-5-16 Toranomon, Minato-ku, Tokyo 105. (03) 503-6181.

Covers Japanese patent abstracts in English. Approximately 18,000 abstracts are added monthly to the database. Contains over 1.5 million abstracts of unexamined, Japanese patent applications. The database was established in 1976. English-language abstracts are available for approximately 91 percent of the unexamined patent applications. Delay between publication of the unexamined patents, and appearance in JAPIO should not exceed three months. Vendors: Maxwell Online.

466. JiJi Press. JiJi Press Ltd., 1-3 Hibiya Koen, Chiyoda-ku, Tokyo 100. (03) 591-1111. (03) 592-1947 Fax. In U.S., contact Jiji Press Ltd., 30 E. 42nd St., S, New York, NY 10017. (212) 986-8250.

Updated daily, this full-text English-language news service covers economic, business, and financial information from Japan. Jiji is the major economic news agency in Japan with 80 bureaus in Japan and 50 correspondents in 25 major cities worldwide. Covers trading markets in Japan and provides information on stocks, bonds, commodities, futures markets, company performance, and other news of interest to the business and finance communities. Vendors: Mead Data Central, NewsNet, and Reuters.

467. JICST-E (JOIS Online Information Service). Japan Information Center for Science and Technology, 2-5-2 Nagata-cho, Chiyoda-ku, Tokyo 100. (03) 581-6411. (03) 593-3375 Fax.

This science and technology database is updated monthly with approximately 15,000 citations from 4,000 periodicals, reports, and conferences. This is about 70 percent of the total number indexed in the Japanese-language version. Approximately 33 percent of the coverage is in chemistry and life sciences; electrical and electronics engineering accounts for about 8 percent. In Japan the JOIS system offers access to a number of different files: JICST File on Science and Technology, JICST File on Medical Science in Japan, JICST File on Current Science and Technology Research in Japan, JICST File on Government Research Reports in Japan, Nikkan Kogyo File on New Technology and Products in Japan, JICST Thesaurus File, JICST Holding List File, and JICST Training File on Science and Technology. To date, only the first two are available in English as the JICST-E file. The JICST-E file contains only Japanese-language publications. Vendors: STN and NTIS.

468. Kyodo English News Service. Kyodo News International, Inc., 2-2-5 Toranomon, Minato-ku, Tokyo 105. (03) 584-4111. (03) 584-6445 Fax. In U.S., contact Kyodo News International, Inc., 50 Rockefeller Plaza, #816, New York, NY 10020. (212) 586-0152. (212) 307-1532 Fax.

Contains all English-language newswires from Kyodo News Service, Tokyo. It includes the *Japan Economic Daily* and the *Kyodo English Language News* newswires. Kyodo News Service, the producer of this database, is the largest Japanese news agency and a cooperative of the Japanese press. Coverage includes general and business news from Japan and international news that relates to Japan. It covers Japan's financial, economic, high-tech, industrial, and government news, including financial statistics from the Tokyo Stock Exchange and government statements. Cultural and feature articles are also included. The database is available from a number of vendors in a variety of forms. The name of the database varies from host to host, depending on coverage from a daily newswire service to the full retrospective database.

Vendors: Data-Star, DIALOG (as Japan Economic Newswire Plus), Mead Data Central, and NewsNet.

469. Moody's Corporate News-International. Moody's Investor's Service, Inc., 99 Church St., New York, NY 10007. (212) 553-0857. (800) 342-5647.

Provides weekly coverage of 3,900 public companies from over 100 countries. Information available includes financial statements, earnings statements, balance sheets, bankruptcy financing, mergers and acquisitions, joint ventures, new products, contracts, stocks and bonds, and rate changes. Vendors: DIALOG.

470. New Era: Japan. Telecommunications Association, 1-12-1 Yurakucho, Chiyoda-ku, Tokyo 100. (03) 201-7811. (03) 201-6015 Fax.

Updated biweekly, this database covers the recently deregulated Japanese telecommunications industry. Research and development, equipment and systems applications, and procurement needs of Japanese companies are covered for database, VAN, and network fields. Vendors: Data-Star (as part of PTS Newsletter Database), DIALOG (as part of PTS Newsletter Database), and NewsNet.

471. Newswire ASAP. Information Access Co., 11 Davies Dr., Belmont, CA 94002. (800) 227-8431. (415) 591-2333.

Contains indexing and full text from Kyodo's Japan Economic Newswire as well as PR Newswire and Reuter's Financial Report. Kyodo's Japan Economic Newswire covers Japanese finance, high technology, industry, and government. Updated daily, Newswire ASAP contains full text. A companion file Newsearch, also updated daily, contains the index portion of each Newswire record. While the full text cannot be searched on Newsearch, a full record from Kyodo and PR Newswire stories can be displayed using format nine. Vendors: DIALOG.

472. NRI/E: Japanese Economic & Business Data Base. Nomura Research Institute (NRI), 1-11-1 Nihonbashi, Chuo-ku, Tokyo 103. (03) 276-4762. (03) 276-4787 Fax.

Weekly, monthly, quarterly, and yearly data on economic and business trends in Japan. Provides macroeconomic data on Japan's economy, financial data, Japanese industries and products, forecasting, and a monthly economic review. Vendors: GE Mark III network and Mead Data Central.

473. NTIS. U.S. Department of Commerce, National Technical Information Service (NTIS), Office of Product Management, 5285 Port Royal Rd., Springfield, VA 22161. (703) 487-4642.

Database of U.S. government-sponsored research, development and engineering, and analyses prepared by federal agencies or under government contract. Report literature from non-U.S. countries is also included. A cooperative agreement with 18 Japanese organizations provides access to the report literature of these companies. Vendors: BRS, CISTI, Data-Star, DIALOG, SEA-IRS, Maxwell Online, and STN.

474. PTS International Newsletter Database. Predicasts, 11001 Cedar Ave., Cleveland, OH 44106. (216) 795-3000. (800) 321-6388.

Updated daily, this database covers approximately 150 specialized industry newsletters full-text, 25 of which are from Japan. Provides information on industry news, company activities, world business events, government funding programs, and regulatory activities. Vendors: Data-Star and DIALOG.

475. PTS Promt. Predicasts, 11001 Cedar Ave., Cleveland, OH 44106. (216) 795-3000. (800) 321-6388.

Through a collaborative arrangement with ODS Corporation, Tokyo, the Comline database has been merged into the PTS Promt file after a 30-day time embargo. Retrieval can be limited to Comline records by a single command. Sources of the information are major newspapers, government-funded research and development reports, corporate press releases, and proprietary market research. Focus is on new and applied technologies, new products, planned production, new facilities, and other market information. Areas covered include biotechnology, chemistry, computers, electronics, machinery, telecommunications, and transportation. Vendors: BRS, Data-Star, and DIALOG.

476. PATOLIS. Japan Patent Information Center (Japatic). 1-5-16 Toranomon, Minato-ku, Tokyo 105. (03) 503-6181.

This is a Japanese-language database. For full details see under chapter on Patents. Vendors: Direct access via Tymnet.

477. Pharmcast. Drugbase Online, Japan Information Processing Service Co., Ltd., Database Services Division, 2-4-20 Toyo, Koto-ku, Tokyo 103. (03) 5690-3202. (03) 5690-3227 Fax.

Database of drugs, of which one-third originated in Japan. Descriptive information is included on 3,800 drug products (2,500 are new chemical entities) which are currently being developed worldwide. Some 1,200 of these entries are for products originating in Japan. This is the machine-readable version of *Pharmcast Japan* and *Pharmcast International.* For details of *Pharmcast Japan*, see entry in the Directories and Handbooks chapter. Subscribers to the print version receive a discount for online usage.

478. World Patents Index. Derwent, Inc., #500, 6845 Elm St., McLean, VA 22101. (703) 790-2400.

For details, see under this title in the Patents chapter. Vendors: DIALOG and Maxwell Online.

479. World Translations Index. CNRS/INIST, Chateau du Montet, 54514 Vandoeuvre-les-Nancy Cedex, France. (01) 835-32900. (01) 835-76309 Fax.

For full details, see under chapter on Translations. Vendors: DIALOG and ESA-IRS.

Chapter 12
Patents

Because much important information can be gained from patents, a separate chapter has been devoted to them. Other than their use for the protection of intellectual property, patents provide an early warning of new technological developments, often not published elsewhere.

The Japanese patent system is somewhat different to that of the United States. Whereas one patent may be applied to an invention in the United States, several patents may be granted in Japan to cover a similar technology. The Japanese Patent Office, overwhelmed by the volume of applications in that country, is trying to change that pattern, but change will not come quickly.

The sheer volume of Japanese patents, along with the language barrier, present very real problems for the researcher attempting to use the patent literature for its technical content. Divided into printed sources and online databases, the entries in this chapter open access to the patent literature of Japan for the English-speaking user. The PATOLIS database has been included, even though it is in Japanese, because it is the most comprehensive index to Japanese patent literature. Searches of the database and translation into English are available. Details of this database are noted in the PATOLIS entry, 476.

A few selected commercial companies have been included because they will provide patent services on a customized basis. This is not meant to be an exhaustive list. Rather, they are included to alert the reader that there are companies that can provide such services for a fee.

PRINTED SOURCES

480. *Chemical Abstracts Service.* Chemical Abstracts (CA), 2540 Olentangy River Rd., PO Box 3012, Columbus, OH 43210. (614) 421-3663 or (800) 848-6538.

Chemical Abstracts (CA) has indexed patents filed by Japanese nationals since 1918 if they were in the subject area of chemistry as defined by the CA editorial policy. Since 1967, a machine-readable version of CA has been made available in addition to the printed publication.

481. *Examination Manual for Patent and Utility Model in Japan.* Aippi-Japan, Toranomon Denki Bldg., 2-8-1 Toranomon, CPO Box 1457, Tokyo 105. 1986. Looseleaf.

Published for the Japan Patent Office, Tokyo, this is a translation from Japanese of the procedural manual used for examining patent applications. About 10 percent of Japanese patents are filed by non-Japanese nationals.

482. *Glossary of Japanese Patent Law Terms: Japanese-English-Japanese.* Wilds, Thomas. Marlin Publications International, Inc., PO Box 649, Plandome, NY 11030. (516) 365-3788. 1979. 80 p. ISBN 0-930624-01-7. $30.00.

A special dictionary of patent law terms, covering about 900 terms used in Japanese Patent Office Publications, Patents, Utility Models, Designs, and Trademarks and in related actions and litigation. Part 1 is an alphabetical listing of romanized Japanese terms; and part 2 is an alphabetical listing by English terms.

483. *Guide to the Japanese and Korean Patents and Utility Models.* Drazil, J.V. British Library, Science Reference Library, 25 Southampton Bldgs., London, WC2A 1AW. (071) 323-7472. 1976. 135 p. ISBN 0-902914-21-9. $15.00.

This guide will assist researchers and librarians who need to deal with Japanese and Korean patent and utility model specifications but who have no knowledge of the Japanese or Korean languages. It is also a useful aid for translators unfamiliar with patents and the patenting process. Providing an interesting introduction to the history of industrial property protection in Japan and Korea, the guide focuses on Japanese patents although Japanese utility models and Korean patents and utility models are included.

484. *Industrial Property Rights in Japan.* Japan External Trade Organization (JETRO), 2-2-5 Toranomon, Minato-ku, Tokyo 105. (03) 582-3518. (03) 587-2485 Fax. 1981. 56 p. (JETRO Marketing Series 15). Gratis.

Describes the Japanese Patent Office and advises on the Japanese patent process including utility models and trademarks.

485. *International Guide to Official Industrial Property Publications.* British Library, Science Reference and Information Service, 25 Southampton Bldgs., London WC2A 1AW. (071) 323-7472. 2d ed. 1988. Unpaged. Looseleaf with binder. ISBN 0-7123-0754-0. 50 pounds.

An excellent guide to official literature of industrial property that covers patents, designs, and trademarks. Information is grouped by country with Japan and China grouped under Far Eastern countries. Information includes history—brief details of early legislation including details of significant changes; current legislation—important changes since the last version of the industrial property laws; specifications—serial numbers and related dates with a description of current document and publication procedure; official gazette—principal content; patent indexes—availability and coverage; designs—scope and presentation of published information; trademarks—scope and presentation of published information; reports of legal judgments and decisions; and early publications—historical publications prior to the establishment of the patent office. Several illustrations are provided as examples of the various Japanese publications for patent specifications. Two useful tables are provided: concordance of subject group to the International Patent Classification scheme, and concordance of subject group to Japanese class.

486. *Japanese Laws Relating to Industrial Property.* Goto, Haivo, ed. Aippi-Japan, Toranomon Denki Bldg., 2-8-1 Toranomon, CPO Box 1457, Tokyo 105. (03) 591-5301. Rev. ed. 1972. $50.00.

Published originally in 1966 for the Japan Patent Office, this revised edition includes the changes in the industrial property laws effective January 1971. These revisions were so extensive that they practically constituted a new law.

487. *Japanese Patent, Utility Model and Trade Mark Classification.* Patent Information Worldwide Services Invention Association, Tokyo. Available in U.S. from Derwent Publications Ltd., 6845 Elm St., #500, McLean, VA 22101. (703) 790-0400.

Provides a brief English translation of the Japanese patent classification system.

488. *Japanese R&D Monitor.* Sumitomo Corporation of America, 345 Park Ave., New York, NY 10154. (212) 207-0565. (212) 207-0813 Fax.

This service monitors and publishes patents and patent applications. For a full description, see under this title in the chapter on Industry Reports.

489. *Patent Abstracts of Japan.* Japan Patent Information Organization (JAPIO), Bansui Bldg., 1-5-16 Toranomon, Minato-ku, Tokyo 105. (03) 503-6181. (03) 580-7164 Fax. U.S. agent: IFI-Plenum Data Co., Plenum Pub. Co., 233 Spring St., New York, NY, 10013-1578. (212) 620-8000 or (800) 221-9369. Monthly. $20.00 per issue (approximate).

JAPIO publishes the Patent Abstracts under commission from the Japanese Patent Office. This abstracting publication in English covers unexamined Japanese patent applications. There are four series: O: Chemical, 75–80 issues per year; E: Electrical, 100–105 issues per year; P: Physical, 105–110 issues per year; and M: General and Mechanical, 105–110 issues per year. Each issue contains 500 abstracts arranged in numerical order, including drawings. These series do not cover the Japanese patent literature exhaustively but tend to cover patents in technical fields where there is noticeable foreign country activity. It also contains only patent applications filed by Japanese nationals. There is a two-month time lag between publication in Japanese and the appearance of these English-language abstracts. See PATOLIS entry 476, for the online machine readable version of this publication.

490. *The Patent and Trademark Laws of Japan.* Foster, Richard, and Ono, Masao, trans. Foster-Ono, c/o Marubiru Jimoki K.K., #284, Marunochi Bldg., Chiyoda-ku, Tokyo 100. 2d ed. 1970. 121 p. $10.00.

The revision of the Japanese patent law, effective January 1971, necessitated this new edition. Revision was closer to a new law. Many English translations are available of Japanese patent and trademark law, but it is very difficult for foreign readers to locate specific information needed and impossible to ascertain whether other sections are also relevant. This book is carefully indexed, so references to any subject are quickly found. There are a number of cross-references. This translation combines viewpoints of a U.S. and a Japanese translation. No attempt is made to translate patent terms used in Japan. Instead, these terms are used, but a glossary is included as well as notes on usage.

491. *Patents & Licensing.* Japan Engineering News, Inc. Sun Mansion #202, 1-1-11 Azabudai, Minato-ku, Tokyo 106. (03) 589-4749. (03) 291-3764 Fax. Bimonthly. ISSN 0388-7081. $100.00.

Journal devoted to current news related to patenting in Japan. Section of news briefs gives information on current company news and new patenting ventures. Articles pertaining to current laws and practice follows. Brief reviews of current court decisions are listed. Articles from foreign correspondents and licensing news follow. Because the journal accepts advertising, it is a good source for addresses of patent attorneys in Japan and for those practicing outside of Japan who are familiar with Japanese patent law.

ONLINE DATABASES

492. CA Search (Chemical Abstracts). Chemical Abstracts Service, 2540 Olentangy River Rd. PO Box 3012, Columbus, OH 43210-0012. (614) 447-3600. (614) 447-3709 Fax.

The Chemical Abstracts database monitors some 10,000 titles per year. This information is taken from journal articles, technical reports, dissertations, conference proceedings, new books, and patents. Patent information is included from the European Patent Office, the United States, West Germany, the U.S.S.R., Japan, the World Intellectual Property Organization, and 23 additional patent offices worldwide. In 1988, 53.8 percent of the 80,795 patents added to the database were of Japanese origin. Vendors: STN, DIALOG, and Maxwell Online.

493. INPADOC. International Patent Documentation Center, A-1040 Vienna, Mollwaldplatz 4, Austria. (222) 65-8784. (222) 65-3386 Fax.

This database provides full coverage of Japanese patents along with patents from most other major patenting countries. Only bibliographic information is included. Unlike the JAPIO database, no abstracts are provided. Coverage includes both unexamined (kokai) and examined patent documents. Vendors: Maxwell Online.

494. JAPIO. Japan Patent Information Organization, Bansui Bldg., 1-5-16 Toranomon, Minato-ku, Tokyo 105. (03) 503-6181. (03) 580-7164 Fax.

Online database in English of Japanese published patents which includes unexamined applications (kokai), this is the only comprehensive source of Japanese patents in English offered online. Examined patents are not included, nor are utility models or design patents. As well as bibliographic information, JAPIO assigns company codes, keywords from a controlled vocabulary, and subject codes. The abstracts from Patent Abstracts of Japan are also included. Currently, approximately 90 percent of the entries have English-language abstracts. Data online lag approximately three months behind publication because data for the online service are taken from the printed publication *Patent Abstracts of Japan.* A monthly COM microfiche index service is also available for unexamined patent applications. These indexes can be arranged by Document Number, Applicant Name, or International Patent Classification code. These indexes contain the following data elements, in English: kokai number, international patent classification, title, foreign priority, applicant and the volume, and number and page in the corresponding section of *Patent Abstracts of Japan.* Vendor: Maxwell Online.

495. PATOLIS. Japan Patent Information Organization (JAPIO), Bansui Bldg., 1-5-16 Toranomon, Minato-ku, Tokyo 105. (03) 503-6181. (03) 580-7164 Fax.

Complete coverage in Japanese of Japanese patents, utility models, trademarks, and design patents, throughout all stages from application to granted patent. Legal status data are provided. Bibliographic data, abstract, and drawings are included. INPADOC (Vienna) will search this database on demand and translate the results. INPADOC markets a kanji terminal emulator which enables you to search the Japanese language PATOLIS database without special kanji terminals and provides automatic translation into English of the constant data elements, common to all patent applications. This can be useful for displaying and printing out current Japanese-language patent information from the database. Automatic translation is provided for bibliographic data, legal status, and important applicant names. The translation can therefore be confined to the free text information, thereby reducing the translation costs. Vendor: INPADOC.

496. World Patents Index. Derwent Publications 6845 Elm St., #500, McLean, VA 22101. (703) 790-0400. (703) 790-1426 Fax.

Coverage of Japanese patents in this database is uneven depending on the subject required. Coverage is as follows: from 1963—pharmaceutical; from 1965—agriculture and veterinary medicine; from 1966—polymers and plastics; from 1970—all chemistry; from 1982—electrical; and from 1984—mechanical. Examined and unexamined patents are covered for chemistry, but subject indexing of the abstracts is restricted to subscribers of the Derwent print publications. No abstracts are available for electrical and noncore chemical patents. Vendors: DIALOG, Maxwell Online, and Questel.

COMMERCIAL SERVICES

497. International Science & Technology Associates (ISTA, Inc.), 11 Beatrice Dr., Bryn Mawr, PA 19010. (215) 527-4538. (215) 527-2041 Fax.

Can search the Japanese-language database PATOLIS which covers Japanese patents, utility models, designs, and trademarks. Translation and document delivery services are also offered on a fee basis.

498. Japan Association for International Chemical Information (JAICI). Gakkai Center Bldg., 2-4-16 Yayoi, Bunkyo-ku, Tokyo 113. (03) 816-3462.

Will supply and translate Japanese patents. Orders can be placed online via DIALOG's Dialorder facility or STN International's Order command. Orders can also be sent via telefacsimile. An excerpts option is also available for translation of Japanese patents into English. This option provides translation of bibliographic heading, claim, and the first example.

499. Japan Patent Data Service Co., Takashima Bldg., 1-17-6 Nishi-Shinbashi, Minato-ku, Tokyo 105. (03) 580-9681. (03) 580-5648 Fax. U.S. agent Norman Ross Pub., Inc., 1995 Broadway, New York, NY 10023-5896. (212) 873-2100.

This company, a subsidiary of Chuo Kogaku Shuppan Co., Ltd., one of the largest patent microfilm publishers in Japan, offers a complete service for Japanese patent and utility model information. Most of their services such as an SDI service and microfilm publications have been in Japanese. However, the company is investigating publication in English of a *Kokai Watching Report*, a one-subject, one-page summary sheet service for Japanese patents. The check sheets would be offered on a subject basis, with the 26 industrial fields according to the International Patent Classification being offered. The company will provide full translation of patents and can supply copies of any Japanese patent.

Chapter 13
Translations

This chapter is not a listing of available translations from Japanese to English. Rather, it is a collection of publications and services that will help in locating existing translations or will provide direction for commissioning the services of a translator or translation agency.

Because machine translation is often suggested as an answer to the problem of procuring translations from Japanese into English, a few recent reports that may shed some light on current developments in this area are included.

PRINTED SOURCES

500. *Commercial Translations: A Business-Like Approach to Obtaining Accurate Translations.* Harris, Godfrey, and Sonabend, Charles. The American Group, 9200 Sunset Blvd., #404, Los Angeles, CA 90069. 1985. 135 p. ISBN 0-935047-02-6. $15.95.

Designed as a handbook for businesspersons needing to obtain accurate translations, this book alerts the reader to some of the pitfalls inherent in obtaining a translation of a foreign document into English. Although this is not devoted to translation from Japanese to English, the suggested checklist for choosing a translation service is useful in the Japanese to English arena.

501. *Directory of Consultants and Translators for Engineered Materials.* Materials Information, ASM International, Metals Park, OH 44073. (216) 338-5151. (216) 338-4634 Fax. 2d ed. 1990. 60 p. $60.00.

A directory compiled to assist individuals and companies wishing to locate translators or specialists in the field of advanced materials. Emphasis is placed on identifying the expertise of the individuals listed in relation to materials science. The experts listed come from the fields of advanced polymers, ceramics, and composites, and coverage is international in scope. The directory is divided into separate listings for consultants and for translators who are listed in three separate sections by geographic area, by language expertise, and by corporate or individual name index.

502. *Directory of Metallurgical Consultants and Translators.* Materials Information, ASM International, Metals Park, OH 44073. (216) 338-5151. (216) 338-4634 Fax. 4th ed., 1990. $60.00.

Similar to the *Directory of Consultants and Translators for Engineered Materials* but lists consultants and translators skilled in metallurgy.

503. *Journals in Translation.* British Library Publications Sales Unit, Document Supply Centre, Boston Spa, Wetherby, West Yorkshire LS23 7BQ. (0937) 54-6080. 1988. 218 p. ISBN 0-7123-2038-5. 48 British pounds (including airmail).

Published in association with the International Translations Centre, Delft, this is the fourth edition of a work first published in 1976 as a guide to journals in translation. It replaces the earlier titles published by each organization: *Translations Journals*, 1974, and *Journals in Translation*, 1976. Listed are journals translated cover to cover or selectively, as well as journals that publish translations selected from a variety of source journals. Titles held by the British Library are indicated. The alphabetical list of journals is indexed by keywords and an original title index. A number of appendixes provide outlines of major translation series.

504. *Journals with Translations Held by the Science Reference Library.* Alexander, B.A. Science Reference Library, 25 Southampton Bldgs., Chancery Ln., London WC2A 1AW. (071) 323-7472. (01) 405-8721. 1985. 65 p. ISBN 0-7123-0717-6. $10.00.

Covers biology, physical and information sciences, technology, and inventions. Lists journals both current and ceased that are translated cover to cover or selectively. Also includes journals that publish translated articles collected from a variety of sources. Arrangement is alphabetical by translation journal title. A list is also provided of original titles. Two indexes are provided. Section A is alphabetical by Science Reference Library subject headings, and Section B is arranged in alphabetical order of Science Reference Library classes. Although Russian is the major language, there are a number of Japanese translation journals listed.

505. *Translation Services Directory.* Learned Information, Inc., 143 Old Marlton Pike, Medford, NJ 08055. (609) 654-6266. 6th ed., 1986. 157 p. ISBN 0-938734-16-4. $20.00.

Published for the American Translators Association, this is a directory of registered translators. Alphabetical listing of translators gives name; address; citizenship; country of birth; native languages; languages translatable into English; subject areas of expertise; other foreign-language services offered such as interpreting, word processing, etc.; and education and relevant experience. There are useful indexes by language pairs, subject area, and geographic area. The introductory section provides helpful advice on hiring a suitable translator.

506. *Translations Index.* Materials Information, ASM International, Metals Park, OH 44073. (216) 338-5151. Quarterly. $110.00.

Index of the translations available from the Materials Information Translations Service (MITS). Listing includes translations available through MITS as well as those completed by other services commissioned by Materials Information.

507. *Translations of Scientific and Technical Literature: A Guide to Their Location.* Wright, Kathleen. Special Libraries Association, Aerospace Division, 1700 Eighteenth St., NW, Washington DC 20009. (202) 234-4700. 1987. 27 p. $20.00.

Useful guide to locating scientific and technical translations in English. Strategies for locating translations are provided in an appendix. Major providers of existing translations are enumerated. Procedures for ordering a custom translation are also provided. A bibliography (Appendix B) provides information on specific sources, discusses transliteration problems, provides information on locating and using commercial translators, and discusses searching for translations and suggestions for locating foreign publications.

508. *Translator's Handbook.* Picken, Catriona, ed. Aslib, Information House, 26/27 Boswell St., London WCIN 3JZ. (01) 430-2671. 1983. 270 p. ISBN 0-85142-173-3. $49.85.

Although primarily a handbook for translators, this is also a useful source for those who use translations and the services of translators. Covers types of translations, quality, specifications, national and international translation organizations, relations between languages, and a bibliography of technical translations and sources of information.

509. *World Translation Index.* International Translations Centre, 101, Doelenstraat, 2611 NS Delft, Netherlands. (015) 14-2242. 10 issues per year + cumulation. Vol. 1, 1987. ISSN 0259-8264. 1,150 Dutch guilders.

Formed by the merger of World Transindex and Translations Register Index, this is a joint publication of the International Translations Centre, Commission of the European Communities, the Centre National de la Recherche Scientifique, and the National Translations Center, formerly at the John Crerar Library, University of Chicago, and now at the Library of Congress. It lists translations from east European and Asian languages into Western languages in science and technology. There are three sections: References, Source Index, and Author Index. The source and author indexes are also published separately as an annual cumulative volume. A machine-readable version of the database can be accessed on DIALOG and ESA. For details see Chapter 11 on Online Databases.

OTHER SOURCES

510. American Translators Association (ATA). Japanese Language Division, 10,000 S. Claremont, Chicago, IL 60643. (312) 779-3009. (312) 779-9843 Fax.

The Japanese Language Division of the ATA accredits Japanese to English translators in the U.S. Maintains a directory of Japanese translators. At the annual ATA conference, the Japanese Language Division presents a program of speakers.

511. Japan Translation Association. Nichijukin Shibuya Bldg., 1-24-4 Shibuya, Shibuya-ku, Tokyo 150. (03) 409-4702.

The association promotes standards in the translation industry, evaluates translators, and licenses suitably qualified translators. It maintains a listing of translators and translation agencies in Japan and will provide a referral service to suitably qualified individuals. Publishes a directory of member translation companies.

512. Materials Information Translations Service (MITS). Materials Information, ASM International, Metals Park, OH 44073. (216) 338-5151.

Materials Information, a joint service of the American Society of Metals and the Institute of Metals (U.K.), offers a translation service. Selected articles from journals, conferences, and the patent literature are translated into English. Over 25 source languages are covered including Japanese. Subject coverage is metallurgy with the exception of extractive metallurgy. Recently engineered materials, including polymers, ceramics, and composites, have been added. A weekly translations list is produced by MITS to announce new translations. About 1,000 titles are added each year. Currently they hold about 25,000 translations. The weekly lists cover the following areas: Series A—Nonferrous Metallurgy; Series B—BISITS Ferrous Metallurgy; and Series C—Engineered Materials (polymers, ceramics, and composites). A subscription to the weekly list costs $17.00 per year per series. A standing order arrangement is offered whereby companies can obtain multiples of 25 at a discounted rate. A free subscription to the quarterly *Translations Index* is included for standing order customers. An exchange arrangement is also offered.

513. U.S. Patent and Trademark Office (PTO). Translation Division, Crystal Plaza 3-4, #2C15, Washington, DC 20231. (703) 557-3193. (703) 557-9564 Fax.

Requests for translation are accepted from PTO staff only. However, the public can purchase copies of any translated Japanese patents. Fee is $0.50 per page.

MACHINE TRANSLATION

514. *Chinese and Japanese Language Translation by Computer.* U.S. Department of Commerce, National Technical Information Service (NTIS), 5285 Port Royal Rd., Springfield, VA 22161. (703) 487-4650. (703) 321-8199 Fax. 1989. NTIS Order No. PB89-868913/LAK. $55.00.

List of citations from the INSPEC database covering machine translation of Chinese and Japanese. Citations cover the period June 1975 to August 1989.

515. *Computer-Aided Translation: An Industry Survey.* Ingall, Martin. Associated Technical Services, Inc., 855 Bloomfield Ave., Glen Ridge, NJ 10728-1394. (201) 748-5673. Undated. 57 p. $135.00.

This mimeographed report was prepared for the Middle East Language Corporation. It assesses machine translation systems worldwide. The first section covers commercially available sytems. Along with a narrative description of the system is the name, address, and contact person for each company. The second section covers government and university research into this technology. The final section covers commercial products which can be used with existing machine translation systems to enhance their effectiveness.

516. *Current Status of Japanese to English Machine Translation. Report to Congress.* Kusada, T. U.S. Department of Commerce, Japanese Technical Literature Program, #4817, H. C. Hoover Bldg., 14th & Constitution Ave., N.W., Washington, DC 20230. (202) 377-1288. (202) 377-4498 Fax. 1988. 18 p. NTIS Order No. PB89-128276. $13.00.

This report to Congress assesses the present status of Japanese to English machine translation. The machine translation process is discussed as well as current developments in the U.S., Japan, and Europe. Optical character recognition is discussed as an input device.

517. *Japanese View of Machine Translation in Light of the Considerations and Recommendations Reported by ALPAC.* Japan Electronic Industry Development Association (JEIDA), Kikai Shinko Kaikan, 3-5-8 Shiba Koen, Minato-ku, Tokyo 105. (03) 433-1941. (03) 433-6350 Fax. 1989. 187 p. Gratis.

This report is based on a survey conducted by the Machine Translation System Research Committee of the JEIDA. This committee has been researching machine translation for the past 10 years. The survey looked at various machine translation systems in current use in a number of countries. The study also looked at the translation industry in Japan today and ways in which machine translation is being used in the industry. The report concludes that the situation is very different today from that in 1966 when the ALPAC report was written.

518. *Machine Translation: Foreign Language Translation and Natural Language Understanding.* U.S. Department of Commerce, National Technical Information Service (NTIS), 5285 Port Royal Rd., Springfield, VA 22161. (703) 487-4650. (703) 321-8199 Fax. 1989. NTIS Order No. PB89-867931/LAK. $55.00.

List of citations from the NTIS database covering January 1970 to July 1989.

519. *Machine Translation of Online Searches in Japanese Databases.* Sigurdson, Jon, and Greatrex, Roger. Research Policy Institute, Lund University, Box 2017, S-220 02 Lund, Sweden. Available from U.S. Department of Commerce, National Technical Information Service (NTIS), 5285 Port Royal Rd., Springfield, VA 22161. (703) 487-4650. (703) 321-8199 Fax. 1987. 124 p. ISBN 9-1860-0262-7. NTIS Order No. PB88-230073. $23.00.

Originally published by Research Policy Institute (RPI), Lund University, it was reprinted and made available through NTIS. Subtitled "A Way to Facilitate Access to Japanese Techno-Economic Information?" Provides a good overview of the information industry and online databases in Japan. Machine translation of Japanese is explored, followed by a description of the major Japanese databases. The major machine translation systems currently under development are explained in some detail with experiences of those using the systems. Examples of machine translation are included. Conclusion offers suggestions for using machine translation to improve access to Japanese information.

520. *Machine Translation Summit.* Nagao, M., ed. IOS, PO Box 2848, Springfield, VA 22152-2848. (703) 323-9116. (703) 250-4705 Fax. 1989. 224 p. ISBN 4-274-07445-5. $65.00.

Published proceedings of the Machine Translation Summit held in Japan, September 16–18, 1987.

APPENDIX A: Booksellers

Listed below are some of the booksellers and agents both in Japan and the United States who handle Japanese publications, particularly the scientific, technical, and business sources referred to in this handbook. Although many nonspecialist booksellers may be able to obtain Japanese publications, it is generally more expedient to use those listed. Publications listed as gratis or unpriced should be obtained directly from the publisher.

Associated Technical Services, Inc. (ATS, Inc.)
855 Bloomfield Ave., Glen Ridge, NJ 07028-1394
(201) 748-5673 • (201) 748-5560 Fax

Established in 1949, this company specializes in scientific, technical, and general dictionaries; translation aids; and books of abbreviations and acronyms. They are particularly strong in Asian languages. To keep information, particularly price information, current, ATS, Inc. does not publish a catalog. Instead they will send flyers covering specific fields of interest. This is an excellent source for Japanese scientific and technical dictionaries, many of which are kept in stock. This company also provides a translation service for over 40 languages, including Japanese, specializing in scientific and technical translations.

Government Publications Service Center (GPSC)
1-2-1 Kasumigaseka, Chiyoda-ku, Tokyo 100
(03) 504-3885 • (03) 504-3889 Fax

Supplier of official Japanese publications including those of the government bureaus, offices, ministries, councils, and related organizations. This is the main office, but there are a number of branches throughout Japan.

Intercontinental Marketing Corp.
CPO Box 97, Tokyo 100-91

Sales agent for books and publications on Japan. Also publishes a number of directories of the Japanese book trade.

International Specialized Book Services, Inc.
5602 NE Hassalo St., Portland, OR 97213-3640

Distributor for North, Central and South America, and Oceania for publications from the Japan Scientific Societies Press (JSSP)/Gakkai Shuppan Senta. The JSSP is an independent publisher of English-language scientific and medical books in Japan. It publishes in cooperation with the Center for Academic Publications Japan (CAPJ), a publisher of academic and scientific societies publications. JSSP produces a *Catalog of English Editions* covering books and journals.

Japan Publications Trading Co., Ltd.
IPO Box 5030, Tokyo International, Tokyo 100-31
1-2-1 Sarugaku-cho
Chiyoda-ku, Tokyo 101, (03) 292-3751

Exporters and sales agents for many Japanese publications.

Kinokuniya Book Store Co., Ltd.
3-17-7 Shinjuku, Shinjuku-ku, Tokyo 160-91, (03) 354-0131
Offices in the U.S.:
1551 Webster St., San Francisco, CA 94115, (415) 567-7625
110 S. Los Angeles St. #12, Los Angeles, CA 90012, (213) 687-4447
10 W. 49th St., New York, NY 10020, (212) 765-1461.
(212) 541-9335 Fax

Major Japanese bookseller. This is the main store, but there are a number of locations in Japan and the U.S. Sells Japanese books and journals as well as books on Japan published in English.

Maruzen Co., Ltd.
2-3-10 Nihonbashi, Chuo-ku, Tokyo 103
Export Department, PO Box 5050, Tokyo International, Tokyo 100-31
(03) 278-9223 • (03) 274-2270 Fax

Major bookstore in Japan. Carries large number of English-language publications. Also supplies journals to libraries on subscription basis. Maruzen International Co., Ltd., New York is an export office only. All orders for books from Japan must be handled through Maruzen, Tokyo.

Nihon Faxon Co.
4th Fl., Kurihara Bldg., 7-8-13 Nishishinjuku, Shinjuku-ku, Tokyo 160
(03) 367-3081 • (03) 366-0295 Fax

Periodical subscription agent and bookseller.

Overseas Courier Service (OCS)
OCS America, Inc., National Press Bldg., #1186, 14th and F Sts., NW, Washington, DC 20045
(202) 347-4233
2-9 Shiba-ura, Minato-ku, Tokyo 108

Distributor of many Japanese publications. The Washington office is the only OCS office in the U.S. that handles Japanese publications.

Pacific Subscription Service
PO Box 811, FDR Station, New York, NY 10150
(212) 929-1629

Agent for many Japanese books and periodicals.

Pan Asian Publications
PO Box 131, Agincourt Station, Scarborough, Ontario M1S 3B4
(416) 292-7544

Supplier of books in Asian languages. Provides a cataloging service, also acquisitions lists in the vernacular and in transliterated format.

Want Publishing Co.
1511 K St., NW, Washington, DC 20005
(202) 783-1887 • (202) 393-5106 Fax

Distributor for a number of Japanese book publishers and some magazines. Specializes in publications that deal with Japanese trade and technology.

APPENDIX B: Libraries

This highly selective listing of libraries includes only those collections that have a high proportion of Japanese scientific, technical, and business publications. Many of the excellent, very extensive East Asian collections in the United States do not cover science and technology. Holdings of current sci-tech journals from Japan, particularly those in Japanese, are not held extensively in the United States. Of the 10,000 titles currently published in Japan very few are held in any publicly accessible library in the United States.

Many of the more generalized directories and handbooks listed in this sourcebook will be found in libraries in the United States because they are in English. Some of the more specialized directories, and many of the reports, will not be easily located. The libraries listed in this appendix will, however, provide a good starting point.

British Library
Japanese Information Service, Science Reference and Information Service,
25 Southampton Bldgs.
Chancery Ln., London WC2A 1AW
(01) 323-7924 • (01) 323-7495 Fax

Collects current Japanese business information as well as science and technology. Excellent collection of directories and ready reference sources, also market reports, patents, and numeric data. The collection numbers over 3,500 journals, six million patents, and all Japanese industrial property publications. Linguistic aid service available to assist with determining relevance of Japanese-language material prior to arranging custom translation services. Can also search Japanese-language databases for a fee. Provides a referral service to alternative sources of information, where necessary.

Center for Research Libraries (CRL)
6050 S. Kenwood Ave., Chicago, IL 60637
(312) 955-4545

This is a research collection supported by a consortium of large U.S. research libraries. The collection focuses on expensive, often esoteric, research materials that individual research libraries may not be able to justify purchasing for their own collections. Over the last few years, CRL has endeavored to increase its holdings of current Japanese-language journals covering science and technology, not held in U.S. libraries. Holdings of CRL are listed in the OCLC Inc. union catalog.

Chemical Abstracts Service Library
PO Box 3012, 2540 Olentangy River Rd., Columbus, OH 43210
(614) 447-3600 • (614) 447-3709 Fax

Chemical Abstracts Service (CAS) can supply copies of documents listed in the Chemical Abstracts database. For a listing of titles held, consult *Chemical Abstracts Service Source* (*CASSI*) *Index* (See Chapter 4, Bibliographies). CAS is a good source of Japanese-language serials in chemistry, broadly defined.

Japan External Trade Organization (JETRO) Library
2-2-5 Toranomon, Minato-ku, Tokyo 105
(03) 582 5511

In U.S. contact

JETRO, Library
1221 Avenue of the Americas, New York, NY 10020
(212) 997-0432

The Tokyo library is open to the public Monday through Saturday from 9:30 a.m.-4:30 p.m. It contains marketing information, particularly trade statistics, international company reports, some market research reports, and company and telephone directories. Although much of the information is in Japanese, there are a number of English-language publications in the collection. Helpful staff are available to assist with inquiries. There are 30 branches of JETRO throughout Japan, all with their own libraries. The U.S. office aims to study the U.S. market and assist in promoting trade between the U.S. and Japan. The office can be helpful in providing information.

Japan Information Center of Science and Technology (JICST)
Library, 2-8-18 Asahicho, Nerimu-ku, Tokyo 176
(03) 976-4141
Administrative Office
2-5-2 Nagata-cho, CPO Box 1478, Chiyoda-ku, Tokyo 100
(03) 581-6411
In U.S. contact
1550 M St., NW, Washington, DC 20005
(202) 872-6370 or (202) 872-6371 • (202) 872-6372 Fax

The JICST libraries in Japan are open to anyone wishing to use the collections. JICST also offers document delivery and translation services for foreign users via mail or telefacsimile. The main JICST collection comprises over 14,000 journals, technical reports, conference proceedings, and patents. Collects foreign as well as Japanese material. Currently, about 48 percent of the collection is of Japanese origin.

Japan Studies Centre Library
University of Sheffield, Sheffield, South Yorkshire S10 2TN
(0742) 78555

Although predominantly aimed at serving the university's Japan Studies Department, there are also significant holdings of Japanese business materials. The librarian, a Japanese linguist, can help in locating relevant information.

Library of Congress
10 First St., SE, Washington, DC 20540
(202) 287-5639

Holdings include 600,000 books and 16,000 serial titles in Japanese. The Library of Congress (LC) is a depository library for Japanese government publications. Although the holdings of Japanese serial titles look impressive, the number of current titles in science and technology is not extensive. Because of budget restraints, LC is unable to add substantially to their holdings of current serials in science and technology. Many of the titles held are not purchased but are received as gifts or under exchange agreements. Such arrangements are less reliable than receiving titles by subscription. Since 1989, the National Translation Center (NTC), formerly housed at the John Crerar Library, University of Chicago, has been relocated to the Library of Congress. A number of translations from Japanese scientific and technical journals are included. Very recent articles will generally not be found in the NTC collection. For further information on translations, call (202) 707-0100.

Library of Japanese Science and Technology
24 Duke St., Whiteley Bay NE26 3PP
(0632) 53-3479

Private collection containing over 3,000 Japanese journals in science, technology, and business. Articles will be photocopied and mailed for a modest fee. A scanning service, literature searches, and SDI services will be conducted for a fee. The collections are housed at the University of Newcastle upon Tyne, but the office is at Whiteley Bay, where all inquiries should be sent.

Linda Hall Library
5109 Cherry St., Kansas City, MO 64110
(816) 363-4600

This is a private library for science and technology. It houses approximately 700 current Japanese journals. Document delivery of needed articles is provided for a fee. Although a private collection, the library is open to the public.

Massachusetts Institute of Technology
Library, 14S-216, 77 Massachusetts Ave., Cambridge, MA 02139
(617) 253-5651

This collection focuses on engineering, technology, and the physical sciences. Supports the Japan Science and Technology program at MIT.

National Diet Library
1-10-1 Nagato-cho, Chiyoda-ku, Tokyo 100
(03) 581-2331 • (03) 581-0989 Fax

Like the Library of Congress in the United States, this is the largest collection in Japan. Designed to serve members of Japan's Diet, it also is open to anyone over 20 years of age.

North Carolina Biotechnology Center
Box 13547, Research Triangle Park, NC 27709
(919) 541-9366

This private, not-for-profit, center promotes biotechnology research in North Carolina. The center's library is open to the public, Monday through Friday, 9:00 a.m. to 4:30 p.m. A document delivery service is available for a fee. The staff will also search its catalog, available online for a $25.00 fee.

North Carolina State University Japan Center
NCSU Box 8112, Raleigh, NC 27695-8112
(919) 737-3450 • (919) 737-3686 Fax

Collection numbers over 300 scientific and technical journals from Japan. The center offers a referral service for translations of technical information.

Ohio State University
University Library, 1858 Neil Ave. Mall, Columbus, OH 43210
(614) 422-2073

The collection numbers over 36,000 volumes in Japanese and numerous volumes in English on Japan. The library holds subscriptions to 506 periodicals on Japan, 349 of which are in Japanese. It also subscribes to four Japanese-language newspapers and four newspapers on Japan in English. Of particular interest is the collection of Japanese government white papers, works on the history of science and medicine in Japan, and Japanese company histories.

U.S. Patent and Trademark Office
Scientific Library, Crystal Plaza, 3–4 #2C01, Washington, DC 20231
(703) 557-3545

Holds Japanese patents from 1880 to the present. For translations of Japanese patents see under chapter on Translations.

University of California, San Diego
International Relations and Pacific Studies Library, La Jolla, CA 92093
(619) 534-1413

Although the focus is on business and political information for all Pacific Rim countries, Japan is a particular strength of this collection. Although a relatively young collection, there is an excellent selection of directories for business information from Japan. Current business journals and newsletters from Japan are also held. Science and technology is not a primary focus although some current material is held because these impact Japan's economy.

University of Chicago
East Asia Library, 1100 E. 57th St., Chicago, IL 60637
(312) 702-8434

The Japanese collection is strongest in humanities and social sciences; however, it does contain excellent resources for researching the history of Japanese companies, history of science, reference materials, and technical journals from Japan in both Japanese and English. The University of Chicago's science library also holds many journals with scientific and technical information from Japan in English.

University of Hawaii
Thomas Hale Hamilton Library, 2550 The Mall, Honolulu, HI 96822
(808) 948-8263

The University of Hawaii, Asian collection, is strong in Japanese vernacular materials, although science and technology is not a primary focus. Their reference collection is a good source for Japanese materials, many in English as well as the Japanese-language materials.

University of Maryland at College Park—Libraries
McKeldin Library, College Park, MD 20742
(301) 454-3011

The Gordon W. Prange Collection holds 10,000 books and 1,000 journals that are concerned with Japanese science and technology.

APPENDIX C: Other Sources of Information

The listings in this section are for noncommercial organizations that provide information on Japan. Many have been referred to throughout this guide because many are publishers of information about Japan.

No attempt has been made to cover the numerous cultural societies that exist to promote U.S.-Japan relations. These can be found in many of the directories and handbooks referenced in these pages.

American Chamber of Commerce in Japan
#701, Marunouchi, 3-chome, Chiyoda-ku, Tokyo 100
(03) 433-5381

Serves business interests for U.S. companies interested in trade with Japan. Publishes a variety of informative reports and journals.

Embassy of Japan
2520 Massachusetts Ave., NW, Washington, DC 20008
(202) 234-2266

Can provide much useful information or suggest a more appropriate source to handle particular inquiries.

Infosta-Nipdok (Information Science and Technology Association)
Japan Information Desk, Sasaki Bldg., 2-5-7 Koisikawa, Bunkyo-ku, Tokyo 112
(03) 813-3791 • (03) 813-3793 Fax

Somewhat like the U.S. National Federation of Abstracting and Indexing Services (NFAIS), Infosta is an organization representing Japanese science and technical database producers and other information providers. The Japan Information Desk is provided for English-speaking users of Japanese databases. Will put requesters in touch with the appropriate Japanese information source. Will also locate information for a fee. This is not a library, and it does not provide a document delivery service.

Japan External Trade Organization (JETRO)
2-2-5 Toranomon, Minato-ku, Tokyo 105
(03) 582-5511

Acts on behalf of many Japanese trade associations. The Japanese office is open to the public. U.S. offices are very helpful in trying to locate business information from Japan. JETRO holds a number of directories that it will consult to answer telephone inquiries.

In U.S.:
725 S. Figueroa St., #1890, Los Angeles, CA 90017
(213) 624-8855 • (213) 629-8127 Fax

401 N. Michigan Ave., #660, Chicago, IL 60611
(312) 527-9000 • (312) 670-4223 Fax

1221 McKinley, One Houston Center, #2360, Houston, TX 77010
(713) 759-9595 • (713) 759-9210 Fax

2100 Stemmons Freeway, World Trade Center, 1st Fl., Dallas, TX 75258
(214) 651-0839 • (214) 651-1831 Fax

360 Post St., Qantas Bldg., #501, San Francisco, CA 94108
(415) 392-1333 • (415) 788-6927 Fax

245 Peachtree Center Ave., #2102, Atlanta, GA 30303
(404) 681-0600 • (404) 681-0713 Fax

1200 17th St., #1410, Denver, CO 80202
(303) 629-0404

Japan Information Center of Science & Technology (JICST)
2-5-2 Nagata-cho, Chiyoda-ku, Tokyo 100
(03) 581-6411
In U.S.:
1550 M St., NW, Washington, DC 20005
(202) 872-6370 • (202) 872-6372 Fax

Collects and disseminates information on science and technology from Japan and foreign countries. Producer of abstract journals in various fields of science and technology and the JICST online information system (JOIS). JICST will perform searches of its database, both retrospective and on a continuous monthly cycle (SDI). Also provides document delivery service, for a fee, and translation services.

Japan Tariff Association
Jibiki Daini Bldg., 4-7-8 Kohji-Machi, Chiyoda-ku, Tokyo 102
(03) 263-7221 • (03) 263-7345 Fax

Collects and publishes guides for import to and export from Japan.

Japanese Technical Literature Program
#4817, H. C. Hoover Bldg., 14th & Constitution Ave, N.W.,
Washington, DC 20230
(202) 377-1288 • (202) 377-4498 Fax

Will provide searches on request of Japanese-language databases as well as the English-language version of the JICST database (JOIS-E). Produces a newsletter covering areas of interest to those tracking Japanese science and technology. For details see *Japanese Technical Literature Bulletin* in Chapter 1, Guides to Sources of Japanese Information.

MIT—Japan Science and Technology Program Office
Massachusetts Institute of Technology, #E53-447, Cambridge, MA 02139
(617) 253-2449

Offers Japanese language training for science and engineering students at MIT as well as to scientists and engineers in industry.

Ministry of International Trade and Industry (MITI)
Information Office, 1-3-1 Kasumigaseki, Chiyoda-ku, Tokyo 100
(03) 501-1657

Publishes useful statistical and economic data. Helpful source for the foreign businessperson.

U.S. Department of Commerce
U.S. and Foreign Commercial Service, Office of Japan, #2318,
Washington, DC 20230
(202) 377-3808 Japan Desk Officer • (202) 377-4527 Business Counseling and Economic Information

The U.S. and Foreign Commercial Service forms part of the Department of Commerce, International Trade Administration. It is aimed at the marketing information needs of U.S. exporters and importers. There are 50 district offices and 17 branch offices throughout the U.S. There are also 125 posts in 66 countries throughout the world, including Japan.

APPENDIX D: Online Vendors

Addresses follow for the online vendors listed in Chapter 11, Online Databases.

BRS
BRS Information Technologies
(a division of Maxwell Online)
1200 Rt. 7
Latham, NY 12110
(518) 783-1161
(800) 289-4277
(518) 783-1160 Fax

CISTI
Canadian Scientific Numerical Database Service
National Research Council Canada
Ottawa, Ontario K1A OS2
(613) 993-3294
(613) 952-7158 Fax

Comline International
Shungetsu Bldg.
3-12-7 Kita Aoyama
Minato-ku, Tokyo 107
(03) 486-0696
(03) 400-7704 Fax
In U.S., contact
InfoCorp
20833 Stevens Creek Blvd.
Cupertino, CA 95014
(408) 973-1010

Data-Star
D-S Marketing Ltd.
Plaza Suite
114 Jermyn St.
London, SW1Y 6HJ
(01) 930-7646
(01) 930-2581 Fax
In U.S., call
(800) 221-7754

DIALOG Information Services, Inc.
3460 Hillview Ave.
Palo Alto, CA 94304
(415) 858-3810
(800) 334-2564

U.S. Field Offices:

Cambridge, MA	(617) 494-1114
Chicago, IL	(312) 726-9206
Houston, TX	(713) 789-9810
Marina del Rey, CA	(213) 827-0055
New York, NY	(212) 682-4630
Arlington, VA	(703) 553-8455
Philadelphia, PA	(215) 977-8161

Representatives outside the U.S.:

Australia/New Zealand	(02) 212-2867
Japan	(03) 439-0123
Canada	(416) 593-5211
Europe	(865) 73-0275
Korea	Telex 28311

Dow Jones News/Retrieval
Dow Jones and Co., Inc.
PO Box 300
Princeton, NJ 08543-0300
(609) 520-4000

ESA-IRS
Esrin
via Galileo Galilei
00044 Frascati
Italy
(06) 94-1801
(06) 94-180361 Fax

Other offices worldwide:

Austria	(02.254) 80-3850
Belgium	(02) 519-5643
Denmark	(42) 88-3088
Finland	(0) 4356-4410
France	(01) 4278-7203
Ireland	(01) 370-101
Netherlands	(020) 223-955
Norway	(07) 59-5120
Spain	(01) 247-9800
Sweden	(08) 790-8970
United Kingdom	(071) 215-6578

Fiz-Technik
Ostbahnhofatrasse 13
Postfach 60 05 47
6000 Frankfurt am Main 1
West Germany
(69) 4308-225
(69) 4308-200 Fax

GE Mark III Network
General Electric Information Services Company (GeNie)
401 N. Washington St.
Rockville, MD 20850
(301) 294-5405
(301) 340-4488 Fax

Maxwell Online
8000 Westpark Dr., #400
McLean, VA 22101
(703) 442-0900
(800) 456-7248
(703) 893-4632 Fax

Mead Data Central, Inc.
PO Box 933
Dayton, OH 45401
(513) 865-6800
(800) 227-4908

National Technical Information Service (NTIS)
U.S. Department of Commerce
5285 Port Royal Rd.
Springfield, VA 22161
(703) 487-4822

Needs-Net
Nihon Keizai Shimbun Inc. (Nikkei)
Databank Bureau
1-9-5 Ohtemachi
Chiyoda-ku, Tokyo 100
(03) 270-0251
(03) 270-8555 Fax

Newsnet, Inc.
945 Haverford Rd.
Bryn Mawr, PA 19010
(800) 345-1301
(215) 527-8030
(215) 527-0338 Fax

Offices outside the U.S.:

Japan	(03) 463-7181
Israel	(03) 494444
Singapore	(16) 296-8080
U.K.	(0990) 29-1072
Denmark	(06) 18-2844

Reuters Information Services, Inc.
1700 Broadway
New York, NY 10019
(212) 603-3300

STN International
c/o Chemical Abstracts Service
2540 Olentangy River Rd.
PO Box 3012
Columbus, OH 43210
(800) 848-6533
(614) 447-3600
(614) 447-3713 Fax

Offices outside the U.S.:

Germany	(7247) 808-555
	(7247) 808 666 Fax
Japan	(03) 581-6411
	(03) 581-6446 Fax
Australia	(03) 418-7253

VU/TEXT Information Services, Inc.
325 Chestnut St., #1300
Philadelphia, PA 19106
(215) 574-4400
(800) 323-2940
(215) 627-0194 Fax

Index of Authors

Index of Titles

Index by Subject

by Linda Webster

Numbers in regular type refer to item entry numbers. Numbers in italics refer to page numbers.

Index of Publishers and Related Organizations

by Linda Webster

Numbers in regular type refer to item entry numbers. Numbers in italics refer to page numbers.

DAWN E. TALBOT

Dawn E. Talbot is a librarian and the manager for information services at the Center for Magnetic Recording Research at the University of California, San Diego. She received her B.A. from Monash University and completed graduate studies in librarianship at the University of New South Wales. Prior to moving to California, she held positions at the University of Sydney, Australia. As manager for information services at the center, an industry/university consortium, she established a model for acquiring and translating selected information from Japan for the recording industry. Active in this area since 1984, she has spoken at national meetings and acted as a consultant to government and private groups.

DUE	RETURNED	DUE	RETURNED
1.		13.	
2.		14.	
3.		15.	
4.		16.	
5.		17.	
6.		18.	
7.		19.	
8.		20.	
9.		21.	
10.		22.	
11.		23.	
12.		24.	